M

BIRTH CONTROL LAWS
SHALL WE KEEP THEM
CHANGE THEM OR
ABOLISII THEM

A Da Capo Press Reprint Series

CIVIL LIBERTIES IN AMERICAN HISTORY

GENERAL EDITOR: LEONARD W. LEVY

Brandeis University

BIRTH CONTROL LAWS

SHALL WE KEEP THEM
CHANGE THEM OR
ABOLISH THEM

BY

MARY WARE DENNETT

DA CAPO PRESS · NEW YORK · 1970

A Da Capo Press Reprint Edition

BIRTH CONTROL LAWS

SHALL WE KEEP THEM
CHANGE THEM OR
ABOLISH THEM

BY

MARY WARE DENNETT

One of the Founders of the National Birth Control League,
Formerly Director of the Voluntary Parenthood
League, Author of "The Sex Side of Life"

FREDERICK H. HITCHCOCK

The Grafton Press

NEW YORK   MCMXXVI

INTRODUCTION

THE scope of this book does not include any general discussion of the merits of birth control, or its sociological and racial ramifications. That has been amply undertaken in recent years by many able people; and the birth rate in all high-grade communities and groups clearly indicates that the subject, per se, is not now to any extent a moot question. Birth control is not an if. It is an actuality.

But what does need further discussion and thinking through to a sound conclusion is the question as to whether laws affecting birth control are necessary in the United States, and if so, just what the provisions of those laws should be. We have laws on the subject already, and have had them,—the same ones,—for over fifty years. They are increasingly unenforced, and are generally acknowledged to be unenforceable. But it is not wise to wait their slow and complete dissolution from disuse, because the diseased and dying body of these laws creates a most unsanitary morale in this fair land of ours.

The question is shall they be done away with altogether, or shall they be modified, and if so, how? This is a matter which potentially affects every family in the country. The theory of laws in a democracy is that they reflect the wishes of the people. This book therefore raises the question as to what they really want, and tries to answer it, or at least to give to the public in condensed and convenient form the facts on which an answer may be based.

In this field at present, there is much muddled reasoning, much jumping at conclusions, much substituting of emotion for thought, and much general assumption that reformers who agitate for birth control must necessarily also be wise law-makers on the subject. To help clarify public thought, and to help crystallize public responsibility as to the legislation which is inevitably a part of the birth control question so long as the present statutes remain on the books, is the aim of this volume.

The book is presented to American citizens in the hope that it may be a useful service. It makes no pretense at literature and it is not propaganda. It is not a legal brief nor a piece of academic research. It simply talks over the subject in an untechnical fashion, from the human standpoint, with the idea that most thinking, well-meaning people want our laws to represent common sense, justice and practicability; and that they want them to harmonize with our heritage of American ideals of freedom and self-government. Although informal in its presentation, every effort has been made to include only statements for which there is authority from original sources. The main points are given in the body of the book, and the appendices give detail and authorities, for the use of those who are interested to check up and be more thorough in their consideration.

The first part of the book explains just what our present laws provide, and how they happened to be the way they are. The second part analyzes the various propositions that have been made for changing the laws, and the reasons offered by their advocates. The third part makes an effort to show the basis on which to differentiate between sound and spurious legislation, and the tests by which it may be determined what the people really want, underneath their upper layer of careless acquiescence, inhibition or inertia. If the author did not have an abiding faith in the fundamental sound sense, good intentions and latent ideality of the average American citizen, this book would not have been written.

New York City   M. W. D.
   1926.

CONTENTS

PART I

WHAT SORT OF LAWS HAVE WE NOW?

PART TWO

WHAT CHANGES IN THE LAWS HAVE BEEN PROPOSED?

for restoration of American freedom to acquire knowledge, which
was taken away 50 years ago—Birth rate in United States proves
that people want and get some information in spite of law—Catholic
speakers discuss birth control, not the bill—Wages of government
employees quoted as reason for passing bill—Prof. Field shows
historically that suppression does not suppress—Mrs. Glaser argues
for freedom for scientists to learn and teach regarding control of
human fertility—Mrs. Carpenter shows how federal law operates
to prevent Chicago Clinic—Prof. Johnson gives eugenic view-point—
Hearing reopened at request of Catholics—Lengthy irrelevancies—
Congressman Hersey heckles the witnesses—Report of Senate Sub-
Committee a sop to the workers for the bill—Unique effort to get
vote of full Committee before adjournment, as aid to reducing inhibition in next Congress.

No one answer covers all reasons—Quiet request to Congress for
repeal might have succeeded twenty years ago, before sensational
law-breaking created prejudice—Laws defied without first attempting their repeal—Speeches and writings of early agitation not calculated to induce Congressional initiative—Struggle announced in
advance as likely to be long and bitter "fight"—Shortage of funds
for publicity on behalf of bill the second reason for slowness of
Congress—Third and most dominant reason found to be general embarrassment over subject—Distaste, inhibition and fear, in varying
degrees almost universal among Congressmen—Striking instances—
Fears covered careers, colleagues, families and constituents—Fear on
behalf of young girls greatest of all—Political opposition to birth
control legislation misinterpreted by "radicals"—Abortive attempt in
Harding presidential campaign to use his tentative interest in this
bill against him—Club women afflicted with inhibitions similar to
those of members of Congress—It is leaders, not members, who hold
back endorsement by large organizations—Organized labor women
endorse repeal ahead of club women.

"Doctors only" federal bill followed straight repeal bill just as
limited bills in states followed straight repeal bills—Advocated on
Margaret Sanger's initiative—Provides medical monopoly of extreme
type—Arguments in its behalf analyzed and answered—Proponents
of "doctors only" bill do not live up to own demands for limiting
contraceptive instruction to personal service by doctors—Birth control
periodical carries thinly veiled advertisements for contraceptives—
Improved type of "doctors only" bill drafted by George Worthington—Not so many loopholes and inconsistencies as in first bill pro-

sonal medical instruction?—Proponents of "doctors only" bill admit that they do not—English birth control organizations disapprove "doctors only" stand—Best known English authority on birth control is biologist, not M.D.—Are laws to curb improper advertising of contraceptives practicable?—Average citizen too occupied to analyze legislative proposals—Proponents of limited legislation backward about explaining their bills to the public—They refuse to debate openly or confer privately with proponents of freedom bill.

Congress will do what the people want if the request is made clearly and forcibly enough—Inhibitions are waning—Later generations will not bless birth control workers or Congress if legislation is bungled now—Danger of blundering as Comstock blundered—Those who mean well regarding legislation must do well—Present laws unconstitutional—First class legal opinion deems all "doctors only" laws unconstitutional also—Time to discard governmental distrust of the people.

PART ONE

WHAT SORT OF LAWS HAVE WE NOW?

CHAPTER I

THE SITUATION

The actual situation under Federal and State law: Not even parents can lawfully inform their married children about how to space their babies: No doctor can lawfully or adequately study the control of conception: Present provisions of Federal law: Scope of State laws: Clinics under State laws: Access to birth control information not only criminal but classed with obscenity: Control of Conception confused with abortion: Precise meaning of term birth control in modern application: Not a crime to control parenthood, but a crime to find out how: What if that principle were applied to some other scientific knowledge, making automobiles for instance?

IT is a crime under the Federal law for a mother to write to her daughter a letter such as this:

DAUGHTER DEAR:

It wrings my heart to know that you are so terribly worried. I have felt for a long time, that something was troubling you. You are absolutely right in your determination to know all there is to be known about how to have your babies when you want them and not otherwise. Now that your own doctor has failed to give you practicable advice, I realize more than ever that I should have raised heaven and earth to see to it that you had adequate information when you were first married. Somehow I blindly hoped that you would never have to go through what I did, that you would be sure to find out what I never properly knew in my married life, and that you would be spared the terror of living in fear that the love which brings you and your husband together should bring your babies so rapidly that you can not possibly take care of them. I blame myself that I let my inhibitions stand in the way of finding help for you long ago, so that now you could help yourself.

But I will do my best to make up. There must be no more worry and uncertainty for you in this crisis. Now that he has

3

lost his job and his health at the same time, you must be sure that no more babies are started for, say four years. I hope and believe that by that time you may be able to have your fourth child in safety. But until then you and he will need every atom of your vitality to make the little bank balance tide you over to better times.

Now here is help. (It makes my blood boil that your doctor should have been so helpless when you took your problem to him, but there is no use berating him, for it is probably not wholly his fault that he knows so little on this subject. The laws won't let him study the matter.) I am sending you a wonderfully clear explicit pamphlet which tells the best and simplest methods for regulating conception. It is written by Doctor ——— who has made a business of studying this problem, law or no law, for over twenty-five years. The methods recommended in it are practically the same as those taught by the best authorities abroad.

I am not stopping to tell you how I got the pamphlet. But I was a "criminal" according to our State law when I got it. And I am a "criminal" again according to Federal law, now that I am mailing it to you. But I am willing to be that kind of a criminal a thousand times over if only I can at this late date make up for letting you go so long uninformed, and if only I can now put your poor tormented mind at rest.

With boundless love,

MOTHER.

For writing such a letter and for sending the pamphlet to which it refers, this mother could be sent to jail for five years and fined $5000. That she would not be discovered is probable. It is also likely that if discovered she would not be indicted. But that would be due, not to the law but merely to the fact that the authorities are almost wholly negligent in enforcing the law. The Federal law makes no exceptions whatever. It is a crime for any one, even for the best of reasons and in the greatest need, to send or to receive by mail anything that tells "where, how or of whom" information may be secured as to how conception may be controlled. The number of unarrested "criminals" of the type of this mother is beyond knowledge or computation, but they are everywhere. Many of them could not tell exactly what the law is. They simply know that the whole subject is under a cloud, that doctors are mostly unsatisfactory when asked for instructions, and that whatever one learns has to be learned secretly.

Here is another kind of letter which it would be a crime to mail. A Philadelphia physician writes to an Iowa physician:

DEAR DOCTOR:

I can not answer your letter as I ought, because of the fool laws, but I will do the best I can. I sympathize most heartily with you in your need for authoritative data on the control of conception. My experience has matched yours precisely, in that patients are asking more and more for advice on methods. After some very humiliating and disastrous experiences several years ago because my patients acted on the half baked instructions I gave them, those being all I then knew,—I determined to study the subject as thoroughly as I could. Fortunately my trip abroad stood me in good service at the time, for I was able to visit several of the scientists who have made a special study of the subject and whose research covers a period of many years. I got most of my material in England and Germany. By sheer luck on my return, the customs officials did not inspect the books and the notes I had on the subject. But they could, and indeed they should under the law, have seized and destroyed them. The most comprehensive of the books is by Dr. ———* of London, a biologist of note who has done some exceptional research work. The book is printed by the well known medical publishers, ———. You might try ordering a copy, but the chances are that it would not come through, and that you would be only wasting your time and money. So I will send you my copy by today's mail, insured, parcel post, and wrapped very securely. Let me have it back inside of a month if you can, for it is much in demand here. I am also sending with it a copy of some particularly useful items from my notes based on the experience of Drs. ——— and ———, also a pamphlet which you may find more helpful than any other one thing, this latter being the work of an American physician, Dr. ——— of ———. It can't be signed of course on account of the laws, and it has to be circulated secretly. I find it excellent not only because of its brevity and soundness, but because

---

* To give the name, would make this book "unmailable" under the law.

it serves very well as a handbook of information for my patients, to supplement the instructions I give them personally. I think you will find yourself wanting a quantity for distribution, especially among your patients who ask your advice by letter, and who do not live near enough to come to your office.

Of course you realize that I am a deliberate law-breaker in sending you this letter and parcel, but I would rather take a chance on being held up for it than to have you repeat my experience of advising people without adequate knowledge as to method. According to the law you will be just as bad as I, when you "knowingly" take from the mail the parcel I am sending. And worse yet, your State of Iowa has a law which makes it a crime to *have in your possession* any instructions for contraception! So be cautious.

Let me know if I can be of any further use.

With best wishes, as ever

(Signed) ....

Another bit of human "crime" is an actual instance which occurred in the experience of a Washington man who has been active in the campaign to change the laws regarding birth control knowledge. It was several years ago, when the effort to introduce a bill into Congress was still new. He dropped into the office of a certain Congressman whom he knew well, his errand being on another matter, but in passing he mentioned the work of the organization which had proposed the first Federal bill on this subject, and inquired if he had yet met the Director. Instantly the Congressman was alert. "No, but I would like to, and you are just the man I want to see right now. I want you to tell me how to get all the best information there is on this question of regulating the growth of a family. I need it." He outlined his own situation. He had four splendid youngsters, all of them wanted and welcomed. But since the birth of the last one his wife had not been well, and it was far from wise for her to have another one soon, certainly not for several years. Also he was not a man of means. He could not afford to rear a very large family. The question of control had never been pressing before. Now it was imperative. Strange as it might seem he was practically without reliable information as to methods. Would Mr. ———— be so mighty kind as to put him in the way of getting proper instruction? He would, and did. But it was utterly unlawful. However he was a cordially willing criminal, and the Congressman likewise cordially appreciated the friendly criminality. "Of course you can count on me to vote that bill when it comes up in Congress," he said with emphasis that was most sincere.

It is obvious from the foregoing examples, which might be multiplied indefinitely, that the present status of our laws is profoundly at odds with the beliefs and the needs of the people. What then do the people need or want in the way of laws, if they need any at all, on this subject? A necessary preliminary to answering that question is to take account of the stock of laws we already have, to inspect them open-mindedly, and then to add or subtract from them whatever common sense, justice and self-respect may require.

First of all we have the Federal law which affects the whole country. Then we have State laws in all the States but two, which either directly or by inference form a legal barrier between the people and this knowledge. In just half of the forty-eight States there are specific prohibitions. In all but two of the other half, the same prohibition is feasible under the obscenity laws, by virtue of the precedent of the Federal obscenity law and the obscenity laws of half the States, for it is in these obscenity laws that the prohibition of the circulation of contraceptives is found. The Federal law was passed first and is the model on which all the State laws are framed.

The Federal Criminal Code contains five separate sections dealing with the subject, as follows. They are given in sequence according to Section numbers, not according to the date of their enactment.

Section 102 penalizes any government employee who aids or abets anyone who violates the law which forbids the "importing, advertising, dealing in, exhibiting, or sending or receiving by mail obscene or indecent publications or representations, or means for preventing conception or producing abortion, or other article of indecent or immoral use or tendency." Note the word "tendency," and consider the scope and power which it gives to government officials with a penchant for suppressions.

Section 211, the parent of all the United States obscenity laws, declares unmailable any information or means for preventing conception. The prohibition is well nigh limitless in scope, for it forbids any information whether given directly or indirectly, and even includes any "description *calculated* to induce or incite a person to use or apply" any means for the prevention of conception.

Section 245 covers the same ground, but applies to transportation by express or any other common carrier, from one state to another or to or from any foreign country.

Section 312 applies to the District of Columbia, which is under the direct control of Congress. It is one of the most sweeping of all the laws. It forbids any one to lend or give away any published information, or even to "have it in his possession for any such purpose," or to write where, "how or of whom" information may be secured. Some of the extraordinary infringement of this section by members of Congress and officials at the Capitol will be described later in the book.

Section 305 of the Tariff Act of 1922 prohibits the importation from any foreign country of any contraceptive information or means. Any such may be "seized and forfeited."

The maximum penalty for infringements of these Federal statutes is five years in jail or a fine of $5000 or both.

The wording of all these laws is very similar, and like

most laws from the view-point of the layman, very repetitious and involved. It is hardly worth while to reproduce them here in full, but it is well for the reader to take the trouble to wade through the disagreeable verbiage of one of them, in order to realize the essential factors in the question under discussion. The now notorious Section 211 is the most representative one. It is the unfortunately prolific parent of the mass of legislation which has come to be called the Comstock laws, because it was Anthony Comstock who saddled them on to the United States, beginning in 1873 with this original Section 211. It reads as follows:

Every obscene, lewd, or lascivious, and every filthy book, pamphlet, picture, paper, letter, writing, print, or other publication of an indecent character, and every article or thing designed, adapted, or intended for *preventing conception* or producing abortion, or for any indecent or immoral use; and every article, instrument, substance, drug, medicine, or thing which is advertised or described in a manner calculated to lead another to use or apply it for *preventing conception* or producing abortion, or for any indecent or immoral purpose; and every written or printed card, letter, circular, book, pamphlet, advertisement, or notice of any kind giving information directly or indirectly, where, or how, or of whom, or by what means any of the hereinbefore-mentioned matters, articles or things may be obtained or made, or where or by whom any act or operation of any kind for the procuring or producing of abortion will be done or performed or how or by what means *conception may be prevented* or abortion may be produced, whether sealed or unsealed; and every letter, packet, or package, or other mail matter containing any filthy, vile, or indecent thing, device or substance and every paper, writing, advertisement or representation that any article, instrument, substance, drug, medicine, or thing may, or can be, used or applied, for *preventing conception* or producing abortion, or for any indecent or immoral purpose; and every description calculated to induce or incite a person to so use or apply any such article, instrument, substance, drug, medicine, or thing, is hereby declared to be a non-mailable matter and shall not be conveyed in the mails or delivered from any post office or by any letter carrier. Whoever shall knowingly deposit or cause to be deposited for mailing or delivery, anything declared by this section to be non-mailable, or shall knowingly take, or cause the same to be taken, from the mails for the purpose of circulating or disposing thereof, or of aiding in the circulation or disposition thereof, shall be fined not more than five thousand dollars, or imprisoned not more than five years, or both."

Now as to the State laws. They are very similar in import and phraseology to the parent Federal law, Section 211, but they deal with other ways of circulating contraceptive knowledge and means than transportation by mail or express. The 24 States which have specific prohibitions, variously forbid publishing, advertising or giving the information. Fourteen States prohibit any one to tell. (Fancy trying to enforce such a law!) In most of these States the statute is similar to that in the District of Columbia, which even forbids the *telling* of anything that "will be *calculated* to lead another" to apply any information to the prevention of conception, and also makes it a crime to have in one's possession any instructions to lend or give away. That is, the most ordinary channels for human relationship,—private conversation and the sort of help one friend or relative naturally gives to another,—become criminal where this subject is concerned. In several States private property and personal belongings can be searched by the authorities for "contraband" instructions. Colorado forbids anyone to bring contraceptive knowledge into the State. (The hold-up of traffic on the State line if that law were enforced, would be amazing to contemplate.) But Connecticut surely deserves the booby prize, for it has the grotesque distinction of being the one State to penalize the actual utilization of contraceptive information; in other words, the Connecticut law makes it a crime not only to find out how, but actually to *control* conception. The enforcement of that law fairly staggers the imagination. What could have been in the minds of the legislators who passed it is a question.

New York has a unique sort of post-script to its State law, passed in 1881, eight years after the first law. The main statute (Section 1142 of the Penal Code) is of the most sweepingly suppressive variety. The added provision (Section 1145) declares that "An article or instrument used or applied by physicians lawfully practicing, or by their direction or prescription, for the cure or prevention of disease, is not an article of indecent or immoral nature or use." Just how an *article* can have an immoral or indecent *nature* has never been explained. However, this section has within the last few years been judicially interpreted to mean that the giving of contraceptive advice by a physician to a patient who was diseased or seriously threatened with disease is not an act of criminal indecency. And under this interpretation a Clinic has been established in New York City by the American Birth Control League. It is now (1926) in its third year of service and reports that during its first year it gave contraceptive instructions to 3000 patients. Similar service is creeping gradually into a few of the New York Hospitals, but it is being rendered quietly, indeed almost furtively, so pervasive is the effect of the general legal taboo. As recently as 1919 thirty of the chief hospitals in the city officially stated that no preventive instructions would be given even to seriously diseased women.

These prohibitions, in the 24 States where they exist, are a part of the *obscenity* statutes, just as is the case in the Federal statutes. They appear under such headings as "Obscene literature" and "Indecent Articles." In California the prohibition comes under a general chapter heading, —"Indecent Exposure, Obscene Exhibitions, Books and Prints, Bawdy and Other Disorderly Houses." None of the laws define contraceptive information as, per se, obscene, indecent, immoral, lewd, lascivious, filthy, or any of the other revolting things named in the statutes, but they list it along with these things, in most cases there being no more separation from them than that which a comma affords. Section 102 of the Federal law makes a still closer connection of idea, for it prohibits "importing, advertising, dealing in, exhibiting, or sending or receiving by mail obscene or indecent publications or representations or means for preventing conception or producing abortion, or *other* article of indecent or immoral use or tendency." This knowledge is thus definitely classed as one among "other" things of indecent or immoral use.

Science and indecency are in fact hopelessly jumbled in the whole mass of law affecting this subject. There is not the slightest differentiation between what is scientific truth, —a part of the world's store of knowledge, and things which are the expression of sexual depravity and perversion.

To add to the mess, the laws link contraceptive knowledge so closely with instructions for abortion that in some of the statutes there is not even a comma between the two. In California the prohibition of contraceptive information occurs in a statute entitled "Advertising to produce miscarriage." Of course the two ideas are actually separated by an abyss that has no bottom. To control the inception of life must forever remain a fundamentally different thing from the destroying of life after it exists. Abortion may be birth control, but birth control is not abortion.

Just here it may be well to state precisely what is meant and what is not meant by the term birth control in its modern application. *It means the conscious, responsible control of conception. It does not mean interference with life after conception has taken place, but consists solely in the use of intelligence and scientific hygienic knowledge to determine the wise times for conception to occur, and to limit the possibility of conception to those occasions.* It seems unfortunate that the term birth control was ever popularized, for the more correct term is conception control. However birth control has now become an accepted part of the language, and it is less and less misleading as time goes on.

Another extraordinary factor in our laws regarding this

subject is that (with the absurd single instance of Connecticut) the act of controlling conception is nowhere declared a crime. It is only *finding out how* conception may be controlled that constitutes the crime. To regulate the incidence of parenthood and the growth of one's family is a perfectly lawful procedure. Having once secured the knowledge, which act is unlawful, one may then lawfully utilize it ad infin. The preposterousness of such a principle as a basis for law is satirically set forth in an article in the *Birth Control Herald* * (Jan. 12, 1923) from which the following is quoted:

The futility as well as the hypocrisy of standing for laws that make it a crime to secure knowledge which it is not a crime to use after it is secured, shows up beautifully if one applies the idea to some other phase of scientific knowledge than that concerning the control of conception. Take for instance the principles upon which the mechanism of the automobile is based.

Fancy some obfuscated back-number in Congress, with a violent personal prejudice against the whole notion of automobiles, and who might love to make eloquent speeches about how man was intended by God to be a horse-drawn creature, that come what might, he himself would go about in his own victoria behind his own span of noble steeds; and that moreover he would do his utmost to see to it that everyone else should likewise adopt what he considers Nature's true plan for transportation,—the horse.

Picture him then, as he sees the whole world tending to the ambition to own at least a Ford, introducing a bill a la Comstock, which would make it a crime to circulate any "book, pamphlet, picture, paper, letter print or other publication" showing how automobiles may be constructed, or any "article or thing designed, adapted or intended" to aid in such knowledge, or "anything which is advertised or described in a manner calculated to lead another to use or apply it" to the making of automobiles, or "giving information directly or indirectly how, where or of whom or by what means, any of the hereinbefore mentioned matters, articles or things may be obtained," etc., etc.

And while he could he could not help witnessing the daily in-

* Published by the Voluntary Parenthood League.

crease in automobile traffic, and while he might now and then, when unobserved, use a taxi himself when circumstances made it desirable, he certainly would not let that mar his feeling of righteous loyalty to his general conviction that the spread of knowledge as to the making of automobiles ought never to be sanctioned by the laws of our great and glorious nation.

"Blithering idiot" would be about as complimentary an epithet as such a Congressman, if he existed, would receive from his fellow members.   But because the Comstock law deals with science pertaining to sex instead of science pertaining to motors, some Congressmen do not yet quite recognize the innate stupidity as well as the injustice of any governmental attempt to put a "no admittance" sign over any department of knowledge.

As above stated, we have 24 States in which there is a specific prohibition of the circulation of contraceptive information or means.   Now what is the situation in the other half of the States?   In all but two of them,—North Carolina and New Mexico,—there are obscenity laws modeled very closely upon the Federal laws, but unlike them in that they do not mention by name the subject of contraceptive information or means.   But just because the Federal laws and the laws of half the States do name the subject among the penalized obscenities, these 22 other States have the strongest possible legal precedent for prosecuting, *as an obscenity,* if they so desire, the circulation of any sort of contraceptive information whatever, as something which is against public policy.   And just because obscenity itself has never been defined in law, but can mean all sorts of things to all manner of officials, judges and juries, there could be nearly as much opportunity to prosecute those who give contraceptive information in the relatively free States as in the States which have specific prohibitions.

Indeed this is what has recently happened in the State of Illinois.   The Chicago Parenthood Clinic was organized in the fall of 1923 by a special Committee and Council of well known public spirited men and women of which Mrs. Benjamin Carpenter was the Chairman. Funds were raised to support it; Dr. Rachel Yarros of Hull House was engaged as the physican in charge; a building was equipped; and everything was ready to function when Health Commissioner Bundensen refused to allow a license to be issued. In stating his reasons for holding up the project, Dr. Bundensen indicated that he was actuated not only by his personal disapproval of birth control but that he felt amply justified in his position because of the precedent of the Federal law. He said that "advocating prevention of conception is contrary to public policy, as clearly indicated by ——— act of Congress."

The conservative and humanitarian purpose of the Clinic as outlined by Mrs. Carpenter's committee was "to extend advice and treatment to married people only, and where the conditions are such as to make the bearing of children dangerous or prejudicial to the health and welfare of the wife or child; to prevent in every manner rational and proper, recourse to abortion, now too prevalent, and to avoid as far as is humanly possible, the burdening of the community with defective children, and the ruination of the health of countless mothers." In an interview Dr. Yarros stated that the sponsors of the Clinic were "opposed to sensational methods, and intended to present both negative and positive information (that is to help overcome difficulties which prevented parents from having children as well as to instruct those who needed to avoid or postpone having children) and to inspire ideals of family life and happiness." Dr. Bundensen was adamant, however, and he was backed by a considerable amount of vehement Roman Catholic opposition to the Clinic.

The case was taken to Court, and the decision of Judge Harry M. Fisher of the Circuit Court of Cook County was in favor of granting a license to the Clinic. But the opposition appealed the case. The decision of the higher court in March, 1924, was that the granting of a license was entirely within the discretion of the Health Commissioner. There could hardly be a clearer instance showing the influence of the precedent which the Federal law affords, to suppress contraceptive knowledge in States which have no law against the giving of verbal personal instructions. Had there been no legal precedent outside of Illinois, in the absence of any suppressive law within the State, the Health Commissioner would have had no basis for his action except his personal opinion. That alone would, in all probability, not have been deemed sufficient basis for suppressing the Clinic. However, as it was only because the Clinic was to give *free* service that it required a license, the charging of a small fee enabled the same people to arrange for the same clinical service under the name "Medical Center," and two of these are now operating in Chicago with marked success. Shorn thus of his opportunity to suppress this service through his licensing power, the Health Commissioner apparently does not consider it worth while to institute proceedings against the Medical Center, as he still might do if he wished to press the Federal precedent into use again,—especially as the report of the first year's work of the two medical centers has now been published. (The substance of this report is given in Appendix No. 3,—expurgated sufficiently to avoid making this book "unmailable" under Section 211 of the Federal Criminal Code.)

The question has often been asked why publishers do not sell books on scientific contraceptive methods, in the 24 States where there are no local laws to forbid it. There is great demand for such books, and the present secret way of circulating the relatively few authoritative ones in existence is most inadequate for the people's need. As there are nearly 50,000,000 people in these 24 States, why not give

them what they need and want now, without waiting for
the slow and uncertain action of Congress in repealing the
Federal prohibition? The answer is very illuminating.

This is the situation which a publisher or book seller
would be up against, if he were to consider such a thing
practically. He might think first of importing a stock of
books from England, for instance the well-known little volume by ———— (the law prohibits naming it) which is so
popular over there that it is now in its ninth edition. But
the Federal law would prevent that at the very start. For
the statute reads, "Whoever shall bring or cause to be
brought into the United States from any foreign country
any . . . book . . . giving information directly or indirectly," etc. He could be fined $5000 or jailed for five
years for even trying it. Well then, how about printing a
special edition for, say Illinois, to be sold only in that State?
It sounds hopeful. But just as soon as he got the book
printed the trouble would begin. For he could not mail
any announcement of the book to anyone anywhere. He
could not put a single advertisement in any newspaper or
magazine, because they are mailed to subscribers, and the
Federal law prohibits all mailing. He might put the books
on sale in the larger book shops, say in Chicago, but if he
did so without having them announced or advertised, they
would not sell enough to pay for publishing. However if
they were also on sale in the shops of other cities and towns
of the State the aggregate sale might be worth while from
the point of view of human welfare if not from that of
the publishers' purse.

But even that would be impracticable because the books
could not be shipped from the bindery to any other town
either by mail or by express or freight, or by any sort of
common carrier. The Federal law prohibits all that. So
there would be no way to get those books into circulation,
except for one person to tell another that they could be

bought, and for them to be transported from city to city by private vehicle or messenger; or to advertise them by posters and handbills distributed personally to individuals, which of course is an exorbitantly expensive method.

The conclusion is inevitable that the only practical thing to do is to repeal the Federal prohibition, which is the root difficulty that lies in the way of any adequate circulation of the knowledge, anywhere in the United States.

For a digest of the provisions of the State laws, see Appendix No. 1.

For the effect of Federal law upon State laws, see Chart Appendix No. 2.

CHAPTER II

HOW IT HAPPENED

How it came about that information concerning one item of science became a criminal indecency: Anthony Comstock's blundering bequest to the people: Congress an unwitting partner: States hastily followed suit: United States the only country to class contraceptive information with penalized indecency: Legislation aimed at indecency but hit science: Europe laughs at our "Comstockery": Documentary proof that Comstock and his successor, Sumner, did not expect laws to prevent doctors from giving and normal people from using contraceptive instructions.

"THE evil that men do lives after them,"—likewise their stupidity and blunders. For over half a century the people of the United States have been the victims of a great error which Anthony Comstock and Congress unwittingly committed in connection with their commendable effort to free the young people of the country from contamination by those who were then trafficking extensively in smutty literature and inducements to sex perversion.

Their error in judgment was to include in Section 211 of the Penal Code the two words "preventing conception." In their eagerness to abolish the promotion of the misuse of contraceptive knowledge in connection with morbid and irregular practices, they rashly framed the law so as to forbid all circulation of any knowledge whatever, thus making it in the eyes of the law just as much a crime for high-minded responsible married people to learn how to space the births in their families wisely, as for the low, vicious or perverted few to spread information about how to abuse this knowledge in abnormal, unwholesome ways.

19

The Congressional Record of the short session of Congress which ended on March fourth, 1873, shows beyond any reasonable doubt that Anthony Comstock himself had no intention of penalizing *normal* birth control information. He was simply so bent upon wiping out the shocking commerce in pornographic literature which disgraced that period that he rushed headlong into the question of legislation without due consideration as to the results, which have made the United States the laughing stock of Europeans, and which have even prevented the lawful circulation of medical works for the medical profession.

The Record reveals the fact that the first draft of the bill contained the following exemption after the prohibition of all information as to the prevention of conception or as to abortion, "except from a physician in good standing, given in good faith." Why this exemption was later omitted does not appear in the Record, but its original existence proves that there was at least some glimmering of realization somewhere that a wholesale prohibition was not the aim of the statute. There is wide spread evidence that present day public opinion would not be at all satisfied with any such exemption, even if it had been left in the bill, because contraceptive knowledge is part of general hygiene and education, and not a physician's prescription as for disease, though of course the knowledge emanates naturally from the professional scientists who have made a study of this subject.

A little sober forethought would not only have spared the country from the unique disgrace of this careless legislation, but it would to a considerable extent have spared the country from the need for a birth control movement,—an advantage of no mean proportions!

Not one of our Senators is in Congress now who was in Congress then, not even the most venerable of them, but it would seem that the least which this present Congress can do is to redeem the record of their predecessors with all possible grace and speed.

The Comstock bill was introduced on February 11, 1873, passed by both Houses and signed by President Grant before the close of the session on March fourth.

The chronology of the history of the Bill in both Houses is very brief. There was practically no discussion on the subject matter. There were no speeches delivered, until *after* the bill was passed. The measure was granted unanimous consent action in the Senate, and was passed under a suspension of rules in the House. There was no roll call on the passage of the bill in either House. It slipped under the wire for the President's signature on the very last day of the session. And Comstock went home happy.

The sequence of events was as follows:

The bill was sponsored in the Senate by Senator Windom of Winona, Minnesota, and introduced on February 11th. The measure was referred to the Committee on Post Offices and Post Roads, and reported out without amendment two days later, on February 13th. No public hearings were held.

On February 14th the bill was recommitted to the Committee on motion of Senator Buckingham of Connecticut who thereafter took charge of the bill on the floor. It came promptly back the next day, amended and approved by the Post Office Committee, but neither the bill nor the amendment was discussed. The writer has personally inquired whether there is an official report on the bill in the files of the Post Office Committee, and was told that there is none. Senator Buckingham asked unanimous consent to take up the bill, saying, "I think there will be no objection to it." Senator Thurman of Ohio protested that it was too important to vote on without deliberate investigation, and asked that it go over. It did, for two days.

On the 20th, by unanimous consent the business of the

"morning hour" was extended for ten minutes to permit discussion of the bill. But the discussion was remarkably unilluminating as to the merits of the bill. Senator Buckingham offered an amendment which omitted the clause providing exemption for contraceptive information on prescription of a duly licensed physician, given in good faith. Two Senators asked Senator Buckingham to explain the difference between the amended version and the previous version. He evaded explaining.

Senator Hamlin of Maine urged that the measure be accepted as approved by the Committee and "not to tinker with it on the floor." Senator Conkling of New York insisted that the bill be printed as amended, "in order that we may know something at least of what we are voting upon." He said, "For one, although I have tried to acquaint myself with it, I have not been able to tell, either from the reading of the apparently illegible manuscript in some cases by the Secretary, or from private information gathered at the moment, and if I were to be questioned now as to what this bill contains, I could not aver anything certain in regard to it. The indignation and disgust that everybody feels in reference to the acts which are here aimed at may possibly lead us to do something which, when we come to see it in print, will not be the thing we would have done if we had understood it and were more deliberate about it."

When Senator Conkling thus cautioned the Senate to be careful in the framing of the Comstock bill, he had what might be called almost feminine intuition. For as history has conclusively proved, the Senate did precisely that thing. It prohibited what it had no intention of prohibiting,—the spread of scientific education of the wise spacing of births in the human family.

But the warning was unheeded and there was no further discussion. The next day, February 21st, the bill was called up and passed.

The history of the bill in the House is even more brief. On February 22nd a message was received from the Senate that the bill had been passed and the concurrence of the House was requested.

On March first Representative Merriam of Locust Grove, New York, moved to suspend the rules and "take from the Speaker's table and put upon its passage the bill (S. 1572)." Mr. Kerr of Indiana moved its reference to the Judiciary Committee, saying, "Its provisions are extremely important, and they ought not to be passed in such hot haste." Mr. Cox of New York inquired if debate was in order. The Speaker ruled that it was not. Mr. Merriam moved to suspend the rules and pass the bill. The necessary two-thirds vote to suspend the rules were polled, and the bill was passed without a roll call.

After the passage of the bill, Mr. Merriam obtained leave to print remarks on it in the Congressional Record.

Can any candid reader of the record of how this measure was presented to Congress and passed by the members without debate, possibly assume that the bill was aimed at the complete suppression of access to scientific knowledge for normal use?

If that had been the aim of the bill, surely some of the members would have been more insistent than they were upon discussing the provisions of the bill. It is interesting in this connection to note how John S. Sumner, Comstock's successor, has attempted to refute the criticism that the Comstock bill was passed in careless haste. In a letter which he wrote to Senator Cummins on January 23, 1923, protesting against the Senator's bill to repeal the Comstock blunder, he gives as his first proof that "this bill was thoroughly considered by some of the most brilliant members of the Senate at that or any other time," the opening paragraph of Mr. Merriam's "leave to print" remarks, and states that it was "in the House of Representatives on

March 1, 1873" that the Congressman said them. We can
give Mr. Sumner the benefit of the doubt that he read the
Congressional Record so carelessly that he did not notice
that the bill was passed before the Senate could possibly
have read Senator Merriam's arguments urging its passage.
But it is also noteworthy that in this letter to Senator Cummins, he omits to state the date (March first) on which the
bill was passed. He simply says that it was "subsequently
passed by the Senate." It is also significant that Mr. Sumner puts the Merriam (unspoken) speech at the head of
page of excerpts he quotes from the Congressional Record,
when as a matter of fact it was the last occurrence in the
Senate. It took place after the bill was enacted, and was
therefore no factor whatever in its enactment.

For some years previous, excellent publications containing contraceptive instructions of a dignified and scientific
sort had been increasingly circulated in the United States,
notably the book by Dr. Trall which was sold in such quantity in the sixties that it would rank well as a "best seller"
in present days. It would also still rank high as authoritative teaching regarding the control of conception if it could
be published in full today.

The fact that the control of conception was not once
mentioned by any member on the floor of either House is
most convincing evidence that their minds were not taken
up with that question, but that they accepted on faith the
general aim of the measure, which was to suppress gross
indecencies. In this connection a further quotation from
Sumner's letter to Senator Cummins is noteworthy. Although he attempts to convince the Senator that the Comstock bill had ample attention from Congress and was thoroughly understood before it was passed, and that it was
also backed by the press of the country, he was unable to
muster a single quotation from a member of Congress or
from the press that so much as named the control of con-

ception, much less discussed whether information regarding it should be banned in the law. His contention has no more strength than the mere statement that "each time the bill came before Congress it was described as a measure for the suppression of trade in and circulation of obscene literature and articles of immoral use." Nor are the few press items he quotes any more specific. He tried to make them so by underlining the word *articles* in each one. But as there are various "articles" used or usable in abnormal sex practices, the mention of "articles" does not connote the control of conception, and certainly not the use of contraceptives in normal life. So his contention is flimsy to the last degree. Congress knew that it had voted to suppress indecent matter, but it did not know it had also voted to suppress scientific knowledge.

People who well remember Comstock's procedure during the short session of 1873 have described his very effective way of getting support for his bill. He simply showed to the members of Congress whom he interviewed, specimens of the disgusting pictures and publications which were then in circulation and from which the publishers were deriving large profits. The stuff was so obviously outrageous and it was so revolting to know that it was being diligently spread among the youth of the country, that the response of the Congressmen to his proposed bill for making the matter unmailable was immediate. This is the outstanding fact which accounts for the case with which the bill was put through without debate. In writing of his own work afterward, Comstock said, "I am positive I personally presented the full facts to the large majority, both in the Senate and House."

Below are extracts from the *only* speech made in behalf of the Comstock bill, and that speech was *never spoken on the floor of the House*. "Leave to print" speeches have long been a peculiar and questionable characteristic of

American legislation, and this instance is of exceptional peculiarity in that the "speech" was made *after* the bill was passed.

In the whole long document of which only a brief portion is given here, there is only one mention of the words "preventing conception" and that is in a letter which Mr. Merriam quotes from Comstock and this *one mention is solely in connection with indecencies and perversions.*

"Mr. Speaker, the purposes of this bill are so clearly in the best interests of morality and humanity that I trust it will receive the unanimous voice of Congress. It is terrible to contemplate that more than 6000 persons are daily employed in a carefully organized business, stimulated to activity by all the incentive that avarice and wickedness can invent, to place in the schools and homes of our country books, pictures and immoral appliances, of so low and debasing a nature that it would seem that the brute creation itself would turn from them in disgust."

With this, his opening paragraph, Mr. Merriam proceeded to express his confidence that Congress would so act and that "the outraged manhood of our age" would condemn this traffic which sought to make "merchandise of the morals of our youth." Recent revelations had shown that no school or home was safe from these "corrupting influences" and that "the purity and beauty of womanhood has no protection from the insults of this trade."

Mr. Merriam said further that this trade was worse than war, pestilence or famine. Only this subtle influence, now revealed, could explain the "crime and depravity in this our day." He then praised the revelations made by "one young man in New York whose hand with determined and commendable energy is falling heavily upon the workers in this detestable business," referring to his exhibit of over 15,000 letters received by dealers in this literature from students of both sexes in all parts of the country. These and other letters in the Dead Letter Office had exposed a regular circulating library of obscene books and pictures. Most of the book plates had been recently seized and destroyed.

With the object of placing all the facts before Congress and the country, Mr. Merriam placed in the Record as part of his remarks a long letter which he had received from Anthony Comstock of New York. The letter is dated January 18, 1873, and its first paragraphs are as follows:

"Dear Sir: I have the honor to acknowledge the receipt of your favor of the 12th instant in which you ask for a statement from me in reference to the traffic in obscene literature.

"There are various ways by which this vile stuff has been disseminated. First, by advertising in the above named papers. Some weeks there is not a single advertisement in some of these papers that is not designed either to cheat or defraud, or intended to be a medium of sending out these accursed books and articles. For instance, I have arrested a number of persons, one in particular, who advertised a musical album to be sent for fifty cents. I sent the fifty cents, and received back a catalogue of obscene books with the following card attached: 'The album is only a pretense to enable us to forward you a catalogue of our fancy books. Should you order these books your fifty cents will be credited.'

"It is needless to say I ordered, then arrested him, locked him up in the New Haven Jail, and he has been indicted by the grand jury in the United States Court of Connecticut and now is held in bail for trial. In the same way, by advertising beautiful views or pictures of some celebrated place or person, men receive answers from innocent persons for these pictures, and among the pictures sent will be one or more of these obscene pictures and catalogues of these vile books and rubber goods. For be it known that wherever these books go, or catalogue of these books, there you will find, as almost indispensable, a complete list of rubber articles for masturbation or for the professed *prevention of conception*. (The italics are ours.)

"Secondly: The abominations are disseminated by these men first obtaining the addresses of scholars and students in our schools and colleges and then forwarding these circulars. They secure thousands of names in this way, by either sending for a catalogue of schools, seminaries, and colleges, under the pretense of sending a child to attend these places, or else by sending out a circular purporting to be getting up a directory of all the scholars and students in schools and colleges in the United States, or of taking the census of all the unmarried people, and offering to pay five cents per name for list so sent. I need not say the money is seldom or never sent, but I do say that these names, together with those that come in reply to advertisements, are sold to other parties so that when a man desires to engage in the nefarious business he has only to purchase a list of these names and then your child, be it a son or daughter, is as liable to have thrust into its hands, all unbeknown to you, one of these devilish catalogues.

"You will please observe that this business is carried on principally by the agency of the United States mails, and there is no law by which we can interfere with the sending out of these catalogues and circulars through the mail, except they are obscene on their face; and there are scores of men that are supporting themselves and families today by sending out these rubber goods, etc., through the mails, that I cannot touch for want of law. There are men in Philadelphia, in Chicago, in Boston and other places who are doing this business, that I could easily detect and convict if the law was only sufficient."

Mr. Merriam then concluded as follows:

"With the passage of this bill I shall have performed a most uninviting duty. No man even when compelled by a conscientious conviction of official duty, goes willingly down into the gutters of human depravity to act as scavenger to root out moral deformities. He fights to advantage who knows his enemy. The good men of this country who regard their homes as their sanctuaries, warned by this exposure, will act with determined energy to protect what they hold most precious in life, the holiness and purity of their firesides."

So much for the story of how the Federal statutes happened to be fastened upon American law. The example was contagious. A veritable epidemic of State legislation in similar phraseology ensued, until ere long, there were only two States without obscenity statutes which echoed the Federal law and which, in many instances, went much further than the Federal law in suppressive policy. American laws in this regard stand unique among those of the nations of the world. In various countries there are obscenity statutes and regulations, but in none save the United States is contraceptive information, *per se,* classed with penalized indecency. In no other country is science reduced to the level of obscenity in the law. Bernard Shaw said twenty years ago, "Comstockery is the world's standing joke, at the expense of the United States."

Some degree of praise and a deluge of denunciation has been poured upon Anthony Comstock for the legislation he initiated, the arrests and suppressions which he accomplished, and for the spying methods he used, to entrap those whose activities he considered criminal. Any final or complete estimate of his qualities, and the value of his work to the people of the country would be out of place in this book, but it may be of use, in considering what sort of legislation the country should have, to get at something of the *why* of Comstock's efforts. The fairest way to arrive at an unprejudiced conclusion about him would seem to be to let him speak for himself, by quoting from his own books describing his major work, and then to give the reader representative glimpses of his work and his psychology through the words of both his ardent supporters and his adverse critics.

But first it is essential to bear in mind that the dent Anthony Comstock made in American life was considerably due to the fact that he was given special power both by Congress and by the New York State Legislature to act as a government agent in securing arrests. This power, coupled with the almost unparalleled energy of the man, made his career exceptional. Had it not been for these two factors, it might perhaps seem clear that his psychology was not so very different from that of many less well known folk of his day and our own,—the perfectly respectable, and to all outward appearance normal people, who see sex as something innately nasty and dangerous: the only difference being that while Comstock, armed with his governmental power, translated his feeling into prodigious activity in the way of suppressing people, the others, lacking his official power and his energy, have remained rather inert. They have not therefore become conspicuous characters. The Comstock psychology, in modified and milder form, appears to be not at all a rarity.

The way in which Comstock got his special power to enforce the Federal law is described by his biographer, Rev. C. G. Trumbull in his book, "Anthony Comstock, Fighter," as follows: "Immediately after the patience-taking passage of the bill in Congress . . . , Senators Buckingham, Windom, Ramsey, and Representative Merriam united in asking Post Master General Jewell to appoint Comstock a special agent of the Post Office Department to enforce the laws. The Post Office Bill was still pending; the Post Office Committee offered this proposition as an amendment, and it was passed with the bill." The Post Master General agreed to make the appointment, if an appropriation were voted for the salary and per diem expenses. Comstock went before the Committee on Appropriations and opposed the salary, on the ground that the position would thus be kept out of politics. He was appointed and held the office for thirty-three years. The Y. M. C. A. paid him $100 a month "to compensate him for the time lost from his business." He was still ostensibly a grocery clerk. When Cortelyou was Post Master General, he insisted that Comstock should take a salary and be a government employee on a regular basis. At this time also his title of "Special Agent" was changed to "Inspector." This occurred in about 1910. The duties of the office, as given by the Postal Laws, include the following: the "investigation of all matters connected with the postal service," "alleged violations of law" and "when necessary to aid in the prosecution of criminal offenses." Postal employees are "subordinate to post office inspectors when acting within the scope of their duty and employment." "Inspectors are empowered to open pouches and sacks to examine the mail therein." When authorized by the Post

Master General, they are empowered to "make searches for mailable matter transported in violation of law," to "seize all letters and bags, packets or parcels, containing letters which are being carried contrary to law on board any vessel or on any postal route."

Comstock's special power under New York State law was in connection with his position as Secretary of the Society for the Suppression of Vice. This Society was incorporated by the New York Legislature in May, 1873,—within six weeks of the passage of the Comstock bill by Congress. Section 3 of the Act of Incorporation states the object of the society to be "the enforcement of the laws for the suppression of the trade in and circulation of obscene literature and illustrations, advertisements, and articles of indecent and immoral use, as it is or may be forbidden by the laws of the State of New York or of the United States." Section 5 contains an extraordinary provision, which reads this way: "The police force of the city of New York, as well as of other places, where police organizations exist, shall, as occasion may require, aid this corporation, its members or agents, in the enforcement of all laws which now exist or which may hereafter be enacted for the suppression of the acts and offenses designed in Section 3 of this Act." Note that the police force was to aid the Society, not the Society the Police. An almost incredible further provision in the original Act of Incorporation was that "One half the fines collected through the instrumentality of the Society, or its agent, for the violation of the laws in this act specified, shall accrue to its benefits,"—a provision which fortunately was soon repealed.

This unusual sharing of official responsibility for law enforcement between government officials and private citizens was carried still further, by the enactment, two years later, of Section 1145 of the New York Criminal Code, which under the general heading of "Indecency" is subtitled, *"Who may arrest persons violating provisions of this article"* and reads thus: "Any agent of the New York Society for the Suppression of Vice upon being designated thereto by the sheriff of any county in the State, may within such county make arrests and bring before any court or magistrate thereof having jurisdiction, offenders found violating the provisions of any law for the suppression of the trade in and circulation of obscene literature and illustrations, advertisements and articles of indecent or immoral use, as it is or may be forbidden by the laws of this State or of the United States." According to John S. Sumner, the present secretary of the Society, Comstock *"was always deputized"* by the sheriff. "He liked the arresting and all that sort of thing," said Mr. Sumner with a rather tolerant smile; "I don't care much for it, myself."

This special power with which Comstock was vested by the State was questioned, but never with sufficient force to revoke the act which conferred it. Mr. Courtlandt Palmer, a lawyer of distinction, made a most earnest criticism of the Comstock laws in the New York Observer of April 26, 1883, in which he said, "These laws tend to confine administration to certain classes. The district attorneys are the only democratic prosecutors of the cases under consideration by the Society for the Suppression of Vice." He spoke of the Society as endeavoring to "supplement and supplant the regular process of law by confiding the machinery of justice to special and irresponsible associations upon whom is conferred the unrepublican power not only of prosecution but of arrest."

In selecting representative passages from Comstock's own words, space forbids the giving of any large number. Choosing is a bit difficult, because Comstock's style of expression was so redundant, so abounding in detail, that concise quotations are not easy to provide. Selections pertinent for our present use are first those which indicate his general psychology,—the mental background on which he built his career, and then those which show the place he gave in his own mind to the subject of the control of conception.

The titles of his two sizable books are "Frauds Exposed" and "Traps for the Young." They constitute his life story in his own words. He was proud of having arrested 3873 persons, of whom 2911 were convicted. Satan was to him a very live foe. He dramatized the combat with this enemy to the highest degree. His reports of his adventures in making arrests read, not like the recapitulations of a dutiful officer or of a trained welfare worker, but rather like the dime novels which he so roundly denounced. He wound up the story of one of his captures in Boston with the exuberant exclamation, "Then ho for the Charles St. Jail!"

Satan to him was apparently the representative of obscenity; and obscenity, if not completely synonymous with sex, was very nearly so. At any rate the idea of obscenity as an enveloping enemy permeated every other subject that Comstock touched upon. It seems as if he felt that practically all roads led to obscenity, and that it was his duty to block all the roads. In the opening chapter of "Traps for the Young," after describing in detail box traps, fox traps, partridge snares, bear traps, rat traps, etc., he says: "Satan adopts similar devices to capture our youth and secure the ruin of immortal souls . . . the love story and cheap work of fiction captivate fancy and pervert taste . . . rob the child of the desire to study. . . . There are grave questions in the minds of some of our best writers and of our most thoughtful men and women, whether novel reading *at its best* does not tend downward rather than upward. . . . Light literature then is a devil trap to captivate the child by perverting taste and fancy." (The italics are ours.)

Fear was apparently as great a factor in Comstock's make-up as his vigor. He seemed to have little trust in the

self-reliant virtue of people of any age and almost none at
all in young people.   Here is another bit from the "Traps":
"Drop into the fountain of moral purity in our youth the
poison of much of the literature of the day, and you place
in their lives an all pervading power of evil.   A perpetual
panorama of vile forms will keep moving to and fro before
the mind, to the exclusion of the good.   *Evil influences burn
themselves in.*   Vile books and papers are branding irons
heated in the fires of hell, and used by Satan to sear the
highest life of the soul.   The world is the devil's hunting
ground, and children are his choicest game."

The Chapter headings which Comstock chose for the
"Trap" book are indicative of his mental trend.   This is
the list:

    I. Household Traps (light literature)
   II. Household Traps continued (newspapers)
  III. Half-dime Novels and Story Papers
  IV. Advertisement Traps
   V. Gambling Traps
  VI. Gambling Traps continued
 VII. Gambling Traps continued
VIII. Death Traps by Mail (Obscenity)
  IX. Quack Traps
   X. Free Love Traps
  XI. Artistic and Classical Traps
 XII. Infidel and Liberal Traps
XIII. More Infidel and Liberal Traps

In a letter read on the fortieth anniversary of his Society, Comstock said, "Let me emphasize one fact, supported by my nearly forty-two years of public life in fighting
this particular foe.   My experience leads me to the conviction that once these matters (obscenity) enter through the
eye and ear into the chamber of imagery in the heart of a
child, nothing but the grace of God can ever blot it out."
One wonders how lively Comstock's faith in the grace of
God may have been, inasmuch as he was willing to give it

so few chances to function. His own words and his actions
seem to invite the conclusion that his fear was considerably
larger than his faith.

In an interview with Comstock by Mary Alden Hopkins
in Harper's Weekly of May 22, 1915, he asserted that the
"existing laws are a necessity in order to prevent the down-
fall of youth of both sexes. . . . To repeal the present laws
would be a crime against society and especially a crime
against young women." Apparently he felt that young
women were especially weak in their power of resistance to
obscenity. In the same interview, speaking of the Federal
law, Miss Hopkins asked, "Does it not allow the judge considerable leeway in deciding whether or not a book or a picture is immoral?" "No," replied Mr. Comstock, "the highest courts in Great Britain and the United States have laid
down the test in all such matters. What he has to decide
is whether or not it might rouse in young and inexperienced
minds, lewd or libidinous thought."

Here we have at least one key to Comstock's attitude.
It is evident from the passages already quoted and from his
record as a prosecutor of many persons of fine standing,
good taste and high ideals, that the things which he thought
could arouse lewd or libidinous thought were legion, and he
detected that quality in all manner of instances when it was
not at all evident to others. For example, he describes on
page 163 of the "Traps," how he made an arrest at what
he called a "free love convention." He said he slipped into
the hall unnoticed, and "looked over the audience of about
250 men and boys. I could see lust in every face." If ever
anyone had a sturdy belief in the fall of man, it would seem
to be Anthony Comstock. Human nature to him was innately corrupt, or at least so large a part of it was corrupt
that, in his view, it warranted suppressive laws applying to
everyone whether clean minded or depraved. This attitude
was plainly indicated in a later part of the above mentioned

interview with Miss Hopkins. She says, "I was somewhat confused that Mr. Comstock should class contraceptives with pornagraphic objects which debauch children's fancies, for I knew that the European scientists who advocate their use have no desire at all to debauch children. When I asked Mr. Comstock about this he replied,—with scant patience for "theorizers who do not know human nature." "If you open the door to *anything,* the filth will all pour in and the degradation of youth will follow." (The italics are ours.)

That he dramatized himself as a hero and a martyr seems quite evident all through his career. When the Hearing was held on the petition to repeal his laws shortly after they were passed by Congress, he describes the scene thus: "As I entered the Committee room, I found it crowded with long-haired men and short-haired women, there to defend obscene publications, abortion implements and other incentives to crime, by repealing the laws. I heard their hiss and curse as I passed through them. I saw their sneers and looks of derision and contempt. . . . It was not the blackening of my reputation that weighed me down, so much as the possibility that one of the most righteous laws ever enacted should be repealed or changed."

His faculty for reading into things what was in his own mind was never more clearly demonstrated than by his description in "Frauds Exposed," of the work of the National Liberal League, an organization formed in 1876, one of the chief objects of which was the repeal of the Comstock laws. He devoted a long chapter to it, writing in great detail of how "Infidelity" had "wedded Obscenity." At the first convention of this League, Comstock says, they "espoused the cause of nastiness" and "considered means to aid and help the vendors of obscene publications." He asks, "Do infidelity and obscenity occupy the same bed? Are they appropriately wedded?" He declared that at this convention they "proclaimed the banns between Infidelity and Obscenity in the following resolution, which he quotes as overwhelming proof of the nastiness of the organization:

Resolved, that this League, while it recognizes the great importance and absolute necessity of guarding by proper legislation against obscene and indecent publications, whatever sect, party, order or class such publications claim to favor, disapproves and protests against all laws which by reason of indefiniteness or ambiguity, shall permit the prosecution and punishment of honest and conscientious men for presenting to the public what they deem essential to the public welfare, when the views thus presented do not violate in thought or language the acknowledged rules of decency; and that we demand that all laws against obscenity and indecency shall be so clear and explicit that none but actual offenders against the recognized principles of purity shall be liable to suffer therefrom.

Resolved, that we cannot but regard the appointment and authorization by the government of a single individual to inspect our mails with power to exclude therefrom whatever he deems objectionable, as a delegation of authority dangerous to public and personal liberty, and utterly inconsistent with the genius of free institutions."

"Therefore," says Comstock triumphantly, "I charge that they defended obscenity for the love of it."

A welter of adjectives was an outstanding feature of Comstock's books. He gives his reader very little opportunity to judge for himself as to the character of the crimes his prisoners committed, for he does not state concretely what they were, but he uses phrases about them such as "diabolical trash," "carrion," "leprous influences," etc. On only two pages opened at random in the "Traps" book, were noted the following words and phrases: "moral vulture," "terrible talons," "cancer," "damns the soul," "frightful monster," "homes desolated," "whited sepulchres," putrefying sores," "immense cuttlefish," "turgid waters," "jackal," "pathway of lust," "lust is the boon companion of all other crimes." In the light of modern psychology, this choice of language carried to such extreme, betrays fear and sex obsession to a degree that would hardly seem to fit a man for sound service either as a law maker or as an enforcer of the law.

However, now let us take a look at Comstock through the eyes of others. His biographer, Rev. C. G. Trumbull, wrote of him thus toward the close of his career: "Mr. Comstock today likes to dwell upon what he calls the wonderful goodness of God in those early days of the fight for purity. And it *is* a story of God's work, not man's, when we remember that it was an unknown clerk, twenty-eight years old, who had hardihood to go to the national capitol with the idea of getting his own convictions put into legislative action; that finding there two or three other bills pending in the same field (one regarding the District of Columbia instigated by the Washington Y. M. C. A., the other by Gen. Benjamin F. Butler, amending the inter-state commerce law to prohibit sending obscene matter from one State to another) he stuck to it till all were merged in a single bill of five comprehensive sections; that he prayed his bill through both houses in the strenuous closing hours of the winter session, and that he returned home under appointment as a staff officer of a cabinet officer of the United States!" Dr. Trumbull adds that the Y. M. C. A. "gladly paid the expenses of the Washington campaign."

That is the viewpoint of a friend and admirer. Now we turn to the slant from which Comstock was viewed by one of his most severe critics, D. M. Bennett of New York, editor of "The Truth Seeker" and a leader in the agnostic and liberal group known as the National Liberal League. Comstock alluded to this organization as "debauching the public conscience," and as "this pestilence which drags down and never builds up." Comstock secured the arrest and conviction of Bennett on an obscenity charge, and Bennett wrote at great length several articles to prove that Comstock's real animus against him was religious intolerance, and that the obscenity charge was a subterfuge. Bennett served a sentence of several months in the Albany jail. In his pamphlet, "Anthony Comstock,—His Career of Cruelty and Crime," published in 1878, Bennett says: "Far be it from the writer to deny him any of the good he has performed, though the means by which he reaches his ends, and by which he brings the unfortunate to punishment, are not such as good men approve. Among a certain class of vile publishers, he has accomplished a reform that must be placed to his credit, but the system of falsehood, subterfuge and decoy-letters that he has employed to entrap his victims and inveigle them into the commission of an offense against the law is utterly to be condemned.

"The want of discrimination which he has evinced between those who were really guilty of issuing vile publications, and whose only object was to inflame the baser passions,—and those who published and sold books for the purpose of educating and improving mankind, has been a serious defect with this man. While he suppressed much that is vile, he has to a much larger extent, infringed upon the dearest rights of the individual, thus bringing obloquy and disgrace upon those who had a good object in view. And upon those who in a limited degree were at fault, he has been severe and relentless to a criminal extent. He has evinced far too much pleasure in bringing his fellow beings into the deepest sorrow and grief; and under the name of arresting publishers of and dealers in obscene literature, he has caused the arraignment of numerous persons who had not the slightest intention of violating the rules of propriety and morality."

Further on in the same pamphlet, Mr. Bennett says: "Being questioned at a public meeting in Boston, May 30, 1878, where he was endeavoring to organize a branch of the Society for the Suppression of Vice, he was asked the following question by the Rev. Jesse H. Jones, a Congregational minister: (1) 'Did you, Mr. Comstock, ever use

decoy letters and false signatures?'   (2) 'Did you ever
sign a woman's name to such decoy letters?'   (3) 'Did you
ever try to make a person sell you forbidden wares, and
then when you had succeeded, use the evidence thus obtained
to convict them?'   To each of these questions Comstock
answered, 'Yes, I have done it.' "

One of the best known instances of Comstock's decoy
system for securing arrests was that of William Sanger.   As
described by Mr. Sanger in a written statement prepared
for his trial and which the judge allowed him to present
only in part, the circumstances were these.   On December
18, 1914, a man had come to his studio, saying that his
name was Heller, that he was a dealer in rubber goods and
sundries, that he had read Mrs. Sanger's booklets "What
Every Girl Should Know" and "What Every Mother Should
Know," that he had enjoyed reading them and was in sympathy with her work.   He then asked for a copy of the
pamphlet on family limitation.   Mr. Sanger said he had
none.   The man insisted, asked if Mr. Sanger could not find
one around somewhere for him, as he wanted to reprint it
in several languages for distribution among the poor people
he worked with and with whom he did business.   Mr.
Sanger took the trouble to hunt about among his wife's belongings and found a single copy of the booklet, which he
gave to the man.   A month later Anthony Comstock appeared and arrested him for having given contraceptive information contrary to the New York law.   The man who
came to him as Heller, was in reality Comstock's spy.   His
real name is Bamberger and he is still in the employ of the
Society for the Suppression of Vice.   Mr. Sanger stated
that Comstock on the day of his arrest had offered to get
him a suspended sentence if he would plead guilty.   Mr.
Sanger declined and he was sentenced to thirty days in the
workhouse, which sentence he served.

This leads logically to the next consideration, namely,

the place which Comstock gave in his own mind, and thus in the laws he framed, to contraceptive knowledge. And again let him first speak for himself. In a letter which he wrote on April 28, 1915, to Mrs. Clara Gruening Stillman, Secretary of the National Birth Control League (the first national birth control organization in this country) he said: "A letter dated April 23, 1915, purporting to have been sent out by you as Secretary of the Birth Control League, has been referred to this office. In this letter you say, 'The law, both State and Federal at present makes it a crime even for physicians to give information as to methods, no matter how essential such knowledge may be to the physical and economic well-being of those concerned.' There is not a word of truth in this statement, and you cannot find a single case, since the enactment of these laws, to justify such a statement on the part of your League." Further on in the same letter he says: "I challenge your League to produce a single case where any reputable physician has been interfered with or disturbed in the legitimate practice of medicine. Do not make the mistake, however, of classifying the quack, and the advertiser of articles for abortion and to prevent conception, with reputable physicians.

"You cannot safeguard the children on the public streets by turning loose mad dogs, neither can you elevate their morals by making it possible for them to sink themselves to the lowest levels of degradation, by furnishing them with the facilities to do so. . . . I shall be very happy to meet a representative of your League at any time and show the laws in detail and the necessity for their existence precisely as they are; and I can assure you that they will not be changed either by the Legislature or by Congress."

Again in the interview with Comstock by Mary Alden Hopkins, from which quotation was made above, he responded to her question, "Do not these laws handicap physicians?" by this reply, "They do not. No reputable physi-

cian has ever been prosecuted under these laws. .... A
reputable doctor may tell his patient in his office what is
necessary, and a druggist may sell on a doctor's written
prescription drugs which he would not be allowed to sell
otherwise."

This is a baffling sort of mind to deal with. For either
he did not fully realize the meaning of the laws which he
himself framed, or else he hopelessly confused the actual
wording of the laws with his personal choices as to the
people to whom they should apply. For the Federal law
as enacted by Congress and as it stands to this day contains
no exemptions or qualifications whatever, as to the giving
of contraceptive information. It is just as criminal for a
conscientious doctor to send needed contraceptive instructions to a patient, as for a sex pervert to send an advertisement of contraceptive means with his depraved literature.
And in the District of Columbia and in at least seventeen
States it is just as criminal for a reputable doctor to instruct
a patient, even verbally in the privacy of his own office, as
it is for any low-minded person to peddle pornographic stuff
containing contraceptive directions. The language of these
laws is perfectly plain; they are flat, sweeping prohibitions
and apply to everybody alike. It would seem almost incredible that Comstock should have dared to assert that
they did not forbid physicians, or to assume that because
neither he nor the government officials chose to enforce the
laws on all offenders, that the laws, therefore did not apply
to all offenders. But perhaps his mind was so focussed on
the fact that he had not himself prosecuted any physicians
whom he considered reputable, that he assumed the impossibility of their being prosecuted by any one.

However, it seem doubtful that he was quite so oblivious
as to the plain import of the law's words, as to sincerely
think they did not mean what they said. It seems more
likely that in planning laws as he did with their sweeping

prohibition, he was instinctly acting to provide himself and those who were involved in the enforcement of the laws, with an absolutely unhampered opportunity to decide who among the law-breakers were "reputable" and what was "obscene," "immoral," etc., and to pick out whatever offender they chose for prosecution. He knew of course that complete enforcement was utterly impossible, but to be able to make the law effective here and there according to his own will, was a use of power that was very evidently to his liking.

Comstock's moral code on this matter would seem then to boil down to about this, if he had presented it, shorn of all his adjectives and settings: some perverts use contraceptives, therefore the law should not allow any one at all to secure them or know anything about them, and besides, as most of those who are not perverts can't be really trusted anyhow, hearing about or seeing contraceptives would be pretty sure to make them go to the devil, especially young people, so the complete prohibition is after all the safest; however, if you happen to be decent and you can manage to get a doctor to give you some information, I will not have the doctor prosecuted, that is, provided he is *my idea* of reputable.

The question for present day citizens is as to whether they want to retain laws framed by a man holding such a concept, and which laws accurately reflect that concept, or whether they want to revise the laws to reflect the concepts held by the majority of the fairly normal wholesome-minded people of this country who have long ago proved their belief in the control of conception by practicing it,—that is, as best they can under the handicap of the laws.

While Comstock's successor, John S. Sumner, still echoes the Comstock code, it is a considerably fainter echo than it was a decade ago. Sumner's expression of his views is much less hectic and denunciatory than was Comstock's. He concedes more than Comstock ever did, and a good bit more than he did himself, when he first fell heir to Comstock's mantle.   There are many New Yorkers who recall the crowded meeting at the Park Avenue Hotel when Sumner was one of the speakers in a symposium on birth control, and how he asserted that there was no need for birth control knowledge in the world, because if there got to be too many people, there would always be war, famine and disease to counteract overpopulation, and how he was hissed for saying it.   Contrast that attitude of mind with what he wrote some eight years after, in his previously quoted letter of January 23, 1923, to Senator Cummins, in which he said, "There is no disputing the fact that parents should use judgment in bring children into the world.   Questions of health, heredity, environment and economic situations make this desirable. . . .   The ever increasing number of social and medical organizations and combinations of the two that have to do with the welfare of the people are and will be more and more in position to refer the individual family to the proper authoritative sources of contraceptive information, under the present laws, namely to the proper maternity hospital or physician."   Of course Mr. Sumner knows quite well that "under the present laws" in many of the States this information could not be lawfully given as he describes, and he also knows that no physician anywhere in the whole country could lawfully send any such instructions to a patient by mail.   Later in the same letter is this sentence: "The imparting of information regarding this subject should be confined to reputable physicians after personal investigation of the particular case."   (Just how the laws could be expected to operate to compel the persons to whom the information is imparted by the physician to keep it a dead secret, Mr. Sumner does not state.)

These quotations suggest several important points for discussion in connection with propositions for revising the laws, but their usefulness for the moment is to provide documentary evidence that both Comstock and Sumner, the latter more than the former, have not looked upon the present laws as a means of preventing doctors from giving and normal people from using contraceptive information. That they would prevent it, if enforced, they could not deny, but that only proves conclusively that the present laws are very ill-framed, even from the view points of Comstock who initiated them, and of Sumner who, as yet, does not want them changed.

CHAPTER III

IS ENFORCEMENT POSSIBLE?

Relatively few indictments in over fifty years: Ulterior motive in many of those: Post Master General Hays's leaning toward revision: Post Master General Work's gesture of enforcement: Clinic reports and medical research data unlawfully published and mailed: Misleading criminal advertisements go unpunished: Government itself breaks the law: Forbidden books found in Congressional Library: Senators and Congressmen willing to break law, but hesitate to revise it.

AS noted in the last chapter, it was admitted by Comstock that the law as he framed it, was essentially hypocritical with regard to the giving of contraceptive information. According to his own records, relatively few of the many arrests he procured, were for giving contraceptive information, and a very small part of those were for that thing pure and simple, but usually because contraceptive information was involved in other matters or when it was the most convenient means of "getting" a person, whose arrest was wanted for other reasons. Apart from the prosecutions instigated by Comstock and his successor John Sumner, the government officials in over fifty years have made almost no effort to indict those who have broken the law,—certainly no effort that is at all commensurate with the sweeping and unqualified character of the prohibition. Diligent search has been made for a complete list of the indictments in the United States for the giving of contraceptive information, but so far, no such list has been found, and to extract those few cases from the multitudinous court records would be almost a life work. But enough search has been made to amply warrant the statement that prosecutions have been few, and that infringements have now mounted into the millions. And, like Comstock, the regular government officials, have also been prone to utilize infringements of the contraceptive ban as an excuse for indicting people whose arrest was wanted otherwise.

In Comstock's own book "Frauds Exposed," in which he recapitulates his forty years of work in jailing people, the space given to contraceptive cases is only about five per cent of the whole book. His greatest emphasis and the bulk of his effort went to suppressing general obscenity, gambling and fraud. A similar proportion is found in his later book, "Traps for the Young." In D. M. Bennett's pamphlet on "Anthony Comstock,—His Career of Cruelty and Crime," 27 cases of prosecutions initiated by Comstock are chronicled. Of these only 5 are indictments involving the giving contraceptive information. In Theodore Schroeder's monumental volume, "Obscenity and Constitutional Law," which reviews obscenity prosecutions covering several generations, there are found to be less than ten in which contraceptive information was the probable main factor in the case. Appendix No. 4 gives a list of 23 more or less well known cases of prosecutions with the disposition of each case. Several of them were instances where the birth control issue was obviously used as a cloak for an ulterior motive in causing the arrest.

This was notably true in the recent case of Carlo Tresca, the editor of an Italian paper, "Il Martello," published in New York City. The facts in the case were, briefly, these: In the absence of Mr. Tresca the advertising manager of the paper printed a two-line, small-print advertisement of a pamphlet on birth control methods, by an Italian physician, a publication which has been very popular and which has been considerably advertised in other Italian papers; the

Post Office notified "Il Martello" that the advertisement rendered the paper unmailable as it was an infringement of Section 211 of the Federal Criminal Code; the two lines were accordingly deleted and the edition was mailed; but shortly afterwards the advertising manager was arrested and imprisoned for the infringement; Tresca also was arrested, though he had not known of the advertisement at the time it was printed; he was sentenced to "a year and a day" in the Federal penitentiary at Atlanta. During and after his trial some illuminating testimony was brought forth, showing that the birth control charge was merely a handle for political persecution; it seems that Tresca in his paper and otherwise had vigorously opposed the Mussolini regime in Italy, and the Italian Ambassador while making a dinner address in Washington had stated that there was a certain Italian paper in New York which ought to be suppressed; "Il Martello" was subsequently subjected to many petty annoyances from the Post Office, culminating in the arrest of the editor on the birth control charge, *after* the offending advertisement had been promptly deleted in accord with the Post Office notification; during the trial the prosecuting attorney admitted that the complaint against the paper regarding the advertisement had come from the office of the Italian Ambassador.

These facts became widely known. Many letters of protest from well known citizens were sent to the Attorney General and President Coolidge, with the result that the President commuted the sentence to four months.

It is noteworthy that Tresca's original sentence was the longest of any on record in recent years, perhaps in any years, for this sort of offense. The maximum of five years in jail and $5000 fine seems never to have been imposed since the law was enacted. In the 23 cases listed in Appendix No. 4, the imprisonment terms were as follows: one for a year and a day, one for six months, two for sixty days, four for thirty days, three for fifteen days, and seven were freed or their cases were dismissed. As to fines,—there was one of $1000, one of $100, three for $25 and one for $10. It is told of a judge in the middle west that he imposed a fine of *one cent* in a case of this sort; the prisoner was guilty under the law, so the judge did his duty, but he apparently also took occasion to register his opinion of the value of the law. Margaret Sanger, the best known among birth control "criminals," has served but thirty days in jail, all told, though arrested four times. Her nine indictments under the Federal law in 1914 were dismissed. She was freed after arrest in Portland, Oregon, as was also the case when she was arrested at the Town Hall in 1921 in New York when the police broke up the meeting before any one had spoken at all. The charge in this instance was not giving contraceptive information, but disorderly conduct and resisting the police. The one sentence she served was that imposed for opening her "Brownsville" Clinic for giving contraceptive instruction in New York in 1916. For at least ten years past, the local police, the Post Office authorities and John Sumner, Comstock's successor, have known that Mrs. Sanger was infringing both Federal and State law on a more or less wholesale scale, but there has been no prosecution. In a lengthy letter which Sumner wrote to all the members of the U. S. Senate Judiciary Committee on February 18, 1921, and in an almost identical letter which he wrote to Senator Cummins on January 23, 1923, in which he pleaded for the continuance of the present laws without change, he twice mentions the fact that Mrs. Sanger had "published a pamphlet entitled ———— which described various methods and articles for the prevention of conception and their methods and use." Yet he has not had her arraigned, as he would be in loyalty bound to do, if his belief in the present laws were thorough-going, as he assured Senator Cummins it was. In his letter Mr. Sumner gives the title of the pamphlet, which makes him also an offender against the Federal law, Section 211,—which forbids anyone to mail any "written or printed card, letter, circular, book, pamphlet, advertisement, or notice of any kind giving information, directly or indirectly, where, how or of whom or by what means conception may be prevented." Mr. Sumner in his letter told the Senator "of whom," and he did so "directly." He knew he did not risk arrest for doing it even though his act was a "crime.'" In all probability neither should we, if we were to print the title of the pamphlet; but as both the author and the publisher of this book are interested in the discussion of sound legislation on this subject rather than in possibly precipitating one more indictment under this good-for-naught law, we discreetly leave the title blank.

The conclusion seems quite obvious, judging by the light penalties, the few prosecutions, and the blinking at infringements, that the government, like most citizens, takes this law very lightly and has no idea of living up to its obligation to enforce it. There has been one Post Master General however in recent times who has made at least a gesture toward enforcement, and another who made at least a gesture toward a common-sense revision of the laws.

The latter was Post Master General Hays, and had he not resigned his position to go into the moving picture business, perhaps the United States laws on this subject would now be renovated so as to be more a reflection of the people's beliefs and more true to American ideals. The circumstances in the summer of 1921 were most propitious. Mr. Hays had made several public statements that he was convinced that the Post Office should not operate a censorship system. He had put himself on record in unmistakable terms, and his words had been widely published by the newspapers. So in August of that year, an interview with Mr. Hays was secured by the Director of the Voluntary Parenthood League, and the question laid before him as to whether the time was not more than ripe to remove this particular censorship from the laws which govern the Post Office. He received the suggestion with marked cordiality, saying that it was very timely, for he had about reached the conclusion that it was his duty to submit to Congress a recommendation for the revision of all the Post Office laws which had any bearing on censorship. He asked for a résumé of all pertinent data on the laws affecting birth control knowledge, and he also asked for specimens of good books and other publications on the subject such as are used abroad. On being told that it would break the law (Section 211) to mail such publications to him, he said, "Oh no, I wouldn't want that done, send them by express." "Can't be done," was the answer, "because Section 245 forbids that also." "Well then," said the Post Master General, with an appreciative smile, "by messenger." The parcel was forthwith delivered to him by that method. But even that was unlawful, for according to Section 312, it is a crime in the District of Columbia to "lend or give away," or to have in one's "possession for any such purpose, any book, pamphlet," etc. Mr. Hay's plan to submit a revision to Congress was never carried out, perhaps because his retirement from office followed too shortly after to make it practicable. And apparently he was not of a mind to leave his plan behind him as a recommendation to his successor, Dr. Hubert Work, former President of the American Medical Association. Judging by later developments, it would have been futile for him to have done so.

When Dr. Work took office, he lost no time in making his gesture about the enforcement of the obscenity laws; for only a few days after he became Post Master General, the following official Bulletin was conspicuously posted in all the Post Offices of the Country:

IT IS A CRIMINAL OFFENSE

TO SEND OR RECIVE OBSCENE OR INDECENT MATTER BY MAIL OR EXPRESS

The forbidden matter includes anything printed or written, or any indecent pictures, or any directions, drugs or articles for the prevention of conception, etc.

The offense is punishable by a *Five Thousand Dollar Fine or Five Years in the Penitentiary or Both.*

Ignorance of the law is no excuse.

For more detailed information on this subject read Sections 480 and 1078 of the Postal Laws and Regulations, which may be consulted at any post office.

The Birth Control Herald of July, 1922, commented as follows on this Bulletin:

If Dr. Work intends to enforce the laws, it does him credit. But suppose he undertakes to prosecute all infringements? The relatively low birth-rate in well-to-do families indicates wholesale breaking of this law. How is he going to enforce it? Will he trail these several million respectable, influential parents till it is discovered how they learned the science of family limitation?

There are about twenty-five million families in the country and, roughly speaking, ten million of these are the well-to-do—those above the income tax exemption. Suppose a tenth of these can be convicted of having secured by mail or express the contraceptive information on which their own family limitation is based. The authorities would hardly imprison a whole million. It would mean "standing room only in the jails." An alternative would be to fine them. One million law breakers, fined $5000 each would provide Uncle Sam with a handy five billion in these days, when the national debt stands at about eight billion. But, like the jail idea, this might be a bit impracticable! What alternative is there then? The million malefactors might be *acquitted,*—but that would make the officers of the law look silly. So,—there it is, a large problem staring at the new Postmaster-General. How will he meet it?

Dr. Work's Bulletin says "Ignorance of the law is no excuse." Similarly also, difficulty of enforcement is no excuse for him. So long as the law stands he and the Department of Justice must carry it out, or else be unfaithful and inefficient public servants.

Possibly Dr. Work might welcome a practical suggestion, namely, that he promptly request Congress to change this futile law which has encumbered the Statute books since Anthony Comstock got it passed in 1873. Any law that can't be generally enforced should be repealed.

How about the families below the income tax exemption? There are over ten million of these also,—and they are the ones against whom this laws works successfully. Their ignorance and poverty prevent their securing the knowledge which the well-to-do get in spite of the law.

This Bulletin of Dr. Work's may well serve as a reminder that common fair play for these ten million families demands that Congress shall change the laws at once. Perhaps also this Bulletin will rub it into the minds of the well-to-do parents that the knowledge by which they space their own babies and regulate their own family birth rate is legally classed as "obscene and indecent." How much longer do decent people care to submit to this governmental insult?

Several of the best doctors who have done years of research work on methods of controlling conception, are ready *now* to write books. One of the foremost publishing firms of America, with offices in London also, is ready to bring out an American edition of the excellent book on the control of conception, by a famous British scientist,—a book which has gone through five editions in England, and is the generally accepted text-book on the subject. Our law prevents.

It is time to do something beside talk. It is time to *end the need for the birth control movement,* by demanding that Congress change the laws.

However neither under Dr. Work's administration nor that of his successor has there been evidence of any effort even remotely approaching a genuine attempt at enforcement. In fact infringements seem to be blinked at more and more as time goes on. Very significant and interesting recent infringements are the publication and circulation of the reports on contraceptive methods used in the clinic operated by the Research Department of the American Birth Control League (Dr. James F. Cooper, speaking at the recent Hearing on a bill to amend the New York law stated that 5000 copies of this report had been sold to physicians); also the report by Dr. ———— of the research work on contraceptive method, carried on by the New York Committee on Maternal Health, and published in the "American Journal of ——— and ———." The latter report makes a survey of all the chief methods in use at present both here and in Europe, with descriptions, and an estimate of their relative merit. In neither instance has there been any prosecution or suppression, though the publishers are forthright and knowing breakers of the law. If the well known physician who wrote the article in the above indicated medical journal and the also well known medical publisher who issues the magazine can break the law so frankly, and not be arrested, it would seem as if we might well do likewise and give their names, but we leave them blank, not only to avoid the remote possibility of arrest, but to give the reader one more means of realizing that the present laws are legal nonsense.

Another striking feature of the present situation is the blatantly misleading advertisements of publications which contain no contraceptive information, but which are advertised as if they did. Margaret Sanger's book, "Woman and the New Race" has been repeatedly advertised by book dealers who lean to sensationalism, as if it contained instruction in positive methods of birth control. Various garish phrases have been used, such as "This daring woman has at last told the real truth about birth control," etc. The little pamphlet, "Yes,—but," published by the Voluntary Parenthood League, to answer the objections and misunderstandings which were current several years ago, was reprinted by a sensational publisher without permission, and advertised as if it gave contraceptive information. Thousands of poor worried parents have bought these books,—some of them, as the writer well knows, having spent very hard earned pennies to do so,—only to find that they had bought another "gold brick." The book did not give the one thing they wanted, and which was their sole reason for ordering it. One of the worst of such instances is an advertisement which appeared recently in one of the popular humorous weaklies. It is exactly reproduced below:

The writer took the trouble to go to the address given, and to inspect the book. It contained no contraceptive information whatever. It distinctly *did not* tell "all about birth control." The man in charge of the office, and who had been responsible for the advertisement, admitted its deliberately fraudulent character, and frankly said he used this method to make the book sell better, that personally he did not like sensationalism, but "one must make a living somehow." The writer also inquired of the publisher of the paper in which the advertisement appeared, as to how they dared and why they cared to publish this sort of thing. Apart from the question of taste, it would seem as if the advertisement warranted indictment for obtaining money under false pretenses for one thing, and for another that it gave "notice" . . . "directly" . . . "where" to obtain (contraceptive) birth control information. The result of the inquiry was a letter from the publisher's office saying that the contract for the advertisement would not be renewed. It also stated that every advertisement that had ever appeared in their paper had "first had the endorsement of the U. S. Postal authorities." This last is surely an amazing statement. If the Postal Authorities are willing to approve such crass, vulgar and fraudulent advertisement of birth control information under the present laws, it would seem not a wild thing to demand a change of the laws, so that advertisements could be open, dignified and honest, as they may be in England, for instance. One of the largest and most reliable of the British chemists advertises its service by the simple words, "All birth control requirements, ——— and Co. ——— London." One of the best known medical publishers of England announces the important new book on the control of conception by Dr. ———, with the natural straightforwardness that belongs to any scientific subject. One of their advertisements reads as follows (except for the omissions compelled by our laws) :

———

ITS THEORY, HISTORY AND PRACTICE

A Manual for the Medical and Legal Professions

By ——————, D.Sc., Ph.D.,
(Fellow of University College, London)

Contents:
    Author's Preface
    Introduction by Sir William Bayliss, F.R.S.
    Introductory Notes by Sir James Barr, M.D., Dr. C. Rolleston, Dr. Jane Hawthorne and "Obscurus."

Chapter
    I. The Problem To-day.
    II. Theoretical Desiderata—Satisfactory Contraceptives.
    III. Indications for Contraception.
    IV. Contraceptives in Use, Classified.
    V. Contraceptives in Use, Described and Discussed.
    VI. Contraceptives in Use, Described and Discussed. (cont.)
    VII. Contraceptives for Special Cases.
    VIII. Some Objections to Contraception Answered.
    IX. Early History of Family Limitation.
    X. Contraception in the Nineteenth Century.
    XI. Contraception in the Twentieth Century.

Sir William Bayliss says:
"It cannot fail to be a real service."

Dr. Rolleston says:
"I predict a great success for the work, and I wish to record my thanks to the author for her pioneer work in preventive medicine."

This Book Is the First Manual on the Subject and Is Packed with Both Helpful and Interesting Matter, and Much That Is New and Noteworthy.

Order from your Bookseller or direct from the Publishers:

———

Just so long as our laws remain as they are, just so long will they induce and encourage an atmosphere of hectic unwholesome excitement about a subject that should be merely a part of the general fund of hygienic knowledge which humanity utilizes for its welfare. And just so long will that unwholesome atmosphere be reflected in vulgar advertisements, which can not be properly antidoted by dignified decent advertisements of the proper sources for contraceptive information and means.

Our government not only blinks at the numerous infringements of the laws which ban birth control information, but the government itself breaks the law. Government officials themselves are guilty of flagrant violations, but no one puts them in jail. There are some very striking instances.

The Library of the Surgeon General in Washington, which is open to the public, has received and is loaning to readers the November issue of the American Journal of ———— and ———— published by the ———— Company of ————. It contains a report by Dr. ———— on methods of controlling conception. To mail the magazine from ———— where it was published, and to receive and loan it in Washington, are criminal acts under the law.

The Congressional Library has received from England and has loaned to readers the volume entitled ———— by Dr. ————, published ———— London. It is the previously mentioned manual for the medical and legal professions and is considered one of the best and most comprehensive works on the subject in the world. To pass the book through the customs, to transport it to Washington, to list it in the Library catalogue and to lend it to readers are all criminal acts under the law. This same volume has been borrowed by several members of the Judiciary Committee,—again a criminal act. But not a single government employee has been apprehended for these "crimes," although the offenses were clean cut infringements of the law. Dutiful and full enforcement would mean the jailing for a five-year term of a score or so of the government employees who are involved.

A still more significant fact is that members of Congress who have vehemently opposed the Cummins-Vaile Bill (to remove the words "preventing conception" from the obscenity laws) have actually had the presumption to ask the writer of this book (while working for that measure) to get for them copies of "some of this forbidden literature." One of them added, "I'll see that you are not prosecuted." An instantaneous refusal brought a rather shame-faced expression to his countenance. He was a member of the Judiciary Committee, to which the bill had been referred. It would be interesting to know whether this member, who has flatly said he would vote against the bill, would be willing to confess before the Committee that he was quite willing to break the law, but unwilling to change it, and equally unwilling to insist on its enforcement.

Enforcement is all too evidently a farce, and will never be anything else so long as the present laws are retained. A legal house-cleaning seems the only hope for putting the country on either a self-respecting or a democratic basis, so far as this subject is concerned. An editorial in the Washington Post has said what needs to be said on how to have laws respected:

"The enforcement of all law is necessary to the existence of the States and the United States. The alternative is anarchy. But all law must be constitutional, in accordance with the people's expressed will. The first duty of all citizens and of Congress is to ascertain the will of the people. The second is to enforce and obey it."

PART TWO

WHAT CHANGES IN THE LAW HAVE BEEN PROPOSED?

CHAPTER I

THE TWO FIRST FEDERAL EFFORTS

The big repeal petition of 1876 started by National Liberal League: Comstock's obscenity exhibit wins again: Sanger arrests crystallize growing movement for repeal of law: National Birth Control League founded March, 1915, first organization of the sort in the United States: Repeal bills drafted: Petitions circulated: Noted English sympathizers help.

THREE years after Congress enacted the Comstock bill, thousands of citizens started a petition for its repeal. The number has been variously estimated at from 40,000 to 70,000. Comstock credits it with the latter figure in his book, "Frauds Exposed." The petition was initiated and the signatures collected by the National Liberal League. There was much publicity concerning it, and mass meetings were held in various cities. It was presented to Congress, early in 1878 by a Committee of Seven, consisting of Robert G. Ingersoll of Illinois, Chairman, Charles Case of Indiana, Darius Lyman of Ohio, J. C. Smith of Massachusetts, Jonathan B. Wolff of New York City, W. W. Jackson of Washington, D. C. and J. Weed Corey of Penn Yan, N. Y., Secretary.

The petition was a comprehensive protest against the whole spirit and content of the Comstock laws, as un-American, unjust and unwise. Section 4 of the Petition read in part as follows: "Your petitioners further show that they are convinced that all attempts of civil government whether State or National, to enforce or favor particular religious, social, moral or medical opinions, or schools of thought or practice, are not only unconstitutional but ill-advised, contrary to the spirit and progress of our age, and almost certain in the end to defeat any beneficial objects intended.

"That mental, moral and physical health and safety are better secured and preserved by virtue resting upon liberty and knowledge, than upon ignorance enforced by governmental supervision.

"That even error may be safely let free, where truth is free to combat it. That the greatest danger to a republic is the insidious repression of the liberties of the people.

"That wherever publications, pictures, articles, acts or exhibitions directly tending to produce crime or pauperism are wantonly exposed to the public, or obtruded upon the individual, the several States and territories have provided, or may be safely left to provide, suitable remedies.

"Wherefore your petitioners pray that the statutes aforesaid may be repealed or materially modified, so that they cannot be used to abridge the freedom of the press or of conscience."

The petitioners asked Congress for action on the petition, and the Committee of Seven requested a Hearing on it. After more or less prodding, the House Committee on the Revision of Laws, granted a Hearing. Comstock's characteristic version of the insistence by the Committee of Seven on being heard, was: "After six weeks of plotting and scheming they at last secured a hearing."

Comstock and Samuel Colgate, one of the earlier officials of the Society for the Suppression of Vice were the only ones appearing against the petition. Comstock described the event in his book "Traps for the Young," and says that the House Committee reported its belief that the "statutes in question do not violate the Constitution, and ought not to be changed." He also wrote of it in his letter of April 28, 1915, to Mrs. Clara Gruening Stillman, Secretary of the National Birth Control League, from which quotation was made in Chapter Two of Part One. This is the way he pictures it: "When the National Defense Association in 1876, secured a petition 2100 feet long, containing 60,000 names, and presented it to Congress, following it up with the most infamous attacks upon the efforts to enforce, all that was required, in the face of all their opposition, supported as they were at that time by the public press throughout the country, was to lay the facts before the Congressional Committees and submit to them the circulars which showed to them the system of the business then being carried on, cursing the boys and girls of this country and leading them from the paths of virtue, and both committees reported against any repeal or change whatever." This decision of the Committee was made on May 1, 1878.

If it was true, as Comstock says, that the press of the country at that time was with the petitioners for the repeal, it is a point worth bearing in mind. Evidently the actual sight of a collection of smutty circulars describing sex depravity stampeded the Committee on the Revision of Laws in the same way that it had the Committee on Post Offices and Post Roads, when it reported favorably on the Comstock bill three years previously, so that it blotted out of mind every other consideration, except that obscenity must be made unmailable. It prevented any serious thought about the injustice of depriving the normal majority of access to scientific knowledge. All sorts of strange things are done under the impetus of alarm, and fear can upset the judgment of the best of men on occasion. But now that the country has had the benefit for over half a century of the fears which Comstock so successfully planted in the Congressional mind, the question is how quickly can there be a restoration of calm judgment, and of democratic faith in the people.

After the failure of this petition, many years elapsed be-before any concerted effort was again made to have Congress correct the Comstock blunder. In the meantime, of course the laws were increasingly broken and increasingly unenforced, so far as the circulation of contraceptive information was concerned. Comstock utilized the laws for his campaign to suppress fraud and general obscenity, and he occasionally included a prosecution against someone for giving contraceptive information, but that offense, per se, and uninvolved with obscenity or liberalism, formed a very small part of his total activity. However it was two of these latter arrests which touched off the park that flamed into what has been called in late years, the American birth control movement. These were the arrests of Margaret Sanger and of William Sanger, her husband. In September, 1914, Mrs. Sanger was indicted on nine counts under the Federal law, for mailing her pamphlet on family limitation. Mr. Sanger was arrested the following January, by means of Comstock's decoy system, for giving away a single copy of the pamphlet, as already described in Part One of this book. Previous to Mrs. Sanger's arrest, there were many people who had become tremendously interested in her activity and who were deeply stirred by her righteous indignation that the poor mothers among whom she had worked as a district nurse, were without any sort of adequate scientific information on the control of conception, and by her burst of generous impulse when she determined to get the information to the working people on a large scale, no matter what the laws forbade, and no matter what hardship it might involve for her. Some of the specially interested people helped Mrs. Sanger with funds for her project and by securing mailing lists and so forth. She compiled such information as she could find, and a very large edition of the pamphlet was sent out. She then went to Europe in order to find out more about contraceptive methods in Holland and in England, and to publish some new revised pamphlets before facing trial under Federal indictment.

During this period the conviction was rapidly growing in the minds of many who had been moved by Mrs. Sanger's gallant zeal, that the time had come to remedy the situation fundamentally by organizing a movement to get the laws revised. Mrs. Sanger's arrest added greatly to the strength of this conviction. To tolerate the necessity for a succession of martyrdoms such as appeared likely to occur as the sequel of Mrs. Sanger's spirit and her notable defiance of the law, seemed folly, if by dint of vigorous concerted effort the laws could be changed, so that no one would have to brave martyrdom. This conviction crystallized into action in New York City in March, 1915, when a meeting was held at the home of Mrs. Clara Gruening Stillman at which the National Birth Control League was organized. Mrs. Sanger was then abroad. On her return shortly afterward, she was invited to be a member of the Executive Committee of the League. She declined, stating that she did not think it wise to be officially a part of any organization, as she was likely to have to go to jail, and she did not want her mishaps to involve the activity of others, also that she felt it to be her particular function to break the laws rather than to spend effort at that time in trying to change them. Her point of view was characteristically expressed in her leaflet called, "Voluntary Parenthood," which was published by the League. Describing her feeling at the sight of the suffering due to unintended and unwilling motherhood, she said, "I felt as one would feel if, on passing a house which one saw to be on fire and knew to contain women and children unaware of their danger, one realized that the only entrance was through a window. Yet there was a law and penalty for breaking windows. Would anyone of you hesitate, if by so doing you could save a single life?"

The declaration of principles adopted by the National Birth Control League read as follows:

"The object of the Birth Control League is to help in the formation of a body of public opinion that will result in the repeal of the laws, National, State or local, which make it a criminal offense, punishable by fine or imprisonment, or both, to print, publish or impart information regarding the control of human offspring by artificial methods of preventing conception.

"The Birth Control League holds that such restrictive laws result in widespread evil. While they do not prevent contraceptive knowledge of a more or less vague or positively harmful character being spread among the people, these repressive laws do actually hinder information that is reliable and has been ascertained by the most competent medical and scientific authorities, being disseminated systematically among those very persons who stand in greatest need of it.

"This League specifically declares that to classify purely scientific information regarding human contraception as obscene, as our present laws do, is itself an act affording a most disgraceful example of intolerable indecency.

"Information, when scientifically sound, should be readily available. Such knowledge is of immediate and positive individual and social benefit. All laws which hamper the free and responsible diffusion of this knowledge among the people are in the highest degree pernicious and opposed to the best and most permanent interests of society."

The National Birth Control League then, constituted the first organized and sustained effort in America to concentrate on the repeal of the specific prohibitions regarding the circulation of birth control knowledge. The petition to Congress in the seventies, had included contraceptive knowledge in its protest, but was not circulated for that reason alone. It was a protest against the general content of the

Comstock laws. The National Birth Control League at once set about the publication of literature urging the repeal of the laws, and circulated petition slips for the amendment of both State and Federal laws, which read as follows:

TO THE STATE LEGISLATURE

As a voter of this State, I hereby urge you to secure the amendment of the penal law, so that giving information concerning methods of birth control by the avoidance of conception may no longer be classed as a crime in the laws of this State.

Name ....

Address ....

TO THE CONGRESS OF THE UNITED STATES

As a voter, I hereby urge you to secure the amendment of the Federal Penal Code so that the transportation of information concerning methods of birth control by the avoidance of conception may no longer be classed as a crime in the laws of this country.

Name ....

Address ....

A committee of three lawyers, members of the National Birth Control League, drafted the amendments which the League advocated for the Federal statutes and for the New York State statutes. The provision was similar in both cases. It first removed from the obscenity statutes the words "preventing conception" wherever they occurred; then added a clause to the effect that information as to or means for the control of conception are not, per se, obscene or of indecent use. For Section 211 of the Federal law, this added clause read as follows: "But no book, magazine, pamphlet, paper, letter, writing or publication is obscene, lewd or lascivious, or of indecent character, or non-mailable by reason of the fact that it mentions, discusses or recommends prevention of conception, or gives information concerning methods or means for the prevention of conception; or tells how, where, or in what manner such information or such means can be obtained; and no article, instrument, substance or drug is non-mailable by reason of the fact that it is designed or adapted for the prevention of conception, or is advertised or otherwise represented to be so designed or adapted." (The statutes with the proposed amendments in full are given in Appendix No. 5.)

It was not only within the United States that interest in amending our laws grew apace. The matter got the attention of a very thoughtful and distinguished portion of the British public also. When Mrs. Sanger was in England, she met Dr. Marie C. Stopes (subsequently the founder of the first birth control clinic in England) who was deeply indignant at the situation threatening Mrs. Sanger by virtue of the American law. This feeling found expression in a letter which Dr. Stopes wrote and sent to President Wilson, and which was signed by several other well known English citizens. It reads as follows:

September, 1915.

To the President of the United States,
    White House,
        Washington, D. C.
SIR:
    We understand that Mrs. Margaret Sanger is in danger of criminal prosecution for circulating a pamphlet on birth problems. We therefore beg to draw your attention to the fact that such work as that of Mrs. Sanger receives appreciation and circulation in every civilized country except the United States of America, where it is still counted as a criminal offense.
    We in England passed, a generation ago, through the phase of prohibiting the expressions of serious and disinterested opinion on a subject of such grave importance to humanity, and in our view to

suppress any such treatment of vital subjects is detrimental to human progress.

Hence, not only for the benefit of Mrs. Sanger, but of humanity, we respectfully beg you to exert your powerful influence in the interest of free speech and the betterment of the race.

We beg to remain, Sir,
Your humble servants,

(Signed by) : Percy Ames, L.D., F.S.A., Sec., Roy. Soc. Liter., London

William Archer, Dramatic critic and author

Lena Ashwell, Actress Manager

Arnold Bennett, Author and Dramatist

Edward Carpenter, Author of "Towards Democracy," etc.

Aylmer Maude, Author of "Life of Tolstoy"

Gilbert Murray, M.A. Oxford, LL.D. Glasgow, D.Litt. Prof. Greek, Oxford

Marie C. Stopes, D.Sc., Ph.D., Fellow and Lecturer, U. Coll., London

H. G. Wells, B.Sc., J.P., Novelist.

In this connection it may be added that the nine Federal indictments against Mrs. Sanger were presently dropped. Whether it was due in part to the weight of such messages as this, is not definitely known. But the fact remains that the prosecution for the most forthright, intentional and wholesale defiance of the Federal law that had ever been undertaken up to date was not carried through to a conclusion. A fair interpretation of this act would seem to be that the government itself did not deem the Comstock laws in this regard, as worth enforcing.

CHAPTER II

BEATING AROUND THE BUSH WITH STATE LEGIS-
LATION

Interest caused by Mrs. Sanger's arrest caused much activity despite war-time conditions: First repeal bill initiated by National Birth Control League in New York Legislature: Law makers mostly in favor privately, but publicly opposed or evasive: Dr. Hilda Noyes's experiment in New York village proving that ordinary people want laws changed: Legislator justifies State repressive laws so long as Federal law stands as example: Bills introduced in New York, California, New Jersey and Connecticut: The "doctors only" type of bill appears: Further limitations: Efforts toward freedom stimulate reaction toward stiffer repression in Illinois, Pennsylvania and Virginia: All fail: Fallacy that limited bills win legislators more than freedom bills.

THE year 1915, as noted in the preceding chapter, saw the lines laid down for the repeal of the Comstock blunder. The next four years saw considerable progress in the way of rolling up expressed approval of amending the law, also considerable fumbling around as to just how to go about it. The fact that these four years included the war period had a good deal to do with the latter. All social and civic projects suffered a similar sort of stalling. Sporadic bursts of agitation were easier and more in keeping with the general disorganization of life than was any steady, constructive, fundamental, organized activity. That so much was accomplished under such untoward circumstances, is indication of the vital hold which the idea of doing something about the birth control situation, had upon the thinking public. Or perhaps one might better say the feeling public, for if as much force had gone into thinking as has gone into feeling on this subject, the question of repressive legislation would have been settled long ago.

However, there can hardly be doubt that the great wave of emotional interest which grew apace after the first Sanger arrests, and particularly after Mrs. Sanger's second arrest for opening her contraceptive clinic in 1916, was useful in that it developed a ferment from which presently some clear consistent procedure might be forthcoming which would end the need for agitation. Local birth control organizations sprang up in many parts of the country, many of them being the results of Mrs. Sanger's lecture tours. It was but natural that local groups should tackle State laws first, as most of the associations were loosely or feebly organized and slimly financed, and Washington seemed far away and Congress formidable. The National Birth Control League was somewhat in this status also. Its headquarters were in New York, and most of its active members lived there, though it had members scattered all over the country, and there were co-operating committees in several cities.

So it happened that its first actual legislative move was a State bill undertaken in Albany in the winter of 1917. It was a straight repeal bill to remove the words "preventing conception" wherever they occurred in the obscenity statutes, and to add a new clause providing that contraceptive information, per se, was not to be deemed obscene, and that means used for the control of conception were not, per se, to be deemed of indecent use. (See Appendix No. 5 for the full wording.) The subject of the scientific control of conception was thus to be rescued from its legally formed association with obscenity, and to be safeguarded against the possible assumption that the subject was in itself obscene,— an assumption which judges or juries of certain mental caliber, might well make, in view of its long connection in the

law with indecency.   The bill was introduced both by a
Democratic and a Socialist member of the New York Legislature,—an obvious disadvantage in an overwhelming Republican body.   A Hearing was held, but the bill was killed
in Committee.   The pattern of the reaction of the legislative mind to this sort of proposition, which afterwards
was to become so familiar to those working for the repeal
of these laws, was for the first time clearly visible.   The
reasons for the levity, the stupidity and the irrelevance of
the legislators were not so well understood then as they
came to be a few years later.

But in this very first legislative try-out, the incongruity
which in subsequent legislative efforts become most striking,
was already evident,—namely, that what the various legislators said one by one in conversation with those who went
to Albany to work for the bill, was quite different from what
they said for publication or in the Committee room.   Individually, a large proportion of them readily admitted that
birth control already existed, that the laws were not enforced and could not be enforced, and each one thought
that it would not hurt *him* to know all there was to be known
about the subject; but they were far from willing to say anything of the sort publicly, or to take that stand actively in
the Legislature.   Instead they went far afield with all sorts
of hypothetical conjectures, and professed all manner of
deep convictions that this knowledge, if lawfully accessible
would be dangerous to morals, a menace to the race and an
assault upon religion.   This incongruity will be more fully
dealt with in a later chapter on "Why Congress has been
slow to act."   For the moment, it is enough to give a mere
glimpse of legislative reaction to birth control bills.   The
divergence between private opinion and public action was
again accentuated the following year when the National
League sent a set of queries to all the New York candidates
for Congress and the legislature, regarding their opinion of

the proposed change in the laws. The replies showed many more in favor of the bill than had been found in Albany the preceding year. In fact not a single adverse answer was received. And of those who replied eight per cent were in favor, eleven asked for more light on the subject, and only three side-stepped the question.

Yet that rather encouraging indication did not prevent a repetition of the same incongruous actions when a year later, the National Birth Control League made another effort in Albany. It had to be checked off to educational work, for it did not result even in the introduction of the bill. The Legislators of the majority party, the Republicans, shied off from sponsoring the bill, apparently because, in part at least, it had previously been introduced by a Socialist and because some of the speakers at the Hearing had been "radicals." This served as a first rate excuse, in the days when any excuse was a good excuse. However, the educational work of that session was worth while both for the Solons and for the proponents of the bill. It was particularly illuminating for the latter, as subsequent events will show. The writer of this book had charge of the work in Albany that year, and a picture of the situation there is given in the following extracts from an article she wrote at the time for "The Birth Control Review" (March, 1919).

The Legislators of New York seem to be par excellence the leisure class. They have achieved a six hour week! In these days of battling for forty-eight and forty-four hour weeks, that is something of an achievement.

They convene Monday evening, usually with a two-hour session, and on the three succeeding mornings, with sessions from one and one-half hours to ten minutes in length. When out of session some few of them are in committee but the majority are fled—it is hard to know where.

For the ordinary citizen with a bill in hand which it is desired to have introduced, such a situation is a problem. The whole session is only ninety days—and with legislative week-ends lasting from

Thursday noon till Monday evening, the time available for interviewing members and securing desirable sponsors for the bill is reduced to an appalling minimum.

However, like the public, the legislators are surely moving on toward an understanding of what the Birth Control movement really means. Out of the twenty-seven members interviewed in the last few days, only one declared himself positively opposed to the bill, and he decided after ten minutes' discussion, that he might perhaps be open-minded after all.

It seems to take about three-quarters of an hour to answer all the objections the average legislator can think of, and leave him wondering what he can do next to live up to his preconceived notion that he was opposed. More often than not, they end by cordially admitting that they really have no arguments against the bill— merely a vague aversion to the consideration of the subject as a matter of public or legislative responsibility.

They mostly ask the same questions and voice the same fears about removing the law which tries (so vainly) to suppress birth control information.

They say, "Yes, but if everybody knows how to avoid having children, there won't be any children!"

Then we carefully iron out their fears by showing them that prophecies as to how it *might* work out are not worth so much as testimony on how it *does* work out. We tell them of Holland and New Zealand, the two prize birth control countries of the world,— how Holland has had a ratio of increase in population next to that of Germany and Russia—that New Zealand is a garden country for babies, that they make a fine art of motherhood there, with their wonderful chain of maternity hospitals, and that Holland and New Zealand have the lowest general and baby death rates in the world.

With the race suicide bogey out of the way, they go on to their next fear, which is that there will be a terrifying drop in moral standards if contraceptive information is easily available. Then again we reassure them by citing the other countries which have no shocking repressive laws like ours, but which nevertheless do not show any records of general promiscuity and unbridled excess, or of sexual laxity among the young. We go further, and remind them that if it be true that the mass of our American young people would have so little moral anchorage that we should fear to trust them with knowledge, then something is awfully the matter with us of the older generations who have reared them, and that it is for us to hasten to develop a keener sense of responsibility for the education of *all* young people, as well as those of our families. And they all respond to this appeal. They would obviously feel ashamed not to.

Another idea they advance with confidence is that "practically everyone can now get the information who really wants it." And we reply, "Well if that be true, and the law is already so much of a dead letter as that, then why hesitate a moment to repeal it?" But we tell them, of course, that it is not true that everyone has the information who wants it, as is proven by the incessant stream of desperate, ill and unhappy people who clamor for it, also that much of the information which is now illegally and secretly circulated, especially that which is verbal, is inadequate, unscientific and even harmful, and that it is bound to be so till the medical schools include this subject in their curricula and until the doctors can give the information without evading the laws.

Then they resort to the cynical conclusion that it wouldn't do much good to repeal the laws anyway, because the rich who oughtn't to use the information would do it even more than they do now, and the result would be still fewer children, while the "ignorant poor," who ought to use it, wouldn't, and the horde of "undesirables" would go on increasing just the same.

And again we present the instance of Holland where the rich average larger, and the poor, smaller families than any other country in Europe. And we gently remind them that the use of contraceptives can never be made compulsory, nor can anyone frame legislation which will open the eyes of the selfish rich to the joys and values of parenthood. These results can come from education, not from legislation. All that the laws can do is to give freedom of access to knowledge, but the wise use of knowledge is a matter of mental, moral, and spiritual growth.

And they admit that too.

They look very serious and responsible by the time they arrive at saying, "Yes, but what methods do you propose to teach?" Some of them even assume that somehow or other we think the law itself can *establish good methods!* Whereupon we make it plain that the question of methods is the sphere of the medical scientists, that it is not for us laymen to presume to teach, and much less is it possible for the laws to determine methods. All the laws can do is to give freedom to the scientists to give the world the knowledge that has been locked in their brains and only given out surreptitiously on occasions. And all we ask is the opportunity to help to make the knowledge of the scientists accessible to all who need it.

Their final question is "who wants these laws changed, where is the demand?" We tell them that practically everyone wants it who understands it, and that brings up a most significant phase of the birth control movement, which has a unique psychology, in that the mass of people who want information and want the laws changed so they can get it, do not and will not shout their wishes from the housetops. The nature of the subject is one which largely inhibits an *articulate* demand. But that the majority of the people want it, and are ready to say so, if they can do it without being conspicuous is remarkably well proven by the article elsewhere in this issue, entitled: "Do the People Want It?"

We never fail to impress it on the legislative mind that in the last analysis the present laws are absolutely inconsistent with the principle of freedom to know, to think and to do, on which this country is supposed to be founded and that it is outrageous that the government should attempt to place any barriers between the people and knowledge; that the government may rightly discipline people whose abuse of knowledge infringes upon the rights of others, but there it must stop. It can not curb the freedom of citizens to know all there is to know.

And they admit that, too.

They are amusing in their demands upon us as to the proper way of winning the change of the laws. Some tell us, "You just show us enough demand for this thing and it will go through. If the people want it, let them speak up." Others say, "Now, if you would only see that this thing is *quietly* accomplished, with no noise, no public hullabaloo, no newspaper headlines, no publicity, etc., it would be a simple matter for us to put this bill right through as a matter of obvious public welfare."

At a guess, probably two-thirds of those already interviewed will vote in favor of our bill.

In the light of much subsequent experience with the workings of the legislative mind the writer considers that last sentence an innocently rash prediction. It should have said "are in favor of our bill," rather than "will vote for our bill." For this has proved to be one of the questions on which belief and voting, also private practice and public statement, can be poles apart.

There could perhaps be no more fitting place than here

to quote the above mentioned article "Do the People Want It?"

Here is a slice of public sentiment out of the middle of New York State.

Dr. Hilda Noyes, an expert on eugenics and baby feeding, and incidentally the mother of six splendid intentional children, went to a district in Oneida County, where she did not personally know the people, chose at random two streets at right angles to each other and visited fifty married women in succession.

She explained to them just how the New York law reads which prohibits Birth Control information. Most of them did not know that it is a part of the obscenity laws and is entitled "Indecent Articles" or that it is utterly sweeping in its provisions, so that even a mother can not legally inform a daughter on her marriage as to how to have her children come at intelligent intervals. They only knew in general that whatever one knew about this subject must be learned secretly.

She told them how it was proposed to change this law, and asked them if they preferred to let the law remain as it is and has been for over forty years, or to change it.

Forty-eight out of fifty said "change it."

By far the most significant bit of experience gleaned from the legislative effort of that year was what one of the more thoughtful members of the New York Legislature said, when he was asked to consider introducing the bill. "Why do you come up here asking us to consider a bill of this sort when our National laws set us the example they do on this subject? You say yourself that Congress decided that this information was not 'fit to print'; very well then, go down to Washington and get Congress to reverse itself, and then you will have a talking point when you come to us." It may have been merely his particularly clever form of excuse for not doing anything, but there is no gainsaying that he hit upon a rather unanswerable point. It was undeniably true that the action of Congress in passing the Comstock bill in 1873 had influenced practically all of the States to follow suit. The fact that the New York law on this subject preceded that of Congress by a year, only indicates that Anthony Comstock happened to live and do his work in New York. Both he and his biographer, the Rev. C. G. Trumbull, said emphatically that his campaign of suppression would have been a relatively futile effort without a comprehensive Federal law. Comstock used keen sense when he determined to secure not only the particular power to suppress the transportation of obscene literature that a Federal law would give, but also the very great impetus to his whole campaign which the Federal example would stimulate in the States, for further means of suppression.

The seed thus planted bore fruit within three months, by the organization of a new association, the Voluntary Parenthood League, the immediate object of which was the repeal of the Federal prohibition. And within six months the Congressional work was started in Washington. The story of the Federal bill is however the subject of the next chapter.

The purpose of this chapter is to survey the attempts at State legislation which have been made both before and after the work on the Federal bill was begun, and to make an appraisal of their value toward the securing of freedom of access to contraceptive knowledge.

More endeavors have been made in New York than in any other State. The efforts which preceded the campaign for the Federal bill have already been noted. Following that time, Committees, acting under the leadership of Mrs. Sanger, went to Albany, during the legislative sessions of 1921, 1923, 1924 and 1925. Bills were introduced in the three latter years, and the ones introduced in 1923 and 1925 reached the stage of a Hearing. No bill came to a vote on the floor of either the Senate or the Assembly.

This series of bills beginning in 1921 initiated a marked change in the policy of the legislation. Instead of a straight repeal act, limited bills began to appear, that is with qualifications which would restrict those who could give contraceptive information to certain groups only, and those who could receive it to certain classes only. And another very striking change appeared also, namely that the subject of the control of conception was not removed from its classification with indecency, but the bill was framed to permit certain people to give and to receive the information without being subject to the penalties for indecency that would still apply to all others who give it. That is, the right of access to knowledge as a fundamental principle was abandoned and was replaced by the idea of permits and privileges; and the platform that scientific truths are not per se indecent was replaced by the inference that scientific facts are decent only when stated by certain people and are otherwise indecent, or are at least classed with prohibited indecencies.

This is the proposed legislation which has come to be called, for short, the "doctors only" kind of bill. But other limitations than those applying to doctors have been included. With these successive efforts in the New York Legislature, restrictions were added almost every year that a bill was introduced. The measure first put forward in 1921 limited access to contraceptive information to that given by physicians or registered nurses; then the nurses were dropped out, and no doctor could give information unless the individual applied to him personally for it; and by 1923 the still further restriction was added that access to the knowledge was lawful only for those who were married or who had secured a license to marry. These later New York bills were drafted by Prof. Samuel McCune Lindsey of the Legislative Bureau of Columbia University. The full wording of the latest draft is given in Appendix No. 6. All of them leave the main body of the obscenity statutes just as it stands with its blanket prohibition of the giving of contraceptive information by anyone to anyone, in any way whatever; the amendment in each of these bills is an addition to the release act of 1881, Section 1145 of the Penal Code, which states that an article prescribed by a physician to cure or prevent disease is not "of indecent or immoral nature or use"; these added parts merely declare the doctor's act in giving information or in making a prescription for a preventive to be "not a violation of this article." In other words the old law of 1881 whitewashed the thing prescribed by the doctor, and the proposed amendment whitewashes the doctor for prescribing it. But it leaves the whole subject of knowledge about the control of conception, still in the category of crime and indecency. The doctor merely becomes a privileged character within this category.

Under the same leadership, similar bills have been introduced into the legislatures of Connecticut in 1923 and 1925 and of New Jersey in 1925. In Connecticut the bill, beside restricting access to information to those who get it directly from a doctor or a registered nurse, contained a section to repeal the old law which forbids the *use* of contraceptives, the law which has been the prize joke of the American birth control movement. Appendix No. 7 gives the wording of the Connecticut bill. The wording of the New Jersey law is notably absurd, in that it forbids anyone to be obscene "without just cause," and then adds a clause forbidding anyone even to make a recommendation *against* the use of contraceptives, or to give information in any way as to how or where "any of the same may be had or seen or bought or sold." The amendment proposed by the American Birth Control League merely adds this sentence: "The contraceptive treatment of married persons by duly practicing physicians, or upon their written prescription, shall be deemed a *just cause* hereunder." Appendix No. 8 gives the wording in full. Hearings were held in both Connecticut and New Jersey but in neither State was the bill allowed to reach a vote in the Legislature. In Connecticut the Committee advised against changing the laws "at this time."

In California, a bill was introduced in 1917 by Senator Chamberlain and Assemblyman Wishard to remove the words "prevention of conception" from Section 317 of the Penal Code, which is entitled "Advertising to Produce Miscarriage." Dr. T. Perceval Gerson was head of the citizens committee which initiated the effort. A hearing was held, but the bill died in Committee, although it had excellent endorsement from some of the women's organizations and from the Los Angeles Obstetrical Society, which passed the following resolution:

Resolved, that it is the sense of the Los Angeles Obstetrical Society that the effort being made in California by intelligent men and women on behalf of scientific birth control is worthy of support by all having the best interests of society and its individuals at heart.

Resolved, that the attention of the public be strongly drawn to the fact that this movement for scientific birth control has no relation to the production of abortion or miscarriage, which in fact it aims to eliminate.

Resolved, that this Society composed of physicians and surgeons earnestly engaged in discussing those aspects of medical science chiefly in the domain of obstetrics, gynaecology and pediatrics, respectfully petition the California Legislature to amend by elimination that portion of Section 317 of the Penal Code, reading, "or for the prevention of conception."

Further be it resolved, that this Society at this date, go on record as unqualifiedly approving such propaganda for birth control by scientific contraceptive measures, because of the universal benefits that will accrue.

It is noteworthy that this Resolution by doctors did not take a "doctors only" stand. A loop-hole in the California law has allowed the establishment of a "Mother's Clinic." It started its service in Los Angeles early in 1925 with Dr. H. E. Brainerd, former President of California State Medical Association as Medical Director, and a clinical and consulting staff of eight other physicians. The California statute forbids anyone to *offer* his services in any way, to aid in the prevention of conception, but it does not forbid the giving of information if *asked*.

In three states effort has been made to introduce laws when none existed before, forbidding the giving of contraceptive information, or to make existing laws still more repressive. Illinois and Virginia were instances of the former, and Pennsylvania of the latter sort. These bills all died in Committee, thanks to the strong protests they aroused from representative and influential citizens.

The Illinois measure was modelled upon the New York law, and was introduced in the winter of 1918. Professor James A. Field of Chicago University and Dr. Charles Bacon of the Chicago Medical Institute, both of them representing the Chicago Citizens Committee (for birth control) appeared at the Hearing against the bill. The Illinois Medical Society also sent Dr. C. L. Taylor and Dr. Deal to oppose it. Effective lobbying was done before the Hearing, and by the time that was held, the interest was so great that the session was carried over into the evening. In conversation with members of the Legislature individually, it was evident that they had no idea that the passage of the measure would mean that it would be unlawful for anyone, even themselves to get the simplest and most commonly used sorts of preventive such as are sold at all drugstores. Professor Field and the physicians enlightened them on this and many other points, with the result that the bill was not reported out. It is significant that the way a measure of this sort is presented to a legislator makes such a difference in his opinion of its merit. A proposition to make obscenity less prevalent wins sympathy at once, and if there is no mention made of the fact that it also will forbid the securing of scientific hygienic information for utilization in normal private life, the obscenity point carries the legislator along to approve of the bill. But when he sees the real facts about such legislation, he thinks twice, and thinks sanely. It seems like a sound guess that Congress would likewise have thought sanely, if Comstock and those who rushed his bill through had given the members a chance to know the actual scope of the bill, and think twice. What a pity that no Professor Field and no level-headed doctors were on hand at the time to have saved the day in Washington in 1873, as they did in Illinois in 1918!

The effort to put Virginia into the black list of states which prohibit contraceptive knowledge and means, was a very recent one. In the legislative session of 1924 a bill was introduced which, according to the *Birth Control Review,* would make it "unlawful to sell, give away or possess any appliance or instrument for the prevention of conception." The Committee on Moral and Social Welfare to which it was referred received may protests. So also did the sponsor of the bill, Mr. Ozlin, with the result that he withdrew it from the calendar, before it was discussed at all in the House.

In Pennsylvania there have been two attempts to make the law more suppressive than it already was, which was quite bad enough, for Pennsylvania is one of the states which make it a crime to tell any one, to have in one's possession, to publish or to advertise contraceptive information, and it prohibits the circulation of contraceptive means. The first effort was in 1917, the Stern bill, which far surpassed any previous legislation in comprehensive suppression, for it even prohibited "attempting to impart" any "knowledge or information *tending* to interfere with or diminish the birth of human beings." If opinions have differed widely as to what constituted obscenity, fancy how they would differ on what "tended" to diminish human birth. Isador Stern, the sponsor of the bill, told Mrs. Alice Field Newkirk of the Main Line Birth Control League, that he wanted to "make it impossible to discuss birth control anywhere in Pennsylvania,—in parlors or in public halls." The bill was quietly moved along through legislative routine till it passed both houses and it was not until the eleventh hour that many people knew of its existence. Then protests began to pour in to Governor Martin Brumbaugh, urging him to veto it. This he did with a very strong and forthright letter, in which he called it "one of the most reactionary enactments attempted in years." The veto is here given in full, as it contains several points of importance in considering the question as to what kind of laws on this subject Americans may want:

COMMONWEALTH OF PENNSYLVANIA

Executive Chamber

HARRISBURG, JULY 16, 1917.

I file herewith, in the office of the Secretary of the Commonwealth, with my objection, House Bill No. 1643, entitled "An act forbidding the advertising, publishing, selling, distribution, or otherwise disseminating or imparting, or attempting to disseminate or impart, knowledge or information tending to interfere with or diminish the birth of human beings in the Commonwealth of Pennsylvania; defining it as a misdemeanor and defining its punishment."

The bill forbids the publishing or otherwise disseminating of any information by anybody concerning birth control in this Commonwealth. The existing laws judiciously concern themselves with this matter. This bill does not. It is by far the most drastic bill in regard to birth control in this country. It is, by like token, one of the most reactionary enactments attempted in years.

The popular mind is filled—if I may judge this mind from the many letters and telegrams before me—with all sorts of misconceptions concerning the provisions of this bill. It is not a bill to regulate the size of families, but an attempt to prevent anyone from doing anything "to interfere with or diminish the birth of human beings in this Commonwealth." Just how anyone could diminish birth is not made manifest. The language is viciously vague and indefinite in the extreme. The bill might be construed to punish those that oppose the marriage of the insane or feeble-minded. Indeed the Commonwealth's own acts in segregating these unfortunates in institutions like Laurelton would come under the penalties of this bill. It is, in other words, counter to the whole current of modern social endeavor, and as has been pointed out, could be made a convenient club for the black-mailer. It would deny a physician the duty, in defined cases, of advising his patient. It would seal the lips of mothers and fathers in counselling their children. It is an attempt to do by legislation what should be done by education. It would be a law more honored in the breach than in the observation. It is impracticable and unenforceable.

For these reasons the bill is not approved.

MARTIN B. BRUMBAUGH.

While it is not feasible to agree with Governor Brumbaugh that "existing laws judiciously concern themselves" with this matter, one may well forget that sentence in his letter in view of the forceful truth of his last three lines. In differentiating the proper sphere of education from that of legislation, he rendered a signal service. So also when he emphasized the folly of proposing laws which are unenforceable.

Two years later, the very same bill was re-introduced into the Pennsylvania legislature, by Representative Hickernell. But it did not become a law this time either, thanks to the vigorous work of Mrs. Newkirk and some of the Harrisburg members of the National Birth Control League. The bill had been referred to the Committee on Health and Sanitation, of which a physician was chairman. He was of the opinion that such efforts to stamp out birth control belonged in the class of "freak legislation," and he let his opinion be known in the Committee. The bill was never reported out.

Just as limited or "doctors only" bills were proposed after the first freedom bills were introduced in the states, so also were they proposed for Federal legislation after the trail was first blazed to Congress by a Federal freedom bill. The special import of the "doctors only" idea in Federal legislation will be discussed in the next chapter in connection with the story of the Federal bill, through fundamentally the same considerations apply both to state and to Federal law.   At this point it may be clarifying to take a look at certain happenings when the "doctors only" bills were being urged upon the state legislators, and when the public was being urged to support them.

Those who have pushed these efforts to achieve limited legislation have repeatedly asserted that if the giving of information were restricted to physicians, and possibly to nurses, and given only to the married, and only on individual application, the legislators would be much more likely to pass the measure than if it were an "unlimited bill," that is, a bill which would place this knowledge on just the same basis as any other knowledge so far as the law is concerned. But prophecy is one thing and history is another, and the facts in this case do not seem to bear out the prophecy.

When the first of the "doctors only" bills was proposed to the Albany Solons in 1921, two years after the second straight repeal effort of the National Birth Control League, the pattern of legislative objection was not altered one whit. The situation was precisely the same as it was when the bill asked for freedom for all instead of special privilege for a group.   Then and at every subsequent effort in any state, the newspapers have reported the same old set of remarks made by the few articulate objectors,—that it meant race suicide, that it was the same thing as abortion, that it would induce immorality, and that it was against religion.   As late as the Hearing of 1925 the legislators were still offering the objections of "race suicide," and that it would "increase immorality."   But in the later years the race suicide bogey has become rather less prominent,—perhaps because Holland and New Zealand were so often quoted that the legislators were obliged to concede that birth control and large increase in the population were compatible and often coincident.   In every single instance there has been the same vulgar levity on the part of a few legislators, the same noisy objections from another small portion of them, and the same favorable or tolerant opinions on the part of the majority, but privately expressed rather than publicly, and the same hesitation to let their votes in Committee or in the legislatures reflect either the facts in their own private lives or their real opinion.

What is chiefly in the mind of the legislators is not the terms of the bill at all, but the thought, "What will it do to me and my career if I have anything to do with such an embarrassing subject as this?" These reactions are admitted as true and are so reported, even by those who have been working for the limited legislation. For instance, in the *Birth Control Review* of May 1921, the "Legislative Committee formed by the Margaret Sanger group to push a measure or amendment affecting the present birth control laws in the State of New York" reported their effort to secure a sponsor for the "doctors only" bill drafted by Professor Lindsay. The report reads in part, as follows: "The Chairman of the Health Committee seemed the most logical and best informed man to approach and he was also a member of the medical profession. He stated his absolute opposition to the repeal or amendment of the Birth Control laws and his determination to fight any such measure."

So the "Doctors only" concession was quite wasted on him. The report continues: "Several of the important men of the Assembly assured us of their approval of this class of legislation, but did not care to introduce the amendment."

The "doctors only" bait did not tempt them either. But hope was rewarded, the report says, for

On a second visit to Albany, W. F. Clayton of Brooklyn expressed his approval and belief in the great benefit of such measure. . . . He would sponsor the amendment he said. . . . After three weeks' delay and two more visits to Albany, a letter was received from him saying: "I very much regret, but after consulting with some of the leaders of the Assembly, I have been strongly advised not to offer your bill.   I am told it would do me an injury that I could not overcome for some time.   Now, while I am more or less in favor of your bill and if you can get someone else to favor it, and they are able to get the bill out of Committee, I am strongly inclined to think that I would be one to vote for it, providing it had a ghost of a show.   I regret that I have had this bill so long, but I sincerely hope my keeping the bill this length of time will not in any way prevent you from finding someone to introduce it."

So the "doctors only" idea was no help here.   The report proceeds:

Our next effort was to get sufficient and important backing from the medical profession of the State to influence Dr. Smith of the Assembly to sponsor the amendment.   We did get the Health Board of the Academy of Medicine of New York City to endorse it.   (The Academy later denied having endorsed this particular bill.)   Doctors of national reputation wrote urging Dr. Smith to introduce it. Thousands of slips were signed urging the measure.   The amendment in the form of petitions, was signed by doctors, judges, economists, editors, department of health officials, nurses, settlement workers, prominent philanthropists, clubs and club women and many hundreds of voters in the State of New York.   All these data were presented as a background to the lawmakers.   *Dr. Smith refused on the ground of levity from his associates.*

It seems to take more than a "doctors only" inducement to offset the psychology which envelopes any proposition to legislate on birth control.   The report concludes as follows:

Mrs. Sanger and the Committee approached Mr. Jesse of New York, a very able and prominent member of the Assembly and also conversant with the righteous and urgent need of such legislation. He considered the question and finally decided that he could not sponsor the amendment.   This decision was given after he had consulted party leaders in New York.   Personally many of these law makers believe the measure of great benefit, but the party whip cuts too deeply for courageous action.   The Session drew to a close without the introduction of the amendment.

Again when the Connecticut limited bill (restricted to doctors and nurses) was up for its first Hearing, the newspapers were full of the same old pattern remarks from the objectors, and again the *Birth Control Review* reported that the objections were that it "was against the law of nature, that it was atheistic, that it struck at the foundations of Christian family life, and that it was an insult to womanhood." There was no sign that the objectors lessened or modified their opposition in any way because the proposed bill was a limited one.

In 1923 when the Rosenman Bill, the most limited of any yet proposed, was defeated by the Committee on Codes, Mrs. Annie G. Porritt, managing editor of the *Birth Control Review,* made this comment in the magazine:

"How can I wait for the laws to be changed? It means my life now. If I don't get help in a few years I shall be dead." This is the cry that comes to Mrs. Sanger from all parts of the United States. But this cry had no effect on the Codes Committee of Albany, when in executive session they killed the Rosenman Bill only a few minutes after they had heard the most convincing arguments for its passage. If the action of our legislators were swayed by reason there could have been hope for a better outcome; but it is not reason but politics to which the Assemblymen were giving heed.

The alleged persuasive character of the "doctors only" bill over the freedom bill was still undemonstrated, even with a married-persons-only clause thrown in for good measure in the way of limitations. The men were still afraid to stand for that or any other bill on the subject. "Politics" was still afraid. And the cause of the fear seemed clearly not to be that the bill provided this that or the other, in regard to birth control information, but that the bill brought up the question of birth control at all. That is the persistent sticking point with the man in politics,—nothing else. He feels embarrassed by the whole subject. He feels that it may possibly "queer him" or be used against him by his opponents in some way. And if he reaches the point where he admits the reasonableness of amending the laws to make them reflect the actual practice of the people, and decides that he might as well sponsor a bill for that purpose, then his more wary political associates, his party leaders, step in with restraining advice,—not because they have any really profound convictions on the question, or because they have any sincere opposition, but just because, as a very frank member of Congress explained it, "We have plenty of troubles of our own,—why should we add to the complications by queering ourselves with birth control?" And just here lies the crux of the whole legislation problem.

However even if all propositions for the amendment of State laws were straight freedom bills, and even if the State legislators began to lose their fears enough to act there is one outstanding reason why it is folly to try to correct the conditions in the United States by a series of State bills. There are too many states. And even under fairly favorable conditions it would take too long, not to mention the effort and money needed to make twenty-four separate legislatures go through all the motions involved. Laws do not amend themselves. Many people have to work and work hard to get it accomplished. From the view-point of efficiency alone, State legislation is wasteful, so long as the Federal law remains unchanged; State legislation at best would be a slow enough process, but with the precedent of the Federal law still extant, it would be bound to be slower still. From the view-point of human suffering and ignorance, State legislation without Federal action also, is hardhearted and unintelligent; why break down the barriers to information slowly a state or two at a time and keep struggling worried parents in all the other states waiting for the information much of which they might have quickly by the passage of the Federal bill? And why keep scientists waiting all over the country for the right to import and otherwise order from publishers the books which only the passage of the Federal bill will let them secure lawfully, and subject them to picking up information locally or secretly? From the point of view of public morals, legislating a state at a time, even with straight repeal bills, is dabbing at a national blemish instead of wiping it out. All of which considerations point directly to the need for Federal legislation.

CHAPTER III

GOING TO THE POINT WITH A FEDERAL BILL

1919 sees first concerted effort to repeal Federal law: Initiated by Voluntary Parenthood League, an outgrowth of National Birth Control League: Disbanding of earlier organization and merging of forces: Opposition from birth control advocates on "doctors only" basis arises later: The long hunt for a sponsor: Cummins-Kissell Bill introduced in January, 1923: Re-introduced in next Congress as Cummins-Vaile Bill: Survey of six-year struggle in Congress: Significant characteristics of Congressional reaction: Fear and embarrassment inhibit even those in favor of measure: Suggestions for keeping repeal "dark": Alternate appeals to logic and humanity: Public opposition (mostly Catholic) relatively slight: Sponsor in Senate received 20 letters for bill to every one against:

THE chief answer to the query "What changes in the laws have been proposed?" is that in the summer of 1919 a major move toward redeeming the whole United States from the Comstock blunder of 1873 was made by taking the question to Congress and demanding a repeal of the words "preventing conception" from the five Federal obscenity statutes wherever they occur. This move was the culmination of four years of agitational, educational, experimental and more or less handicapped work, first by the National Birth Control League, and then by the Voluntary Parenthood League, which was started in the spring of 1919, with the primary aim of accomplishing this federal action. As described in the previous chapter, the experience for two years with efforts at State legislation was sufficient to demonstrate clearly that the one time-saving, funda-

94

mental act was the revision of the Federal laws on which
all State laws were modelled, and which was originally and
has ever since been the legal source of the disrepute in which
the subject of birth control has been held.

The initiation of this move to take the matter directly
to Congress was a direct outgrowth of the preliminary work
done by the National Birth Control League in circulating
thousands of petition slips, and much literature showing the
need for amending the laws.   The Voluntary Parenthood
League was in fact formed by members of the National
League, and they differed from the Executive Committee
of that organization only in that they felt the time to act
had come, instead of being in the distant future.   They
argued that Washington was only two hours further away
from the Headquarters than Albany, and that convincing
Congress was only a slightly bigger task, numerically speaking, than convincing the New York Legislature, and that
precisely the same motions had to be gone through in either
case; but that the great difference was that for approxi-
mately the same effort, success in the one case would mean
altering the laws of only one state, and success in the other
case would mean altering the law which affects the whole
nation.   That argument won; and within six months the
National League had practically disbanded and most of its
members had joined the Voluntary Parenthood League.

This union of forces into one active national organization lasted until November, 1921, when the American Birth
Control League was organized, of which Mrs. Sanger was
president, and the limited State bills began to appear,
coupled with opposition to the Federal bill.   This opposition
was not officially stated in the platform adopted by the new
League but was obvious from the statements of the leaders,
the refusal to co-operate and from various editorials in the
Birth Control Review, which became the official organ of
the new League.   Appendix No. 10 gives some of the con-

crete indications of this opposition. Presently, however, the opposition was modified to the extent of approving some Federal legislation, that is, a "doctors only" bill which was announced in March, 1924. An analysis of this proposed bill will be made further on, but at this point a condensed story of the Federal repeal bill is in order.

This first concerted practical measure to rescue the whole United States from the effects of the Comstock blunder has involved a six-year struggle in Congress, and at the present writing, the end is not yet. The preliminary interviews with members of Congress and the scouting for a sponsor for the measure began in July, 1919. A sponsor was secured the following March,—Senator H. Heisler Ball of Delaware, who had been a practicing physician before he became Senator. After delaying his promised introduction of the bill for nearly three months, he broke his word and allowed Congress to adjourn without presenting the measure.

The sponsor hunt continued during the next session, the short and last one of the 66th Congress. A succession of Senators all of whom favored the bill took it under consideration. Each thought it better for some one else to do it. Their various delays in deciding carried the sponsor hunt over to the new Congress which convened in December, 1921. Meanwhile the question was carried to Post Master General Hays who seriously considered including this amendment with his proposed recommendation to Congress that all the laws relating to Post Office censorship be revised. His consideration lasted from midsummer to the following March when he retired from the office to go into the moving picture business. His recommendation was never made in Congress.

So the sponsor hunt was again continued, and lasted until January, 1923, when Senator Albert B. Cummins, President Pro-tempore of the Senate, agreed to introduce the measure.

He was the sixteenth Senator who had been asked to sponsor the bill. He made good on his promise promptly, and the bill was introduced on January 10th. On the same day the bill was sponsored in the House by Congressman John Kissel of Brooklyn, who answered what was practically an advertisement for a "volunteer" statesman to render this service. A letter had been sent to each member of the House asking if he were willing to take the lead in the House to correct the Comstock blunder. Mr. Kissel responded at once and with serious approval.

The bill was a simple straight repeal of the words "preventing conception" wherever they occur in the five Federal obscenity statutes, as follows:

Criminal Code,
Section 102, *which penalized any government employee who aids or abets* in the violation of any law "prohibiting importing, advertising, dealing in, exhibiting, or sending or receiving by mail," any obscene publication, etc.

Section 211, *which makes unmailable* all obscene publications, writings, etc., and all articles used for obscene purposes.

Section 245, *which prohibits bringing into the United States or sending by express or any public carrier,* all the obscene things listed in Section 211.

Section 312, *which penalizes anyone who "shall sell, lend, give away, or in any manner exhibit, or shall otherwise publish or offer to publish . . . or shall have in his possession for any such purpose,* any of the obscene things listed in Section 211. (This section applies only to territory under the exclusive jurisdiction of the Federal government).

Tariff Act of 1922, Section 305, *which prohibits the importation* of any of the obscene things, listed in Section 211 of the Criminal Code.

The introduction of the bill was during the short session of Congress with the usual congested Calendar. There was fairly definite reason to believe that a majority of the Judiciary Committee to which the bill was referred were in favor of it, but they were unwilling to vote it out, that is they evaded voting on it. The session ended without action.

The bill was reintroduced by Senator Cummins in the next Congress on January 24, 1925 and on the following day it was introduced in the House by Congressman William N. Vaile of Colorado. (Congressman's Kissel's term of office had expired with the previous Congress, hence the need of a new sponsor in the House.) The bill this time carried an additional section providing that no contraceptive instructions or means could be transported by mail or by any public carrier unless they were certified by at least five lawfully practicing physicians to be "not injurious to life or health." The full wording of the entire bill is given in Appendix No. 11.

Two Hearings on the Bill were held on April 8 and May 9, 1924, before joint meetings of the Senate and House Judiciary Committees. As in the previous year, there was probable majority in both Committees in favor of the bill, but as before there was great hesitation to act; the few opponents were not aggressive enough to want to have the measure reported out adversely; they merely wanted it pigeon-holed in Committee. And those who favored the bill or who took a tolerant attitude about it were not sufficiently energetic to do anything except to acquiesce in the pigeon-holing of the bill.

Some progress was made however during the next session, the last one of the sixty-eighth Congress. For on January 20th the Senate Sub-Committee of three decided to report the bill to the full Committee "without recommendation." Senator Norris was and always has been unqualifiedly in favor. Senator Overman has always heard the arguments for the Bill with sympathy and seems to have no objection to it, other than a lingering fear that access to knowledge may encourage immorality. He did not wish to hold back action on the Bill, and therefore stood for reporting it "without prejudice." Senator Spencer when first interviewed regarding the Bill expressed his general approval of its aim. Later he brought up various points about which he had reservations. He decided, however, that they should not prevent him from joining with the other two members in a report that would make procedure possible. But no report was made by the full Committee before Congress adjourned on March 4, 1925. The bill died, as do all pending bills which are not enacted when the last session of a given Congress adjourns.

So much for a bare outline of the six years of effort in Congress. This book is not the place for a full story of work, with its many interesting ramifications. For the benefit of those who are interested in the actual chronology of the events in this unique struggle, Appendix No. 12 gives a tabloid story of the successive happenings. But it will perhaps be a useful contribution to the basis for an answer to the question as to what sort of laws the people really want, to give the reader some extracts from the mass of recorded material about this Congressional campaign; to turn the search-light upon certain significant bits of it, with a view to utilizing the experience of the past as a guide for the demands made upon Congress in the immediate future.

The aim of the writer is to put the reader in a position to determine whether the trouble is with the bill, or with the way the Congressional mind reacts to the bill, and what factors there may be that have aggravated the situation so as to produce such an absurd incongruity as that a body of men who have themselves achieved family limitation and who represent constituents who likewise have to a great degree achieved family limitation, should fuss around for six years over the simple act of removing a statute that does not represent American life "as is."

The facts submitted in this survey of some of the high spots of the campaign in Congress are for the most part gleaned from the writer's personal experience in Washington, in direct conversation with the members of Congress. Where otherwise it will be so stated. Being director of the work for the entire six years gave an opportunity for first-hand observation of the vital factors in the situation, and especially of those that were behind the scenes.

The outstanding characteristic notable throughout the whole period has been a general acknowledgment of the reasonableness of the bill, coupled with fear to act. This fear has been occasionally admitted frankly, but has mostly been covered over with all sorts of "rationalizing." And it has been almost as evident among the men in Congress who were for the bill as among those who have opposed it, or those who have stayed on the fence. Thorough-going opposition to the bill has from the very beginning been almost nil, that is, in the sense that a man believed in the prohibition of contraceptive knowledge enough to want it applied to *himself*. No such member of Congress has yet been discovered, though there have been a few found who have said they thought the law as it stands is eminently suitable for application to *other* people.

The first man interviewed when the work began in the summer of 1919 was Congressman Andrew Volstead, then Chairman of the House Judiciary Committee, to which Committee the bill would be referred, when introduced. He was instantly alarmed, said the bill could never be introduced; that if it were, the Committee would never report it out; that if they did, no one would ever vote for it on the floor, and so forth. He added however that he would arrange to give the bill a hearing if it should be introduced. He was sure that the only way to accomplish what we wanted was to revise the penal code and "quietly omit it" (the prohibition of contraceptive knowledge).

Later several of the Senators made similar suggestions that a bill be introduced without a specific title, merely a bill to amend certain sections of the Criminal Code, and simply omit the offending parts, without explaining what was being done. Their idea was to let the bill appear to be new legislation to suppress indecency, which would sound commendable, and not say anything about the control of conception, nor bring it up at all for discussion. As put by one of the Senators who was not going to stand for re-election, "Most Congressmen are too lazy to investigate reasons. If the words presented look plausible, they will vote aye,—and let it go without bothering." The members who advised in this vein said that what the men would object to was not so much doing the act of repealing this prohibition as having to discuss it or having any one know they did it. The subject was "disagreeable."

A related phase of fear, and one met with repeatedly, was that they would be made conspicuous in the newspapers if they got "mixed up" with any of this "birth control talk." They had a horror of the possibility of flaming headlines that would somehow drag them into "sensationalism." They had a stiff aversion to "the whole business." Some of them had no other knowledge of the birth control movement than that a woman named Sanger had "made a rumpus" and gotten jailed, and that when they went up to New York for week ends, they saw the sight-seeing automobile man point out "the birth control woman on Broadway," meaning Kitty Marion, who has become a familiar figure selling the Birth Control Review on the New York streets. Some of them confessed to a sneaking desire to get one of those magazines to see what was in it, but they didn't dare. They assumed that it contained contraceptive information,—so little did they know about what the laws really permit.

The fear that they would be exploited in the newspapers was assuaged as far as was possible by the assurance that they were not being interviewed for publication, that what was wanted was the quickest and quietest possible action by Congress, and that if they would simply introduce and pass the bill, a large part of the impetus to and need for agitation would be done away with, and then there would be no "noise" to fear, and they would have the satisfaction of having done a decent, needed act in a dignified way that would greatly redound to their credit. This assurance helped perceptibly in many instances, particularly in making them discuss the bill in private conversation without embarrassment or discomfort.

The policy of not exploiting the views of the individual members of Congress in the newspapers, and especially of not giving the names of the few opponents who have made themselves ridiculous in interviews has been adhered to throughout the work. When they have put themselves on record as some of them did in discussion at the public Hearings on the bill, that is quite another matter. Also when the bill at the end of six years of effort was allowed to die in Committee, a report of the stand of each member of the Judiciary Committees was published in the Birth Control Herald for the information of those who had supported the campaign to pass the bill.

It was not until February, 1922, that any newspaper articles on the work in Congress were sanctioned. Then a feature article was written for the New York (Sunday) Times and reprinted by arrangement in the St. Louis Globe Democrat. The following excerpts from it shed light on the situation as it was reported up to that date:

The initial interviews served two purposes: one to give the Congressmen a realization that knowledge about the control of parenthood is just the same simple human necessity for all the people as it is for themselves and their own families; the other to enable us to find an advantageous sponsor for the measure.

Most members were quite ignorant to the exact provisions of the present law and the way Anthony Comstock had originally lobbied the measure through. They didn't know that his proposition had been the suppression of pornographic literature and pictures primarily, and that there had been no discussion on the floor of the inclusion of contraceptive knowledge in the bill, and that Congress as a whole did not know it had voted for a law to suppress it.

Some members needed to be assured that Congress is not being asked to sanction the interference with life after it has once begun, but merely to free the knowledge as to how the starting of new human life may be controlled. This distinction relieved many Senatorial minds. A fairly frequent worry among the Congressmen has been "race suicide," but they seemed relieved when told such facts as that Holland, with its fifty-two birth control clinics and its established contraceptive instruction which has been going on for more than forty years, had—up to the war—the second highest ratio of increase in population in Europe.

A somewhat common type of Senator is he who fears that making contraceptive knowledge legally accessible will result in its abuse, particularly by the young. But he usually responds quite nobly to such queries as: "If young people are safe only when ignorant, what happens when somehow they get knowledge, as may occur any moment?" "If American young people, as a whole, are prone to go to the devil as fast as they acquire an understanding of this subject, whose fault is it?" "What is the matter with us elders who have reared them so poorly?" "Isn't knowledge on all subjects capable of abuse, and doesn't safety lie on the far side, not on the near side, of education?"

However, the attitude of the large majority of those interviewed is fairly represented by the letter President Harding wrote when he was a member of the Senate Health Committee, in which he said, "I have not had time to study carefully the provisions of your bill, but at first reading find myself very much in its favor."

The one most arresting fact which the Congressmen were asked to face, and which none could deny, was that Congress itself, like any other group of well-to-do men in the United States, already represents the achievement of family limitation despite the laws. The "Who's Who" section of the Congressional Directory does not report Congressmen with families of eight, ten or twelve. Quite otherwise.

A few weeks of quiet but energetic sampling of senatorial opinions brought us to the point of choosing as the desired sponsor one of the only two physicians of the Senate, a man who had heartily indorsed the bill from the beginning and whose cultured dignity would insure right handling for the measure. But it took him nearly three months to reach the conclusion that he was too occupied with other important issues to do this measure justice. Even then he did not refuse, but merely said he could not yet see his way and urged that someone else be asked. This refusal to refuse has been characteristic of nearly all the fifteen Senators who have been invited in succession to sponsor the bill. All of them believed in it, but in their various ways, they have "passed the buck"—some convincingly, some transparently, some gracefully, some awkwardly, but all of them insistent that it was a job better suited to someone else.

Several were "too busy"—among these was one who was not a member of any major committee, who had introduced no public-interest bills, and who, as observed from the Senate gallery, sits for hours on end in undisturbed quiet. One assured us he was "too old," another was sure he was "too ignorant of the subject—it needs a man who can give all the data in debate, as I can't." We promised him a perfect arsenal of material all classified and condensed, but he felt sure he wasn't "equal to doing it well." Another said he was interested, but better not be the sponsor as—"well, candidly, I shall be up for re-election next year, and you see, . . ."

And still another who is considered one of the pillars of the major party in Congress, a physically big man, standing something like six feet three, announced to the relatively small woman who invited him to render this bit of public service,—"Really, I'd be afraid to introduce that sort of bill." On being told that he "hardly looked the part," he spent an energetic five minutes trying to blot out the picture of himself as a coward.

One man assured us that he was not "important enough in the Senate. I don't count," he said. When the task was put up to one of the *leading* men, his answer was, "What you need for sponsor of a bill of this sort is a man who isn't active, someone who has nothing to lose, someone whose bill wouldn't be specially noticed." Other similar advice was to "get a lame duck to do it" in the short session, that is some man who "is going out of politics anyway." This advice is a reminder of what Senator Thomas of Colorado said, in a speech after his defeat, "the only independent Senators are those just defeated or those just elected."

The short sessions being those which allow the "lame ducks" to legislate just as if they had not been defeated for re-election, has been dubbed the "don't-care-a-damn" session, and it is generally considered the heyday for "freak" legislation. This bill is placed in that class by the scornful. But all the while the members were acquiring a better understanding and a more obvious respect for the measure. Almost every one who was consulted responded to our suggestion that, apart from their individual views on the measure, they would do everything possible to insure for the discussion of the question in the cloakrooms, in committee and on the floor an atmosphere of dignity and seriousness which the subject deserved. An influential representative of the old guard Republicans said: "This is a new idea to me as a subject for legislation, and I must give it more thought, but I can see its social importance, and certainly I can assure you right now that I will do my utmost to see that a proper atmosphere for the discussion is established." (This was the Senator who turned the tide of refusals, and introduced the bill the following year, Senator Albert B. Cummins of Iowa.)

More and more men were found whose attitude was like that of a Middle Western leader, who said, "I see no reason why I shouldn't support it." The interviews frequently developed into perfectly good "mothers' meetings." Even the "busy" men often settled down in the big leather chairs of the Marble Room and grew domestically reminiscent. One told how he himself had been "an unwanted baby," a fourth child born when the family lived in one room, and how several of them died, and he became the main support. "And so," he said, "you see there may sometimes be a place for the unwanted ones after all." "Indeed, yes, because brave humans will always struggle to adjust and triumph, but would you, because of that, deliberately perpetuate the ignorance which keeps on producing unwanted babies?" And he answered unhesitatingly, "No, certainly not."

The men with rural constituents have been specially interested in the need of the country people for good reliable books on the control of parenthood. The mothers and fathers who live miles from a railroad, and who find the only doctor in the nearest village unable or unwilling to give them useful instruction as to how to space their babies, are very real characters to them, and it doesn't take much argument to make them see what our Federal measure will do for these pople, and how simple it will make it for them to order by mail, from book stores in the big cities, practical books by the world's best authorities.

The few instances of hot antagonism became more and more exceptional. Our prize enemy even became friendly enough to suggest easy ways of bringing the measure to vote. But in our first interview he had blurted out remarks such as these, gleaned from our notebook: "You ought to be ashamed, an intelligent American woman like you." "You ought to stay at home and take care of your children" (shades of the early suffrage days!). He refused to be diverted from personal abuse by statistics from the Children's Bureau about the high baby death rate where wages are low and families too large. His answer was that statistics lied and he "wouldn't read 'em." He scoffed at the idea that children needed a fair chance for education. "This education business is overdone. What children need is work." He countered all facts and all logic with "I decline to argue."

On being invited to read a booklet giving the main reasons for our measure he replied, "I will not. I don't need to," and he wound up with the stentorian advice, "Young woman, you better go home and pray for a clean heart." But within a day or so he sent the following note:

> "My dear ——:
> " . . . Perhaps I was a little hasty with you when you called this morning. You took me somewhat by surprise. If you should happen over this way again, and could catch me when I am not very busy, I should be glad to talk over matters with you more fully, and get your viewpoint more clearly.
> "Yours very truly,
>
> "————————————."

And lo! the next time he was gentle and receptive. He chuckled over the query as to whether the farmers in his State sowed wheat as thick as the soil would hold it, and whether they planted potatoes 4 inches apart or over 2 feet apart, and if babies didn't need space just like crops. He answered, "That's so, that's so," and presently he was advising us to get the Health Committee to commend the bill to the Judiciary Committee, which would undoubtedly act on the advice.

Our next most spontaneous and unique antagonist was one of the leading orators of the Senate, who delivered this little speech on the mere sight of our card bearing the name "Voluntary Parenthood League": "All these leagues and welfare organizations, no matter how fair they look on the outside or how well they speak or write, are all 'Bolsheviks' at heart, and what they really want is to overthrow the Government of the United States." The mild suggestion that it might be rash to generalize brought a smile and the remark, "Why, yes, that's fair," and he pocketed the offered literature and promised to "investigate."

Speaking of "Bolshevism," here is another item from the interview notebook:

M. W. D.—"Can the country expect level-headed citizenship from the man whose maximum wage isn't over $20 a week, and whose family has increased annually for several years, whose wife is sick, and whose babies are hungry and ailing?"

Congressman X.—"No, certainly not. Those men get desperate. They are ready to take up with any wild ideas."

It was just this point of view, plus the unemployment situation, which led one of the foremost conservatives of the Senate to consider for three weeks the sponsoring of our bill. He became convinced that "when father is out of a job it is no time for mother to have a baby," and while he felt concerned that the rich don't have more children, he thought that was no excuse for victimizing the poor by laws which try to keep them ignorant as to family regulation. However, he begged off from shouldering the bill, saying he couldn't undertake it for so long that in fairness to us we should ask some one else to introduce it. He was the fourteenth Senator asked, and by that time the always sympathetic Chairman of the Health Committee said we reminded him of Diogenes, except that instead of hunting for an honest man we were merely hunting for a courageous man!

An outstanding independent of the Senate, one of the truly "busy" members, frankly explained what ailed most of them. "Congressmen are such cowards," said he. "Believe in it? Of course they do, and privately they will all say so, but that's mighty different from sponsoring the bill. I know. I've been here twelve years."

A Catholic Congressman from an industrial district crowded with mill workers, listened soberly to the figures of the baby death rate in his home town (130 per 1000, as compared with New Zealand's world record of 50 per 1000). The conversation went about like this: "Suppose we look at this thing practically. Do any mills in your district raise a man's wages every time he has a new baby?" "No." "Do you see any legislation ahead that will put wages on that basis?" "I do not." "Don't most mill workers reach their maximum wages at about the age of 30?" "I should say so." "Is it fair, then, for the government to deprive these fathers of the knowledge by which they can keep their families somewhere near in proportion to their wages?" He looked pained and said: "It is surely a serious question. I want to think it over."

Very few Congressmen have even the partial excuse of belonging to a church which disapproves the scientific control of parenthood.

In this connection it is interesting to note that a Catholic member who began by saying, "Even if I had no religion at all I should oppose your outrageous idea," ended by asking for our literature and admitting he was relieved to find that we did not seem to be, as he had thought, an immoral lot who were assaulting marriage and the home; and he recognized the fact that our proposed change in the law was merely to make access to information legal, not to compel people to use it, and that, therefore, the change would not be an intrusion upon any one's religious faith."

Sound argument and indisputable facts made very perceptible headway for the bill as the interviews accumulated. But the one snag which has always entangled the best of logic is the fact that the nature of the subject embarrasses Congress and therefore inhibits action, even though reason urges action. Over and over again have suggestions been made by members of Congress for trying to accomplish the repeal without having it show. Some of these suggestions have already been noted. Another came from one of the Republican leaders in the House who said, "If only you could think some innocuous *other* way to *amend* the present statutes, you could slip your clause *out* at the same time and it would go easily." Another prominent member of the House advised, "Get your action at the same time that the proposed amendment is presented to add moving picture reels to the list of articles proscribed in the obscenity laws. While they add films, you quietly subtract 'preventing of conception.'" A very well known Senator thought it might be "slipped through" as an amendment to the proposed bill to extend Post Office censorship to race track betting news, if that measure should reach the floor. (It died in committee.)

None of these indirect methods has seemed wise procedure, partly because the little subterfuge would not work, and when once discovered would produce a situation even less to be desired than that induced by plain lack of courage to introduce the straight bill, but chiefly because indirection seems inherently unworthy, when it is devised to cover an attitude that is not in itself thoroughly creditable. Very great effort has been made to divert the members of Congress who are suffering from this undue embarrassment by urging them to give impersonal consideration to the justice and wholesomeness of the bill, and by emphasis on the fact that the bill does not deal with a new and untried idea but only reflects a condition in American life that has long been an actuality.

For instance in 1920 it was pointed out to every member of the Judiciary Committee that if the bill dealt with anything which was "advanced" or ahead of the times or out of harmony with the lives of the average person, it would not have happened that one of the largest of the women's magazines (with a circulation of over two million copies, and an advertising rate of $6000 per page) would have published a feature article entitled "Has a Mother the Right to Decide How Many Children She Will Have?"; nor would that magazine have spent thousands and thousands of dollars as it did, to advertise this special article in the newspapers of many large cities, using full and half pages for the advertisements; for the editor of a popular magazine is always canny enough not to give his readers anything which is very far in advance of wide-spread public opinion.

They were told also that this same magazine followed that article with an editorial asking the opinions of the readers on the laws relating to birth control. A digest of the replies was made, and the proportion of those who were in any way opposed to the change of the laws was only sixteen out of a thousand who unqualifiedly wanted them changed.

To help the members of Congress to displace their own sense of discomfort in merely considering this "disagreeable subject" with a sense of the actual suffering of others whose ignorance made them the victims of the present laws, the

Voluntary Parenthood League followed Comstock's own method in Congress for the correction of his blunder, that is by submitting sample instances showing the need for the legislation proposed. The exhibit of 1873 was smut. The exhibit of 1923 was pitiful suffering.

The following petition was sent to every member of both Houses of Congress, and was inserted in the Congressional Record of February 8, 1923, by Representative John Kissel, the Sponsor of the Bill in the House:

TO THE MEMBERS OF THE SENATE AND HOUSE OF REPRESENTATIVES.

Gentlemen:

Just fifty years ago this month, Anthony Comstock showed to your predecessors specimens of the revolting, smutty literature which was then being circulated by conscienceless publishers among the young people of this country.

The Bill he proposed for the suppression of this traffic got almost instant support, as the abuse was flagrant and the proposed remedy a natural one. But by an obvious blunder the Bill was drawn to include all knowledge of contraception, when the aim of the Bill was only the suppression of this knowledge in connection with sex-perversions—a blunder which has meant injustice, hardship and insult to millions of parents ever since.

Now Congress is asked to correct that blunder, and just as Comstock showed your predecessors samples of the disgraceful traffic of the seventies, so we present to you herewith samples of the letters which the League constantly receives in great quantity from suffering parents whose lives are being made miserable by the error that was unwittingly made fifty years ago.

Just as Congress responded to the need presented to them in 1873, we ask you to respond to the need now presented to you in 1923, and to correct the blunder with as much speed as that in which it was originally made.

Yours very truly,
Voluntary Parenthood League."

(The original wording and spelling is given in these letters.)

DEAR FRIENDS:

You have no idea how bad I need your help. I am 38 years old and am the mother of 6 living children and one dead. Have been married twice. I have had a good many mis-carrages and in the last 6 years I have had 4 children and when your letter came I was in bed from a misshap. Now I am a poor woman live out on a farm 7 miles from no one and if ony you could just visit my home you would not hold back the information. Pleas do be kind and tell me just some little thing that would help me out. I will promish not to tell no one about it. I have not been able to leave this house for 2 years now and see hardly no one if ony I could talk to you in person.

We had only two milk cows and one of them brote a calf and died so we have all the children to feed on the one cow and that cows calf. I kno there is no one that needs any more help in this world than we do to save the children we have without more coming. Please write and tell me how much money you want as if I can help myself I must do so at once. I will go hungry for the money to pay you if ony you will help me.

I would love to send $2.00 but am not able to do so but I wont to read and have others read your leaflets. I do beleave that I need the help that I want of you as bad as eny one on earth but I am a poor woman and I gess it hant for the poor to have eny help on this earth.

I beleave it must be stoped and I want to join you. It's the most needed help on earth. Pleas send me all the papers you can spare and I will let my friends kno about you by giving your papers to them to read. Do pleas write and tell me what you want for a little truth and help. I will promish never to give you away so that the law will ever get a hold of you through no falt of mine.

Good by for this time ─────────────.

Dear Friends:

I was just reading a book called the Sex Searchlights and Sane Sex Ethics, and in this book I found your address and seeing that you will give people information on the topic you have in this book, about helping people to keep from becoming mothers. If they increase too rapidly. My case isn't this. I have a little boy and the doctors tell me not to have any more or I will not be here any longer. I asked them how I was going to prevent this. All they said was find out. My baby was taken with instruments and I was between life and death.

Hoping you will send me information on this topic at once,

Yours truly, ─────────────.

MY DEAR FRIENDS:

Will you please tell me some simple remidy to prevent conception. I am the mother of 6 children and soon to become the mother of another. It is sapping my life and breaking down my health. If you cannot give the information please tell me where I can get the information.

Yours truly,

_____.

MY DEAR MRS. DENNETT:

All of the literature received by me from the V. P. L. strikes an answering chord in my heart. I had so hoped that the Federal bill would be passed early enough for me to get and pass on the much needed information to the rural mothers, who are being broken down by child bearing and hard work.

As a Graduate Midwife delivering eight or ten babies a year, in the course of my Public Health work I realize more than most nurses the pressing need of contraceptive information. I came to this work June 1st, 1918, and am leaving March 1st of this year because the doctor has told me I ought not to finish out this year if I'm to keep my own health.

In these four years I have delivered six mothers of two children a piece and one mother of four, twins the 1st June, 1918 and one Oct., 1919, the fourth Feb., 1921. This woman is 23 years old and the mother of six children. Naturally she is already breaking down and the children can't get proper care. It is pitiful! There are three other women who have borne children so rapidly that they are on the verge of physical or nervous break down. If I send them to their family doctors they are given a tonic and told that they "will come around all right." They do, in about nine months with another baby.

If you can devise any way to help us please do so and believe me your grateful friend,

_____.

V. P. L.

Rec'd your pamphlets, thank you ever so much. So sorry you couldn't give me the information I wanted so bad. For God's sake, can't you help me somehow. Am married three years, I have a baby two years old another five months old, and I am pregnant again. Can you imagine anything more awful. If I could only devote the next five or six years of my life to the raising of my darlings I am sure God would reward anyone who would tell me.

I swear if I become pregnant a fourth time I will do something desperate. What I would say about my husband had better be left unsaid. Please, please cant you give me the information I crave, just one little line. I will pray for you every night of my life. May God bless you and help you along in the wonderful work you are doing. I thank you for anything you will tell me, and if you will not I thank you just the same. Once more I ask for our dear Lord's sake please, please help me.

One discouraged mother,

————————————————.

Voluntary Parenthood League:

I have received the literature you sent and wish to thank you although it cannot help me at present. I may be able to help some other poor sufferer. I would like to become a member or be able to send some money but it is impossible at present. We are four months in arrears in our rent, the children have scarlet fever, and my husband was out of work for six months, then he invested the little we had in a business but we cannot keep up with our bills. And now this other expense coming again.

I love little children but don't like to see them suffer from lack of attention and care.

Sincerely yours,

————————————————.

Dear Madam:

I am writing to see if you can help me any. I have two children whom we adore and I am living on the prairie, forty miles from a reliable doctor, and no crops for five years.

Before I married for several years I suffered with rheumatic arthritis terribly, but was free from it for several years. When my baby was two months old (two years ago) we took the "flue." My husband took it first and I struggled around to look after the others. It was 45 below and we would have frozen to death if the fires went out. I was so weak was only able to put on a handful at a time and dare not take off my shoes or undress at all. My husband was inclined to violence and was just crazy. We managed to put out a flag but it was not seen for three days. At last help came after we had been sick about ten days. The neighbors (men) took it in turns to watch and nurse us in twos. Women are scarce here but one would come in now and again as they could. I had pneumonia and dysentry and I was unable to move in bed. Baby was taken away. She was nearly starved to death unable to get any nurse from me and I did not know it, poor little mite. We were able to get a nurse when we were getting better but our kind friends said they had never seen anyone so sick and live.

I had been up a couple of weeks when I was taken with rheumatic fever, every scrap of my hair came off and I've had rheumatism ever since, and I have been unable to do the washing or clean the floors. My husband has had to do it all and he is about run of his legs with his own work. My right arm is crooked at the elbow, my right hand all drawn out of shape and both wrists stiff. Oh if you could only help me. I am terrified of the idea of having another baby when I can so ill look after those we have, besides giving them a share of my ailment.

With my very best wishes for the noble fight you are making.

Yours sincerely,

_____.

MY DEAR MRS. DENNETT:

After a long time that I have been looking for some one to help me, I finally found a friend of mine, whom gave me your address, and hoping you will be of great help to me. I am a girl of 25 years of age. Been married four and a half years. Had two babies, both with critical instrument cases. It meant either the child or my death. So there for I was never able to see either one alive for they were dead before I had opened my eyes, and confined to bed for 4 weeks after. Am not in good health yet. If my last dear one was living it would be one year old the last of this month. It was a little girl, and the first one a boy. But you see I was left empty handed both times. Now the doctor tells me if I should have another, it would mean my life, as my bones are very small and wont give. And yet they wont tell me how to prevent it. All they say is its against the law. And if they would help me its very expensive, they say, as my husband is working and his dayly wages will not permit us to spend to much. So will you please advise me what to do. Of course its against the law. But I don't see why it would be in a case like this.

If you do help me, it will be very much appreciated by me. I'll remain

Yours truly,

_____.

In contrast with the struggles of the ignorant on whom the laws are still an intolerable burden, the members of Congress were asked to consider their own status, as revealed by themselves in the biographies which the members provide for the Congressional Directory.

The biographies in the Congressional Directory are not uniform in the facts presented about the members, but a survey of those biographies which mention the children at all, shows clearly that a restricted and controlled birth rate is the general custom.

The average number of reported births is found to be 2.7 per family. The largest family recorded is 11, and these children were born during a period of 23 years. Successive annual births simply are not found.

In the 225 Congressional families noted, the number of children is as follows:

1 family has	11 children
2 families have	10 children
1 family has	9 children
3 families have	8 children
1 family has	7 children
7 families have	6 children
16 families have	5 children
22 families have	4 children
40 families have	3 children
80 families have	2 children
46 families have	1 child

Many of the Congressional families are smaller than the eugenists usually consider desirable. But however much the members of Congress, like others of the "fit" class, may be open to adverse criticism by students of race progress, the fact remains that the old Comstock law to enforce ignorance as to the control of parenthood, has long ago been frustrated by Congress itself.

Alternation of logic with appeal for simple fairness and human interest has characterized the whole period of work in Congress. No single approach to the subject affects all men alike. And while no appeal has thus far overtopped the towering inhibition which has held them back from acting, the combination of the different appeals has apparently prevented them from being willing to kill the bill outright. Almost no one in Congress wants to go on record against it, but they squirm at going on record for it.

The special reason for giving here some of the specimen appeals that have been made, is in order to better facilitate an understanding of the cause of the inhibitions. For in that understanding lies the clue to their demolition. Toward the close of the session in the winter of 1923, when every effort was being made to bring out at least from the Senate Judiciary Committee a favorable report on the bill, and when there was only one day left on which the committee would meet before the end of the session, the following letter was sent to each member:

To the Members of the Senate Judiciary Committee:

In again urging you to report out the Cummins Bill (S4314) next Monday (February 26th), on behalf of my league, I beg you to think of the request in the most simple and human way possible.

The Bill is *simple* because it merely rectifies a blunder made by Congress 50 years ago. It was contraceptive knowledge in connection with sexual depravity that the original statute aimed to suppress, not the knowledge for normal use. The proof of this statement has previously been submitted to you.

The logic of the measure is also *simple,* for the application of this knowledge in controlling conception is not a crime, therefore it is absurd to maintain a law which deems it a crime to learn what that knowledge is.

I beg you to be *human* about it. Act on this measure as if the need for knowledge were your own, instead of that of millions of poor people. Suppose you were a young man on a small wage, with a frail wife and more children already than your pay could support, would you be patient on hearing that your Senators were "too busy" to spend the five minutes it would take to send this Bill on its way to passage? Suppose you had any one of the many good reasons that millions of parents have for needing desperately to get this knowledge in decent, scientific, reliable form, instead of from here-say and in abominable underground ways, wouldn't you put that need first? Would you stop to debate about the French birth-rate, or any other irrelevant question?

Without speaking personally of individual Senators, it is entirely justifiable to assume what Senators *really* think about this question, for the average birth-rate in their families and their children's families has proven it long ago. Can you then be any longer callous to the needs of millions of your poorer fellow citizens who, unlike you, are struggling with poverty and the whole train of worries induced by poverty?

And most of all, can you not break through the *fear,* which has held many of you back from acting promptly; fear not of public opinion but of each other, the flippant, facetious comment that comes easily to the lips of many men, even good and fine men—in their instinctive effort to cover the embarrassment they feel because this question touches upon sex? Many members have admitted that they were inhibited by this fear. But can you not forget it, through sympathy for the suffering of others? Isn't it more precious to you to be just and generous to your fellow citizens than to further indulge this fear, which in the last analysis could never be a source of real pride to you as a servant of the public?

Gratitude and respect await your favorable action.

Yours very truly,

.

Director of the V. P. L.

What followed is reported in the Birth Control Herald (March 8, 1923).

As soon as possible after the Committee adjourned on the twenty-sixth, we found Senator Cummins and said, "Well, please tell us the worst." He threw up his hands and replied, "I simply could not get it brought up. When they were discussing the constitutional amendment which was the subject of the meeting, I gave notice that as soon as that was settled I should bring up the Birth Control Bill, and by the time the amendment was disposed of they had simply faded away." "Leaving you like Casabianca on the burning deck alone?" "Yes."

We asked what members were present and he told us frankly.

So we know who "faded away." And we know who did not attend at all. The nearest approach to an excuse that any had who were in favor of the Bill, is that some of them were not present at the moment that Senator Cummins announced that he would ask the vote of the Committee. But they all knew beforehand from us that the Senator was going to ask the vote on that day, so the record stands squarely as one of evasion. It is quite true that most of the Judiciary members were genuinely busy, some of them very busy during the last few weeks of the session. But that five minutes could not have been found for allowing the probable favorable majority to vote to report out the Bill is taxing credulity farther than most people are willing to stretch it.

Indeed Senator Cummins was quite candid in saying, "They simply don't want to vote on it." We inquired if it was not chiefly because the subject embarrassed them, and he assented. We discussed a bit with him this curious fact that human sympathy did not overcome embarrassment enough to just vote. We did not ask them to talk, merely to act. The Senator granted that the effort had been very educational. He added, "And, now as the farmers would say, you will have to spit on your hands and go at it again. And next time you will win."

We asked Senator Dillingham if anything mitigating could be said regarding the statement of Senator Cummins that the Judiciary members had "faded away" when they knew the vote on the Bill was to be called for. He said, "No, Senator Cummins was absolutely accurate. That is what they did do, fade away. And yours was not the only Bill they did that to either. They did it to some of mine also." He said he was very sorry for our disappointment, and that the postponement was inevitable in view of the fact that they all had so many other irons in the fire, each one having a lot of special interests of his own that absorbed most of his time, and that on top of their preoccupation with other matters was their sheer distaste for a Bill of this nature.

We reminded both him and Senator Cummins that the "busy" excuse was nothing new, that we had had that hurled at us at the very beginning of the first session of the present Congress. But they both agreed that with our bill introduced early in the next session and a Hearing held we should be in a position to expect results in a fairly short time. That many members of Congress anticipate the efficacy of our persistence is indicated by a chance remark about another Bill that was going hard, "Better get the birth control people to push it!"

While the inhibition which has prevented action on this bill is still powerful in Congress, the maintenance of it has become increasingly awkward for the members, because the demand from citizens for the passage of the bill have been so very much greater than the demands for the retention of the present law. Two weeks after the first introduction of the bill, in 1923, Congressman Kissel, its sponsor in the House was asked, "How about letters in opposition?" Pointing to the pile of letters he had received, he answered, "Not a single one yet." This fact was presently published in the Birth Control Herald and elsewhere, with the result that fifty-six letters in opposition came to the Congressman. Most of them were obviously from Roman Catholics, and a large proportion of these were in stereotyped phrases almost identical in wording. Some half dozen of them were alike word for word, all written in the same writing, but signed with different signatures, and without addresses. When Congressman Vaile introduced the bill, he had a similar experience. One group of such letters came from a middle western city in which the dictation from the shepherd of a church flock had evidently been acted upon with absolute literalness, for the wording was precisely the same in all, though some were on white and some on pink, some on large and some on small sheets. All were hand written, and all were signed by women. The formula for these letters was the following:

DEAR SIR: Believing that the purpose of the Cummins-Vaile Bill is directly antagonistic to all Christian principles inasmuch as it would legalize practices which are a perversion of the divine object of marriage, and a direct insult to motherhood of America, I therefore urge you to do all in your power to defeat this bill.

Respectfully yours,

———————————.

The Birth Control Herald published the above letter with the following editorial comment:

What is the matter with the Catholics? Can't they think or speak for themselves, or can't they be trusted to do so? Must they be dictated to, even to the "respectfully yours"? And what is the matter with the oracle who did the dictating? He seems to have issued his directions without knowing what the provisions of the Cummins-Vaile Bill are. There is nothing in the bill or back of it which is "directly antagonistic to all Christian principle." Quite the contrary inasmuch as the bill merely aims to enable people to find out what is true about the control of conception. And was it not the initiator of Christianity who said, "Ye shall know the truth and the truth shall make you free"? The bill takes no stand whatever on the application of this knowledge. It leaves that entirely to the conscience and judgment of the citizen. Catholics will be free to do as they are taught. Others will be free to do as they think best.

Again the Catholic oracle is in error about the bill, when he says "it would legalize practices that are a perversion of the divine object of marriage." He obviously means the control of conception. But the control of conception is entirely legal now in the United States, everywhere, except in the State of Connecticut. The passage of the Cummins-Vaile Bill will not affect its legal status a particle. The only thing that is now illegal the country over is the circulation of information as to how conception may be controlled. That is, the act of controlling parenthood is no crime, but finding out how is a felony.

The bill a "direct insult to the motherhood of America." How so? Are mothers insulted by having an opportunity to gain knowledge? And conversely, are they honored by being kept in compulsory ignorance?

The Roman Catholics who spoke in opposition to the bill at the Hearings in 1924, claimed to represent several millions of individuals, but none of them gave any evidence that the individuals had been consulted, or had taken any mass action in conventions, meetings or the like. Leaders simply spoke for the members of the church, en masse, and assumed their opposition to the Cummins-Vaile Bill because the Church teaching has been that the control of conception is wrong. They discussed the question of birth control rather than the issue of the bill, which is only the right of the citizen to be able to find out, lawfully, what birth control is. It does not necessarily follow that Catholic citizens, who may most conscientiously believe and act upon what the church teaches regarding the utilization of birth control knowledge, are therefore opposed to freedom of access to the knowledge. Indeed there are some striking examples to the contrary, including a Catholic United States Senator. And the fact remains that the Church as such has not officially taken any stand against this bill. It has merely preached against birth control. It is interesting in this connection to note that in the last Congressional election, one of the leading Catholic clergymen in Denver openly advised his congregation to vote for the re-election of Mr. Vaile as he was valued far more for his stand on some other questions than he was disliked for his stand on this one question.

During the month which followed Senator Cummins' first introduction of the bill, he received but one protest against the measure and that was from Anthony Comstock's successor, John S. Sumner. The Birth Control Herald had this to say regarding the letters the Senator received:

Senator Cummins' Secretary has courteously allowed the Voluntary Parenthood League officers to review the letters which the Senator has received regarding his Bill. It is a remarkably representative collection containing commendation from every sort of American citizen. The letters range from intellectual sociological appreciation to stark human appeal. Some are on important organization letterheads, and others are on poor paper in cramped handwriting. They come from doctors, lawyers, clergymen, educators, social workers, fathers, mothers, teachers, and just folks,—the normal thinking responsible-citizen sort of people. The happy mothers write, who are proud of their wisely spaced families, and they urge the Senator to push his Bill hard so that all the other mothers may have the knowledge that they have. The mothers who have been wrecked by their own ignorant parenthood write too, and say pathetically, "this Bill will help mothers of the whole country." And the one most insistent message in most of the letters, in one form or another, is that the *thinking* people want this Bill passed.

At the bottom of the pile appears the eleven page letter from John Sumner, consisting of elaborate irrelevancies, and many inaccuracies, and, permeating it all is the revelation of his own cynicism regarding the moral character of the mass of the people, particularly the young people, who according to his idea, should be kept as ignorant as possible on this subject, because he is sure they can not be trusted with the knowledge. If John Sumner thinks to inspire the young by thus handing them a wholesale insult, he will perhaps meet an illuminating surprise ere long.

A large batch of the letters Senator Cummins received after his second introduction of the bill were similarly reviewed, and the proportion of letters for the bill to those against it was twenty to one.

CHAPTER IV

THE HEARINGS ON THE CUMMINS-VAILE BILL AND THE AFTERMATH

Delay in arranging hearings analagous to delay in sponsoring bill: Joint Hearings by Senate and House Judiciary Sub-Committees held on April 8 and May 9, 1924: Mr. Vaile in opening remarks pleads for restoration of American freedom to acquire knowledge, which was taken away 50 years ago: Birth rate in United States proves that people want to get some information in spite of law: Catholic speakers discuss birth control, not the bill: Wages of government employees quoted as reason for passing bill: Prof. Field shows historically that suppression does not suppress: Mrs. Glaser argues for freedom for scientists to learn and teach regarding control of human fertility: Mrs. Carpenter shows how Federal law operates to prevent Chicago Clinic: Prof. Johnson gives eugenic view-point: Hearing reopened at request of Catholics: Lengthy irrelevancies: Congressman Hersey heckles the witnesses: Report of Senate Sub-Committee a sop to the workers for the bill: Unique effort to get vote of full Committee before adjournment, as aid to reducing inhibition in next Congress.

THE Hearings on the bill, and the circumstances connected with them offer further light upon the workings of the Congressional mind, or rather the reaction of Congressional feeling concerning this subject. With all due allowance for the fact that the Congressional calendar is always "crowded" and that most legislation in the nature of things under the present system may, and usually does, move very slowly, there has been every evidence that the impulse to postpone committee consideration and action on this bill as long as possible was most compelling in the Judiciary

Committee of both Houses. It was a replica of the hedging about sponsoring the bill, which had characterized the few preceding years, when the various desired sponsors "passed the buck" by saying at the beginning of a session that they were so very busy getting their "important" projects started they could not stop to consider taking on this measure too, and toward the close of a session they were similarly so driven finishing up their "important" projects that they couldn't think of anything else, and in the middle of a session they were just as able to find "alibis" as at any other time. As Senator Cummins has repeatedly said, "The men dislike the thing so!"

The last introduction of the bill was made fairly early in the first session of the new Congress, that is on January 30th. Yet it was not until the middle of March that the Chairman of the Senate Judiciary Committee could be persuaded to appoint the necessary sub-committee in order that a hearing might be held. And it was not till a week later still that the Chairman of the House Judiciary Committee decided as to which of the three standing sub-committees he would refer the bill. The first Hearing was held on April 8th, jointly by the Senate and House sub-committees as a time saving arrangement. The Sub-committee chairman declined to ask their committees for a vote on reporting the bill until after the testimony given at the hearing should be printed. Weeks of delay followed before the printing was achieved. During this time it became obvious that some plan was holding things up and presently it appeared. The hearing was to be reopened at the request of the Roman Catholics. At the first hearing the chairman had made the usual inquiry, "Is there any other opponent of the bill that desires to be heard?" There was no one. The opposition had exhausted its resources with five speakers, so the hearing continued with the testimony of the remaining four out of the ten speakers in favor of the bill.

At the second hearing which did not come till May 9th no new points were made, but a very long paper was read elaborating the Roman Catholic arguments against birth control and emphasizing the fact that the Catholics were not willing to trust their own people if access to contraceptive information were made lawful.   This delay carried over consideration of the bill by the sub-committee so late into the session that they claimed it would not be possible to make a report and have it acted upon by the full Judiciary Committee previous to adjournment. And the relief of some of the members over once more putting off action on "the birth control bill" was plainly evident.   This relief was covered (in many instances unconsciously so) by all sorts of argument which was quite irrelevant to the bill, but which served well enough as a means of making the question seem vastly complicated and one over which a conscientious law maker must ponder long and hard.   In the strenuous effort which was made to secure at least a committee report before the adjournment of Congress, the following appeal to stick to the point was sent by the Director of the Voluntary Parenthood League to every member of the Judiciary Committee:

Judging by conversation with members of the Judiciary Sub-Committee, there seems to be a great temptation to discuss the Cummins-Vaile Bill emotionally rather than logically.   As all the members are lawyers, I hope it will not be taken amiss to urge that, at the meeting to decide on reporting the bill, the discussion will be strictly limited to the LAW points.

I respectfully venture this suggestion because of the short time remaining in which to act during the present session, and not because the ramifications of the subject of the bill are not important. They are indeed.   And we, who are specially voicing the public need for this bill are, in common with the members of the Sub-Committees, deeply interested in the problem of population, sex education, the morality of the young, and all other questions allied to the control of parenthood.   But we realize that they are outside the practicable and legitimate field of legislation.   They are problems in sociology and education. They therefore should not be entangled at this time with the very simple reasons for reporting out this bill at once.

(A brief résumé of the reasons followed which is not given here because a similar and more comprehensive one is to be given later.)

Congress might be excused for not repealing these defunct laws long ago, on its own initiative. But now that large numbers of citizens have, for five years, been definitely asking Congress to act, there can be no tenable excuse for not making an immediate and favorable report.

But the temptation to postpone decision and to befog the issue with irrelevancies won for that session, and the bill had to go over to the short session the following December.

The Hearings Report gives many significant side lights as to the psychology of those who appeared for and against the bill, and of certain members of the Judiciary Committee. It is impracticable to quote lavishly here from the seventy-nine pages of the document. But a few of the remarks which bear most pertinently on the salient points for the bill and some which indicate the attitude of the committee members may well be noted.

The members of the Senate Sub-Committee were Senators Spencer of Missouri, Norris of Nebraska and Overman of North Carolina, and the members of the House Sub-Committee were Congressmen Yates of Illinois, Hersey of Maine, Perlman of New York, Larson of Minnesota, Thomas of Kentucky, Major of Missouri and O'Sullivan of Connecticut. Senator Spencer presided.

Mr. Vaile in his opening remarks said: "These bills do not propose any new or strange legislation, and these bills themselves do not propose to teach birth control." He was at once interrupted by Mr. Hersey who asked, "You said that this is no new matter. Is there any legislation of this sort that has been passed hitherto?" To which Mr.

Vaile replied, "The legislation on this matter consists of our statutes classifying contraceptives as obscene of themselves. We are the only country in the world having this legislation. We did not have it prior to 1873. The bill, therefore, proposes no new or affirmative doctrine. It simply proposes to make lawful what was lawful in the United States prior to 1873. It does not propose to do this by any new or affirmative legislation, but by simply striking those provisions from five sections of our Penal Code."

"Let me, at the outset, refer to a question which immediately bobs up in the minds of everybody with whom you discuss this subject. They say, "It will promote immorality." Let me ask the committee, in all fairness, if the morality of this country is strikingly superior now to what it was before 1873. You can not pick up a daily paper, you can not go into a church, you can not hear a subject of public morals discussed to any great length by any speaker but what you will be advised that we are at a lower stage of morals than we were 50 years ago. Fifty years ago we did not have such a statute on our books. Certainly the insertion of this proviso in our statutes has not noticeably increased the morality of the United States. It is common knowledge that methods of contraception are used by the educated, the well-to-do classes of the community. Would anybody say that these classes are conspicuously less moral than those who can not obtain this information and have no knowledge of it? I think that would be a great reflection on many people, with certainly a highly developed civic consciousness, people prominent in every good work of the community, all of whom as a matter of common knowledge, of which this committee can take judicial notice, do have and use this information. . . .

"I submit, in all fairness, by merely removing the provisions which we put into the code 50 years ago, and which did not exist theretofore, we won't be rushing on a downward path, so far as we can judge by our own experience of that of any other country.

"Now, that raises another question. Is lack of knowledge the best method or even a safe method to prevent vice? Would you insult your daughters by insinuating to them that it is only because they can not get such information as this that they remain good? Of course you would not. Why, then, pass that insult to every other daughter in the United States?

"And, furthermore, if this knowledge can be obtained, though unlawfully—and we all know that it can be obtained unlawfully, or at least without the sanction of law—if it can be obtained, why, then, merely to make it illegal is a very poor way to protect anybody's morality, because they can certainly get the information."

At the close of his remarks Mr. Vaile introduced the writer, who in turn introduced the other witnesses for the bill. Her own remarks included the following:

If agreeable to the gentlemen of the committee, we will divide the testimony that we will present to you under two different categories. One, the direct reasons for the passage of this bill from the point of view of law and the rights of citizens. The other bits of testimony that we are ready to present to you if you desire and if agreeable to you, are certain evidences that the utilization of this knowledge in this country and throughout the world has tended toward racial and individual welfare.

This is not logically and directly speaking necessarily an argument for the passage of this bill, but it is distinctly reassuring, I should say, to Congress when it stands for this measure, to know that the action is in harmony with what has been generally considered by all impartial observers as something which makes for race progress and race betterment.

To begin with the logic, which is less human but possibly more convincing to a committee made up exclusively of lawyers; the continuance of the five statutes which this bill proposes to amend seems to us not tenable, either on grounds of justice or public policy, because first, the majority of the people do not approve of the suppression of knowledge of the regulation of parenthood by the control of conception. When I make this somewhat dogmatic statement I offer to you the best and most conclusive proof there is, namely, the official figures on the birth rate of our country. The birth registration area, if I am correctly informed, covers 22 States, but presumably the population of those 22 States is of about the same character as the population of the remainder of the States, and therefore the birth rate, so far as is recorded, is an exceedingly valid argument.

The birth rate for the country, averaging those States, stands at 22.8 a thousand. A birth rate that I might call natural, that is unguided by the mind of man and simply resulting from instinct and physical impulse, would run from 50 a thousand up, and 50 is an exceedingly conservative figure. Therefore, family limitation by intention has already long been in the world, and for a very long period, in spite of the fact that we have maintained for half a century laws which theoretically keep our entire population in absolute ignorance.

No citizen, so far as I know, has yet come to Congress and said this to his Representative or Senator: "Will you please keep these present laws as they stand now? I personally consider the control of conception rightly classed as indecency. I have no knowledge on the subject, and I don't want any. Moreover, I wish my ignorance legally perpetuated because I do not think I should be trusted with it. I need to have my Government protect me from the temptation to misuse it."

No citizen, I take it, has thus far come to you with that plea on his own behalf. The protests—and you have received some against this measure—have seemed to be wholly on the ground that access to this forbidden knowledge would be dangerous for somebody else, not for the people who themselves protest. Unless it can be proved that there are more citizens who deliberately ask to be kept in ignorance than there are those who want access to this knowledge there can be no justification for not passing this measure. In view of the proof which the birth rate gives, that the majority believe in, because they achieve family limitation, it is hardly likely that those who want to be kept in ignorance can be anywhere near a majority. Asking that others be kept in ignorance is not a valid argument for any legislation.

The abuse of knowledge should be handled in some other way than attempting to maintain ignorance on the part of the population. The present laws as they stand are predicated on distrust by the Government of the mass of its citizens, which is an intolerable principle for laws in a supposed democracy. It is a principle, for instance, which no Member of Congress would care to expound, I think, let us say, in a pre-election campaign. Fancy a Senator or Congressman making a campaign address in which he would state that he deemed his constituents too weak morally to be trusted with scientific knowledge about sex matters. It is incredible. We do not ordinarily cast a wholesale insult upon our fellow citizens. We think too well of the average American to do that, and certainly no such insult should be found in our laws.

Reverend John A. Ryan, speaking on behalf of Catholics in general said:

We regard these practices about which information is proposed to be given as immoral—everlastingly, essentially, fundamentally immoral, quite as immoral as adultery, for instance, or rather a little more so, because adultery, whatever may be its vicious aspects, does not commit any outrage upon nature, nor pervert nature's functions.

We maintain that these practices are detrimental to the family; that they are not in the interest of better families; that they mean the promotion of selfishness within the family and a great reduction in the capacity to endure, the capacity to face hardships, the capacity to do little things, to do the things of life without which there is no consistent achievement or any kind worth while.

Dr. Lawrence Litchfield, former President of the State Medical Society of Pennsylvania, testified that he had

practiced medicine for 36 years. I have been interested in international movements for the control of and the abating of venereal diseases, child labor, and tuberculosis. All of these problems for the benefit of the human race bring us back one after another to the necessity for intelligent birth control. The human race has the same right and need for scientific development that other animals have. We have many laws and many books and many theories that control the breeding of animals, but the breeding of human beings is left entirely to chance.

Senator Spencer: Is there any law in Pennsylvania against a physician freely communicating to his patients?

Doctor Litchfield: Yes. If a patient of mine whom I believe would be seriously injured by not having the information to prevent conception wrote me for such information I am legally unable to send it to her.   If she comes into my office and the doors are locked, I tell her what I think is wise.

Senator Spencer: Do the doors necessarily have to be locked?

Dr. Litchfield: The information can not be given publicly.

Senator Spencer: But I mean, there is no law in Pennsylvania is there, which prevents a doctor from communicating information of this sort to his patients?

Dr. Litchfield: There is, as I understand it.   I might say, further, as a side light on this question, last summer in Europe my wife and I found a book which we read and thought would be a very good thing for our young married daughter to have, and I decided to import some of these books and give them to my patients who were recently married.   I send an order to England and received an answer that the book could not be imported, because it was regarded as obscene.

Mrs. S. J. Bronson, Secretary of the Voluntary Parenthood League spoke for the bill from the practical standpoint of the wage earner, and said in part:

Congress need look no further than to the vast arm of Government employees to find ample reason for the immediate passage of this measure.   The human story revealed in the pages of dry figures of the official register is most compelling.   It shows that in the Federal civil service alone there are 548,531 employees.   The addition of State and municipal employees would carry the figure into the millions for the whole country.   There seems to be no official statement of what the average Government salary is; but the director of the Voluntary Parenthood League has made an illuminating estimate by taking 100 names in alphabetical sequence from the directory in the official register.   (It does not include Members of Congress, the Army or Navy, or post-office employees.)   These hundred employees includes clerks, guards, charwomen, draftsmen, attendants, teachers, firemen, laborers, machinists, accountants, customs inspectors, watchmen, foremen, supervisors, a harness maker, a seamstress, and a judge.   The average salary proves to be $1605.   There were only 5 who get over $3000, and there were 18 getting below $1000.   It is a fair guess that any other 100 names taken from the book at random would tell about the same story.

Now, is it fair play for the Government to retain laws which try to keep its own direct employees in utter ignorance as to how to regulate their families somewhere in proportion to their earnings?

As the Government can never provide unlimited wages for its servants, it ought at least to allow them legal access to the knowledge by which they may, if they choose, safeguard themselves against unlimited families.

Please also bear in mind some representative facts about non-Government wage earners. In the peak of what was called war prosperity the average wage in the shipyards was only $1411, nearly $300 short of the standard set by the War Labor Board. The average wage of the railroad workers in the same period was $1137. Dr. P. P. Claxton, former commissioner of education, gave $630 as the average school teacher's salary in 1918. The average weekly wage of the New York factory workers before the after-war slump was $23.10, and in 169 sorts of factory work in Massachusetts during the first year of the war only a little over one-seventh of the adult males were earning about $25 a week.

At the same time health authorities agree that a growing child should have a quart of good milk a day. Also that there is no adequate substitute for milk. At 15 cents a quart the bill for milk alone for six children would be over $6 a week. Of course, a man earning $25 a week can not provide that and all the other necessities too, and so his babies are puny. Or if they pull through it is at the expense of the parents' vitality, or else charity steps in to save them. And when the children reach adolescence, the age when most of all they need alert, intelligent parents, the father and the mother—especially the mother—are worn out and dull, unfit to take a strong hand in rearing a race that will have brains and brawn and character.

The point I urge is fair play for the millions. These, and other millions to follow, will for an indefinite period make up the actual majority in this country. They can not be left out of consideration. They are "the people."

We are bound to believe that on the whole they are decent, normal, responsible folks, who naturally love children and want as many as they can wisely rear; but they can not afford so very many, nor have them so close together that the family welfare depreciates beyond redemption. That parents and children should be crushed by the very things which ought to be the cause of their deepest happiness is too ironic. Congress surely has the heart to look at this matter humanely.

All too often young married couples start out in life with an inadequate income even for the preparation of the first child, and the young wife finds she must continue working for the first year at least in order to help meet the expense which the birth of a baby involves. No decent, self-respecting woman wants to become the object of charity.

Gentlemen, I ask you in particular to bear in mind the great army of these young married people, who are facing life and parenthood with high hopes and ambitions, and who have no background of financial security, with nothing but their individual earning power to safeguard themselves and their children. It is somewhat the fashion nowadays to decry the young people, and doubtless some of the worry is warranted, but also there are unnumbered thousands who long for and are working for everything that is fine and beautiful, including families of sturdy, well-born, and well-bred youngsters who will make the next generation. On behalf of these young people I beg you to enact this bill, so they may have free and proper access to whatever help science can give them in the vital task that is ahead of them.

The Secretary of the National Council of Catholic Women, *Miss Agnes G. Reagan,* claimed that the bill requested Congress "to open the gates that information ruinous to Christian standards of family life may stream through the mails and flood the land." She asserted that birth control methods are "all contrary to the moral law and forbidden because they are unnatural," that they were "intrinsically wrong,—as wrong as lying and blasphemy." As to the effect upon young people, she said:

I speak from a rather wide and perhaps a sad experience in investigating conditions among young people who have become delinquent, and in many cases their delinquency was due to the fact that they could secure at the present time information concerning such practices; and that that information will certainly be much more widespread if this bill should be passed no one who has had dealings with young people has the slightest doubt. The United States in opening the mails to this sort of literature will do something that would be fatal to our young people.

Professor James A. Field of Chicago University, speaking for the bill, gave some historic proofs that legal attempts to suppress knowledge, especially that connected with sex, only serve to stimulate thought, increase curiosity and promote education. He instanced the situation in England about fifty years ago when obscenity prosecutions were instituted for circulating two hitherto relatively unknown pamphlets (both as it happened written by Americans, "Moral Physiology" by Robert Dale Owen who was a member of Congress from Indiana, and "Fruits of Philosophy" by Dr. Knowlton of Boston). "And then what happened? The case (against Charles Bradlaugh and Annie Besant) came before the greatest and highest court in England.

What would happen if the same high jurisdiction in this country took up a little pamphlet that nobody had heard of and such a pamphlet were taken up and challenged as destructive to public morals? Everybody would want to know what the pamphlet was all about. Well, that is what happened in England. There the pamphlet had sold to a small extent, really negligible in its extent, for 40 years. During the progress of the trial it sold to the extent of 125,000 copies.

The solicitor general prosecuted the case and admitted those figures. He apologized to the jury; he said the case was a mischievous case in its origin and bound to be mischievous in its results. He said he was really sorry he had anything to do with it.

The chief justice, in summing up, said everybody that had followed the case would agree on that, that no more ill-advised and injurious case had ever been brought before a court in his opinion.

A competent observer remarked that that prosecution had put the agitation forward by 25 years; and, in fact, so far as a great many people were concerned, it created the situation as an agitation. A great many people would never have known of it except for this and do not know that except as having this origin.

How about this country? There have been isolated cases, but so far bringing it to the attention of the people generally in the last ten years or so, that is due to what happened in New York within a decade. A nurse was working among the poor in New York and she was shocked to find that the mouths of physicians were stopped from giving advice to women about avoiding the sort of misery into which they had fallen. She found herself against the law. She started to publish what she thought were messages of health for women, but she found that was an infringement of the Federal postal laws, and her publications were suppressed.   She then withdrew to England, which had passed this state of prosecution.   She came back to this country with new enthusiasm, and before the storm was over she started a clinic.   That was against the law of New York.   Her sister was imprisoned in that connection, and they had a hunger strike, and all this appeared on the front page of the papers for 14 days or some such time, and the thing flared over the country.   And out of that has come definite organization, definite propaganda, which I think quite frankly and calmly we should not have at all in this country if it had not been there was legal opposition against which people felt moved to organize.   Now, what has this law, 50 years of it, and of the State laws that have copied it—what have they accomplished in this country?

They have not stood in the way of birth control, which is widely spreading, and a very widely approved practice; they have not stood in the way of the sale of instruments of birth control.   I think it is fair to say that anybody that is aware of what is going on knows that traffic flourishes for whoever chooses to take advantage of it, in spite of the laws.   But the law makes it relatively more difficult, for people who are without reputation or character to get the sort of information and medical advice, and sort of chance to think about these things for themselves which the other people have.

An exceptionally pertinent presentation of salient points was made by *Dorothy Glaser,* who spoke also for her husband, Dr. Otto Charles Glaser, who is the head of the department of biology at Amherst College:

It seems to me that there is a slight misunderstanding on the part of the various religious organizations here represented, especially the Catholics, about the Vaile bill, and I would like to discuss it from the scientific point of view.   I feel that we only stand on our rights as American citizens on this proposition.

We do not object to the teachings of the Catholic faith on this subject for their own people.   But we do feel that it is up to their own priests to advise them, instruct them, and keep them in order. They have no right to ask Federal aid to help the priests in matters of church discipline.   I would make the same reply to any other sect. Suppose, gentlemen, that the Christian Scientists came to you and said that they could not keep their people from using doctors.   Would you then pass legislation to do away with medical knowledge at the request of these Christian Scientists?   We have no objection to their taking any attitude on this matter, but we do object to their method of forcing it on others. We wish to be free to create scientific values without their interference. This is very difficult in the field of birth control, because under the present law the scientist is not free to work in this particular field. In every other than the human species there is freedom. The United States Bureau of Fisheries have a corps of scientists who work across the road from us in the department's laboratories at Woods Hole. They carry on experiments at Government expense with huge tanks of eggs and sperm. They limit the birth of the fish until such time as the temperature, season, and other environmental conditions are right, so that the young fish may have a square deal. But then America wants the best possible fish. The Bureau of Animal Husbandry is carrying on work in fertility, and I have a letter from Doctor Cole, the chief of this department, indorsing the Vaile Bill. Now, however, if some one is very much interested in problems of fertilization in his own species and wants to work in this field, to create new material for the use of the medical profession, what happens? He goes to his laboratory; and suppose he makes a discovery; if he then tells anybody, if he publishes what he has discovered, or whispers it through the keyhole, he is in the position of Galileo, about 400 years ago. He is likely to go to jail for giving his scientific knowledge to the world. In fact, the law tells him that it is obscene. He can, however, publish it in any other country in the world, except the United States.

Of course, we can not agree with the point that has been made this morning, that it is an interference with nature, nor grant that that is a logical argument. For scientific discovery and all medicine is an interference with nature, as are electric lights and plumbing. In fact, it is when we do not know how to interfere with her that many of our worst calamities befall us. The flu came so suddenly that science could not help, and few of us enjoyed letting nature run her course. In the case of yellow fever the Government scientists stepped forward and through birth control of the mosquito, a rank interference with nature, removed one of the greatest menaces to the South.

Again, I would like to emphasize the right of every American to all the scientific information that we can give him and to insist that no group have the right to keep it from him. The scientist has not found that ignorance is bliss. Is it, then, unreasonable for him to ask why his Government, which stands for free education and the public-school system, should write into a law in this instance a faith in man's ignorance about himself? I plead, then, for the removal of this law which would restrict man's knowledge about himself. Have we not faith enough in the people to let them have such information as we possess, or are some fields of science to be kept for the favored few?

Of course, the point of restriction of experimentation, had it come up in other relations, would have been a serious thing for all of us. As an example, the man who discovered insulin, the only known control for diabetes, could never have made this discovery had he been prevented by law from having free access to the material and work done by others before him. There is much valuable material being published in European laboratories. If, however, any scientist or physician brings this material into our country for use in our laboratories that we may advance our knowledge in this field, he is likely to go to jail by reason of the fact that the law tells us it is obscene literature. It can only be done on the boot-legging basis.

We have at present students at Amherst going into all professional fields, many to medical schools, but they may not be given any information in relation to this subject, even though they may ultimately want to use it for the control of venereal disease among their patients. They, like the rest of us, must just find out what they can as best they may.

One other point I should like to touch on in regard to the scientific point of view: We hear a great deal about "interference with nature" and the "right of the child to be born." To speak perfectly frankly, for a scientist this is nonsense, for in the light of the facts it leads to the reductio ad absurdum. I am sorry if I shocked the reverend father, who has just told us that these are things not even to be mentioned among Christians. The scientist must face all facts, sex included. The recent studies of bubonic plague in China have been unsavory and have been made at great personal risk. But some one must have the courage to face all of life, not selected sections of it.

It has been found that every human female has 3600 eggs and every male liberates 2,500,000 sperm at a time. Now, if the "right of the child to be born" means anything at all it must mean, then, the right of the egg to be fertilized, for it does not become a child until it does. Which, then, gentlemen, is the sacred egg? I would say that it is that egg which is fertilized at a time when both parents are in a position to give it a square deal; to give the child food, care, and the sort of environment which goes to the making of a decent American citizen.

I say again, we have no antagonism to the churches. The scientist would simply like to be left free to investigate his material and to put it at the disposal of all the American people, without church interference. We simply want the American people trusted with the best information that we can give them about this matter; that all, not some, may have the right to use it or not, as they see fit.

Mrs. Benjamin Carpenter showed how the precedent of the Federal law had been utilized by the courts to suppress the Parenthood Clinic in Chicago, even though Illinois has no State law prohibiting the giving of verbal information, as elsewhere described in this book. Her closing words were:

I ask you, gentlemen, is it not a shameful thing that when women are anxious to have children, and ask only for information as to how to space their children so that they can recover from one pregnancy before they are plunged into another one; or when they feel that they have had all the children they can possibly bring up as good citizens—and it is the women who bear the children—they want information, and it is refused them; in this twentieth century is it not shameful that any scientific information should be classed as obscene?

The point of view of the eugenicist was vigorously upheld by *Prof. Roswell Johnson* of Pittsburgh University, formerly investigator in experimental evolution for Carnegie Institute, and teacher of biology in the University of Wisconsin and Harvard University:

I wish to call your attention to the very great importance of this legislation for the future American racial composition. In my opinion only the immigration law and the projects for international comity can compare with this bill in so far as they affect the future of this American stock.

There are two kinds of children—welcome children and unwelcome children. This bill will reduce to an important extent the number of unwelcome children. It will increase to a considerable extent the number of welcome children.

Now, if the individual himself will cooperate in this matter, why should we not seize on that opportunity?

We talk in the eugenics movement of coercive legislation, of sterilization, of segregation, and of the regulation of the marriage laws; but here is a case where the individuals themselves, many inferior individuals say, "I won't have this child if you will show me how not to have it."

So I urge you not to continue the present law, which will mean absolutely and certainly a large continued contribution of inferiors to our stock.

Gentlemen, this is an urgent matter. If you let this go over for two years, into the next Congress, you are bringing on a very large number of inferior births that can be avoided. You know the number that are concerned in the immigration bill now pending —367,000 a year; 367,000 a year is no more than you are dealing with here. Now, do you deliberately want to add to the American people 367,000 individuals, we will say roughly, who will be, on the average, inferior?

Mr. Hersey: How do you prevent that—how does this bill prevent that?

Mr. Johnson: This bill will make it possible for individuals who have difficulty in getting access to efficient birth-control literature to get it. At present 80 per cent of the married women are trying one way or the other to achieve birth control. The less-informed women are blundering along with inadequate methods that they employ for lack of better, but which they can not rely on. Therefore by throwing open the distribution of literature, putting this on a scientific basis, like any other science, anybody can go and get material from authoritative sources and thus make it possible for the individual of limited opportunities to get that reliable information.

Mr. Hersey: Do you not think that that information, if admitted, would be found by the bad stock and good stock just the same?

Mr. Johnson: Yes.

Mr. Hersey: And are you not getting the proportion of good stock really lower by this method instead of increasing it?

Mr. Johnson: No; I do not admit that. Take Wellesley graduates, for instance. Their birth rate is already very low. The existence of birth-control methods has already had its effect. The scientific group as a whole knows now relatively reliable methods. What we plead for is their improvement and equalization of methods throughout the population.

The American stock is getting worse to-day, in my opinion, and that is a very serious thing. But in view of the great disparity in birth rates which we have relatively between the superior and inferior stock—

Mr. Hersey (interposing): I want to know the practical side. You claim this bill will increase the population in the matter of superior stock and decrease it in the matter of inferior stock. Now, how can you accomplish this by this bill?

Mr. Johnson: It is accomplished in this way: If you decrease the proportion of inferiors in the population you increase the general economic and social welfare of the whole population.

Senator Spencer: You increase the relative number of superiors?

Mr. Johnson: Yes: and absolutely also. If we increase the social welfare, then the superiors are willing to have more children and will have more children. One of the things that prevents superiors from having more children is the excessive reproduction of inferiors.

The appraisal of the merit of any proposed legislation is often facilitated by an inspection of the objections offered to it, and by consideration of the circumstances under which the objections are made. But to reproduce here the whole fifteen pages of closely printed words that constituted the testimony of the chief opposition speaker for whom the Hearing on the Cummins-Vaile Bill was reopened a month later, would be quite as much of an imposition on the reader as it was upon the Committee who had to listen to it, and upon the government which had to print it. It is estimated that it costs 50 cents a word to print the Congressional Record. Reports cost presumably about the same. But in view of the grave inhibition as to action which afflicted the Judiciary Committee, it may be that they felt grateful rather than imposed upon, for the delay involved and the time consumed; it put off the responsibility of doing anything just so much longer. It may be significant that the Chairman of the Hearing said at the close of this interminable statement, "We are very glad to have heard from you," and no such similar appreciation was expressed to any of the other speakers.

The circumstances under which this second hearing was

held are noteworthy. It came on May 9th. Ten days previous it was discovered that the reports of the first hearing were all ready to print, but were being held on official order. On May 3rd the Director of the Voluntary Parenthood League was told by the Secretary of the Chairman of the House Sub-Committee that the Chairman of the full Committee wished some additional material added to the Hearing Report, and that the printing would be delayed on that account. As several written statements had been filed as part of the testimony which there had not been time to have read at the Hearing, the assumption was that this material was another such statement. But by May 7th it was learned that the Hearing was to be reopened on the 9th. There was no publicity on the announcement and it was only at the eleventh hour that Mr. Vaile himself was notified. Fortunately friends of the bill came on telegraphed call, to be on hand to answer the opposition or the queries of the Committee.

Another noteworthy fact in the circumstances is that the chief speaker for the opposition at this second Hearing was a young Catholic woman, a social worker, Miss Sara E. Laughlin of Philadelphia, who three years previously had joined the Voluntary Parenthood League, with professions of great interest. She had paid regular annual membership dues, which act, according to the membership blanks, constitutes endorsement of the objects of the League, the first of which is the removal of the Federal law which prohibits the circulation of contraceptive information.

Most of her testimony was discussion of the morality of birth control rather than the question of the right of the citizen to have access to the knowledge, which is the point of the bill. It was a general denunciation of the birth control movement and the procedure of its advocates. The following excerpts are characteristic of the whole:

Miss Laughlin: Mr. Chairman, in this instance I am representing the International Federation of Catholic Alumnae. That organization is exactly what its name implies—a federation of the alumnae of the Catholic academies and colleges of the United States and some other countries.

I am here to-day because I am in the position at present of chairman of the bureau of girls' welfare in that organization, and therefore I must be concerned about such matters of public welfare as are involved in this bill.

Because of a difference in training and a belief in the conserving value of a decent reserve, we are not nearly so vocal as the proponents of this bill, but see it as our duty to become more so, as it seems that this is necessary to safeguard the moralities which we believe to be involved in this question.

Partly through the activities of the Voluntary Parenthood League and the Birth Control League, sex relations and allied subjects were removed from their proper place in medical textbooks and necessary instruction in right conduct by proper authorities to each new generation, and have become in many quarters matters of general conversation even in mixed gatherings. As a professional social worker who has dealt with a number of girls, I can not state too strongly the unfortunate effect of this general stimulation of discussion of sex matters, about which everybody admits from a scientific point of view very little is known.

Just as we have never shirked considering any phase of human nature when human interests were to be served, we do not now evade our obligation to state publicly our point of view on the proposed measure, however much we regret the necessity.

You are asked to "redeem the United States from the odium of being the only country to penalize birth control as indecency." We think this is not an odium, but shows a wise concern for the mental and moral health of our people. We think it preferable to the English problem of recalling indecent and improper literature after it has once been released.

We do not advocate the dissemination of this knowledge any more than we would advocate the dissemination of doses and methods of administering deadly poison. This sort of knowledge is in the possession of all physicians. We do not feel that we are discriminated against because it is not made readily accessible to us.

You are told that doctors advocate the passage of this bill because they are not told about the control of conception in a medical school, and their patients keep asking them for this instruction. You are told frequently, too, that doctors are giving this instruction. Yet you are told that they do not have it.

You are told that "millions of self-respecting parents resent the legal insult by which the information as to control of conception is made unmailable." We ask you to give your attention to the millions who are grateful for this provision, because they are convinced of the grave danger which would attend its removal.

If we were concerned only for our own welfare, we would not raise our voices now in opposition, but by refusing to discuss the measure lend our passive assistance to its enactment.

We belong to an organization which has stood the test of time better than any other organization the world has seen.

Mr. Yates: Meaning—

Miss Laughlin: Meaning the Catholic Church. We could assume, therefore, if we could be guilty of such callous indifference to the effect on our fellow citizens, that this was a providential measure intended to enable us to inherit the earth. Following this line of reasoning, we could conserve our efforts and devote our time to keeping our people as free as possible from this pernicious propaganda, and reap the material rewards. Such a procedure would be contrary to the spiritual and ethical principles we have accepted, and abhorrent to any body of Christian people.

I can not, as the organization proposing this measure presumes to do, speak for millions, but I can speak from personal knowledge of hundreds of mothers in whose homes I visit year after year in the course of work with their children. They do not want this information for their own use, and they do not want it circulated to be used as an insidious snare for their children when they have reached maturity.

Compare this last statement about not speaking on behalf of millions, with the seventh item from Miss Laughlin's testimony quoted above in which she asks the Committee to consider "the millions" who are, she asserts, "grateful for this provision" in the present law which denies them access to knowledge.

Compare also her statement of her individual experience with "hundreds of mothers" who "do not want this information" with the experience of both the New York and the Chicago Clinics, in which the proportions of Catholic women who request contraceptive instructions is sizable. The New York Clinic reports the percentage as thirty-two, and the Chicago Clinic as thirty. However, any divergence of testimony that there may be as to whether Catholics want or will utilize contraceptive information is rather beside the point so far as Congress and the bill are concerned. The issue is not as to whether individuals or groups want this knowledge but as to whether anyone who does want it shall have his right to get it recognized by law.

The Chairman of the Hearing allowed a rebuttal to the Catholic testimony by the Director of the Voluntary Parenthood League to be filed as part of the Hearing report. It reads as follows:

The question in the bill is not the control of conception but the right of the citizen to have access to scientific knowledge. The utilization of that knowledge is left entirely to the individual.

Most of the testimony presented by the Catholic speakers is irrelevant. They argued the question of birth control, which is not per se before Congress. If the Catholics could persuade some one to introduce a bill which would make the control of conception a crime, the arguments against birth control would be genuine, but without such a bill they are not.

It would seem doubtful as to whether leaders in the Catholic Church would wish, on second thought, to put themselves on record as opposed to the principles of freedom as to belief and action in private life. As they wish to conserve these principles as applied to their own right to teach and preach their beliefs, they may well take thought about trying to utilize law to suppress the right of others to do the same.

There are about 18,000,000 Catholics in this country. As, therefore, they form less than one-sixth of the population, their protest against the Cummins-Vaile bill amounts to a demand that the laws of the country should be made to reflect the religious creed of a small minority.

Moreover, their protest against the bill implies a distrust of their own church people that will prove embarrassing to the leaders if persisted in. Since the teaching of the church is against the use of contraceptive knowledge, are the leaders to announce thus publicly that they have so little faith in the efficacy of church teaching and so little trust in the moral rectitude of the church members that they would wish to invoke the arm of the law to keep the people in ignorance. If the church people can not be assumed to have the loyalty and strength to live up to their own beliefs, it is surely stretching the bounds of reasonableness for the Catholic leaders to suggest that the non-Catholic population, which is five-sixths of the whole, should go without this knowledge in order to protect the Catholics from their own weakness.

The inappropriateness of the Catholic attitude is well brought out by the following excerpts from a recent letter from a member of our league to the chairman of the Senate Sub-committee of the Judiciary:

"You would not agree that, at the behest of the Methodists, or the Elks, or the Young Men's Hebrew Association there should be passed a Federal law to apply to the whole American public, which law represented merely a belief. You can not then, believe that a law should fail to pass merely because it does not accord with the Catholic belief. A law, being a rule of action, should not stand for what is simply an article of faith. The Cummins-Vaile Bill does not enjoin any action or the refraining from any action. It simply will give legal status to certain scientific knowledge and means which are now proscribed. No one will be compelled to learn the knowledge; no one will be compelled to use the means. No belief will be interfered with; no rule of action will be laid down. The principle of making laws to satisfy a religious group, crystallizing religious beliefs into rules of action for all the people, went out of this Government with the adoption of the United States Constitution."

Various inaccuracies in Miss Laughlin's statements regarding the publications of the Voluntary Parenthood League were answered at the Hearing, but that part of the report is not germane to the subject of this book, except as to the correction on one point which led to a series of question and answers which give light on the working of the minds of some of the Committee.

Mrs. Dennett: There are one or two other inaccuracies that it is worth while to comment upon. One was that this knowledge is already in the possession of all physicians. That is not the case. We have here the president of one of the State medical associations, who will be glad to give you further facts in regard to it. The fact that we receive quantities of letters from physicians asking us to provide them with such knowledge from our headquarters—a thing we can not do legally,—of course, is sufficient to refute that statement.

Mr. Hersey: You have just made a statement denying that this knowledge of birth control, if that is the proper term, is in the hands of the physicians of America to-day?

Mrs. Dennett: On account of the laws, primarily.

Mr. Hersey: Well, some one has got it. What proportion of the physicians of America have that information now?

Mrs. Dennett: It is quite impossible for us to tell. I do not know that any survey has been made.

Mr. Hersey: Who has thorough information upon this subject?

Mrs. Dennet: Nobody, so far as I have yet heard, in the medical profession, or among students of biology, claims to have final and complete information.

Mr. Hersey: Does the organization for birth control which you represent possess the information that you want disseminated now to the public?

Mrs. Dennett: The organization consists of thousands of members. Do you mean all the members, or the officers, or what?

Mr. Hersey: Any part of your organization.

Mrs. Dennett: It has some information, certainly.

Mr. Hersey: Is that information perfect information? Do you know anything about the remedy that you are asking for?

Mrs. Dennett. It is not claimed to be absolutely perfect. No.

Mr. Hersey: Do you know what you are asking this committee to do, madam? You are asking us to do this: To report out a bill here, assuming from evidence before this committee that this committee has definite information that there exists at the present time, in somebody's mind, this information that you say is so precious, to be disseminated among the people, and which we know nothing about. We have no evidence that anybody possesses the perfect remedy for this evil of which you complain—the bearing of children. You do not claim to have it yourself, and your organization does not claim to have that perfect information. You can not point us to a doctor who has it, and to whom we could go for the information. You ask us to say that there is such a thing that the people can have if we pass this bill. You can see the spectacle that we would make of ourselves in the House if Members should get up and ask this committee: "Do you know anything about this matter that you are asking us to adopt; whether it is a remedy for this evil of childbirth, or whether it is simply some quack that wants to sell something, and wants us to remove the bar, which is the United States law, against sending this knowledge through the mail or disseminating it among the people?" You want us to allow that information to be made public, through some one who claims to have it, and you have not even an endorsement of the American Medical Association that there is such a thing as a perfect remedy for the evil of which you complain."

Mrs. Dennett: It would be, from our point of view, the height of absurdity to expect busy committees in Congress to be themselves authorities on questions of science; and for us to demand the passage of a law that will allow scientists to perfect their own knowledge, which now they can not perfect, because of the law—

Mr. Hersey (interposing) : Why not perfect their knowledge?

Mrs. Dennett: Because the law prevents.

Mr. Hersey: No; it does not. Somebody has this knowledge, perfected or not perfected. Is it perfected or not, now?

Mrs. Dennett: It can not be perfected until scientists are legally free to study it.

Mr. Hersey: You must have your remedy before you can send it through the mail. You are asking us to send through the mail something that is not perfected.

Mrs. Dennett: Research work can not be carried on legally on this subject so long as the laws stay the way they are. That is the point.

Mr. Hersey: Then, you claim that the research work has not commenced yet on this matter?

Mrs. Dennett: I do not. It has gone on sub rosa, illegally, and on a bootlegging basis. That is a most undesirable basis for scientific research work. There are no exemptions for the medical profession to these Federal laws—none whatever—and I should be glad to submit to the committee the statement in writing from the solicitor for the Post Office Department, that there are no exemptions for individuals or groups of any sort. The medical profession, therefore, is most seriously handicapped.

Mr. Hersey: Well, why does not the American Medical Association at its annual meetings, recommend that Congress pass a bill like this to relieve them of that difficulty? Why do they not go on record? Why is it necessary for your organization of women to come in here, without knowledge of what you are asking for?

Mr. Vaile: May I make a statement, Mr. Chairman?

Mr. Hersey: Yes; I should be glad to have you.

Mr. Vaile: My understanding is, that there is reliable information at present—not claimed to be very great, but reliable, as far as medical science can get reliability at the present day—which we want to be able to send through the mails.

Mr. Hersey: Where is it?

Mr. Vaile: Mrs. Dennett can tell you, I think.

Mr. Hersey: I wish she would.

Mrs. Dennett: There are admirable publications upon the subject abroad. They can not be legally brought into this country. There are some publications in this country being illegally circulated by well known medical authorities, without the names attached. Their names can not be attached until the law allows. Otherwise they are criminal, indictable under the present laws.

Mr. Hersey: Do you think there is some man of high medical standing in America to-day who has this information?

Mrs. Dennett: There are a great many.

Mr. Hersey: Is it possible for you to find one of those medical men of high standing in the profession to come before this committee and say that his experience has shown that this remedy that he has, even if secret, is all right?

Mrs. Dennett: We have one here to-day, and I will gladly yield to him—Doctor Litchfield of Pennsylvania.

Mr. Hersey: We will be glad to hear from him. This legislation asked for is to make available to the people something that will prevent conception?

Dr. Litchfield: There is not any one thing asked for. We ask for the freedom of the mail to give suitable information to suitable cases of methods that are applicable and desirable.

Mr. Vaile: If the Chair will excuse a suggestion, I understand that it is against the law in the District of Columbia, following and going a little further than the Federal statute, to give, even verbally, information concerning birth-control methods.

Mr. Hersey: I am not asking for the information itself. I am asking this doctor, who is presented here as a witness, as an expert, if he knows—

Dr. Litchfield (interposing): I know several methods of contraception that are reliable, harmless, and desirable in suitable cases.

Mr. Hersey: And you claim that you are about the only man in your profession who has that knowledge?

Dr. Litchfield: Not at all. There are millions that have. I studied in Europe, as a large majority of the profession do.

Mr. Hersey: Then your idea is that most physicians in practice know what you know, is that it?

Dr. Litchfield: No; I would not say that.

Mr. Hersey: The best physicians would know it, would they not?

Dr. Litchfield: Those who have studied abroad, and who have been interested in this phase of preventive medicine, know it.

Mr. Hersey: Is there anything in the law that you understand prevents you from talking with a brother physician and giving him your knowledge?

Dr. Litchfield: Certainly there is. In some states you are forbidden to give contraceptive knowledge to any one, either verbally or through the mail.

Mr. Hersey: Your remedy is effective, is it?

Dr. Litchfield: Certainly; yes.

Mr. Hersey: Are you the only one in Pittsburgh that knows about it?

Dr. Litchfield: I do not know about that.

Mr. Hersey: Where did you get this information?

Dr. Litchfield: I got it in Europe.

Mr. Hersey: How many kinds of information have you?

Dr. Litchfield: I suppose there are a dozen different remedies. Perhaps there are four, five, or six that are approved by those of experience. Most of the methods would be covered by two or three.

Mr. Hersey: Have you tested your method?

Dr. Litchfield: I said I have; yes, sir.

Mr. Hersey: Have you found them all right?

Dr. Litchfield: I found them harmless and desirable. I will not say that they are all right. Nothing is perfect in medical science yet. We are progressing, and we want to progress still further, not only for doctors, but biologists and scientists.

Mr. Hersey: If this legislation is passed removing this ban, would you publish your information?

Dr. Litchfield: It would not be necessary for me to publish it. Others directly interested in that work would publish the information.

Mr. Hersey: Do you not think there would be more money in it for you?

Dr. Litchfield: If I were looking for money, I would not be here to-day.

Mr. Hersey: Who is going to publish the information?

Dr. Litchfield: The physicians have been writing books on this subject, devoting themselves to these particular branches of medicine, and will publish the books as soon as the ban is removed.

Mr. Hersey: Are you a member of the American Medical Association?

Dr. Litchfield: I am.

Mr. Hersey: Why have you not succeeded in getting them to adopt this?

Dr. Litchfield: The medical society has been very busy, but they will do this eventually. The president of the American Medical Association told me so. I met him in conference at Atlantic City, and he said all the members were in favor of birth control, and it was only a question of time that we should have it. I am not authorized to give his name, but he stands as the first man in American medicine.

Mr. Hersey: Where you felt you had a patient bearing a child, who would be in danger of her life, there is nothing in the law at present that would prevent you from pursuing your remedy, is there?

Dr. Litchfield: There is something in the law of my State that prohibits me.

Mr. Hersey: The proponents of this measure contend, as I understand, that some of them do not want to have the trouble with the child, they do not want to have the child on account of the annoyance.

Dr. Litchfield: No; the statement that was made this morning that morality depends on opportunity for conception is an insult to American women. I have been practicing medicine for 25 years, and I do not figure that the morality of the young American women would be influenced in the slightest degree if contraceptive methods become public property. I think morality is something higher, and I do not think Congress is asked to pass statutes in favor of morality any more than they are asked to pass a law that everybody should be a Roman Catholic.

Mr. Hersey: When was this ban fixed?

Dr. Litchfield: 1873.

(For five years Mr. Hersey like all members of Congress had been receiving literature and data frequently, which gave the history of the Comstock law, and all the pertinent facts concerning it.)

Mr. Hersey: And the immediate thing desired here is the repeal of the prohibition of the use of the mails for these methods? If this law were passed you would be confronted by your State.

Dr. Litchfield: We would have to have the State laws changed.

Mr. Hersey: Do you mean to say that at the present time you are prohibited by your State law of advising a patient or communicating through another doctor methods of birth control?

Dr. Litchfield: Yes, sir.

Mr. Major: Do you not think that the main trouble in this country now is lack of children, instead of having too many?

Dr. Litchfield: Too many children in a certain strata is very undesirable.

Mr. Major: I remember the old poem, "There was an old woman who lived in a shoe, who had so many children she didn't know what to do." There was another old poem, "There was a woman who lived in a shoe, who didn't have any children; she knew what to do." I have heard that all my life.

Dr. Litchfield: I do not think that knowledge will prevent the average woman from having children.

Mr. Major: But they do not have many children. I can remember my grandmother and her three sisters, four women married before they were 18, who raised over 11 children and lived to be over 80 years of age. There are seven in my family. I have a daughter with two children. If it keeps on, her daughter will not have any children. That looks to be the trouble; the people that ought to have children do not. A bill like this, to put this information around in news stands, where it can be picked up anywhere, as these women say, I do not know how you feel about it, but I have always felt the very fear of consequences. I have felt that it would promote immorality.

I want to say another thing to you, Doctor. I was State's attorney in my court and my county, which is one of the best in the world, for six years, and during that time I suspect I had at least four seduction cases a year. There has not been a seduction case there now for 20 years. That looks like this information is leaking out in some way.

Dr. Litchfield: It is not getting in the right hands.

Mr. Major: It is getting out. I do not think human nature is changing, but those cases are only heard of when there is pregnancy in a seduction case, and there has not been a seduction case there for 20 years. When you go into different courts you do not hear of it, and it used to be of frequent occurrence, and the only explanation in my mind is that these people are securing from some source the knowledge to prevent conception, and the effect of it is that the people that ought to be having families, and I mean like the lady that spoke this morning—my idea about the best people in this country is that they should not bring up one or two spindley children that do not know how to take care of themselves. They do not have families any more where the girls hand down one dress to another. That is past in this country.

(The English in the above is unedited. It is reprinted exactly as it appears in the government report of the Hearing.)

Dr. Litchfield: I agree; but for every case of seduction there are over 100 cases of worthy, industrious, virtuous, loving mothers who are having their children too close together, and if they had the knowledge to space their children and conserve their own health it would be better than to raise such terribly big families and themselves be broken down in middle life by too frequent pregnancy. We are not working for the profligate who becomes easily seduced and becomes pregnant. They are an inconsiderable number compared with the worthy people that should have the protection that science can give them. The enormous number of women who die before middle life on account of too frequent pregnancy, whose health is broken down, so that they leave a large family of motherless children, could be done away with.

Mr. Yates: Does that frequently occur?

Dr. Litchfield: Yes.

Mr. Yates: I have a daughter who had four babies, and she is fatter and prettier now after having the four.

Dr. Litchfield: She did not have one each year?

Mr. Yates: No. Now, the question I have had in mind that has been troubling me—would it not happen, if we removed the prohibition of the use of the mail—in other words, if the mails were thrown open would it not happen that every cheap publication in the country could advertise to send 50 cents and they would get this information; would not that be an evil, to have these things upon the news stands, in depots, and places like that?

Dr. Litchfield: I do not think so.

Mr. Yates: I am referring to the masses. That is what I am talking about.

Dr. Litchfield: I feel that legitimate sources of information will be the recognized source. I do not think that it will be a thing peddled on the news stands.

Mr. Hersey: What will hinder it?

Dr. Litchfield: If it is peddled on the news stand it will not do as much harm by reaching the immoral as good will be done by the worthy, **well-**meaning, industrious citizens. The people deserve health and protection, and the knowledge of science will give them that protection. I got a book in England that I wanted to send my daughter, and I was forbidden to bring it into the country because of the mails. They would not allow it.

Mr. Hersey: Could not you instruct your daughter without the book?

Dr. Litchfield: No sir; my daughter is a citizen of Holland. I would like to give this book to all young friends, patients of mine who are about to be married.

Mr. Hersey: Why not give it to the members of the committee?

Dr. Litchfield, The custom-house will not let it come in.

Mr. Hersey: I would like to submit it to my home physician whom I trust.

Dr. Litchfield: Would you like me to smuggle a copy in? I know how.

Mr. Hersey: You are asking us to pass something that we do not know anything about.

Dr. Litchfield: We want the freedom to use the mails.

Mr. Hersey: Using the mails would bring it in?

Dr. Litchfield: But we are liable to get caught.

(If the reason for the verbal fencing on the part of the writer under the heckling of Congressman Hersey is not readable between the lines, it is well to say that it was for two reasons, one the natural hesitancy of a layman to make specific claims as to just what the medical profession knows, as such statements should come from the physicians themselves; the other a desire to avoid being led into giving any information which would render the reports of the Hearing unmailable, under Section 211.)

Mr. Johnson: It has been stated that this is a distasteful subject. Gentlemen, it seems to me that even if true it is irrelevant. The Judiciary Committee must deal with many things, distasteful. But I do not believe it is true. How can anything which deals so fundamentally with one of the three fundamental things of life be distasteful? That is an utter inconsequential consideration.

I wish to call attention to the fact that there is in some States a law that says that a refusal to cohabit for one year is a ground for divorce.

A method of control of reproduction, which is sanctioned by a large number of people, that by the "natural" method—that is, abstinence at periods in the monthly cycle—is also prohibited as to dissemination by the mails by this law.

Mr. Hersey: You are giving us the secret?

Mr. Johnson: That is one of the methods, and is considered "natural" and hence not opposed by the opponents of this law.

Mr. Hersey: Known to every woman in the world.

Mr. Johnson: Yes; and it is very unreliable.

Mr. Hersey: Is it as reliable as your method?

Mr. Johnson: No.

Mr. Hersey: Do you know the method advocated here?

Mr. Johnson: Yes; there are several methods.

Mr. Hersey: Better than that one?

Mr. Johnson: Why, of course.

Although Congressman Hersey was the one Committee member at the Hearings who talked at length, his mental processes were by no means representative of the Judiciary Committee as a whole. Most of the others evinced clearer thought and a more wholesome view-point. But many of them were willing enough to let Mr. Hersey "go on." Some confessed to getting amusement from it, and some were apologetic about his "surprising ways," but all of them who preferred postponement to acting on the bill derived comfort from knowing that Mr. Hersey's antagonism would furnish excuse for further "consideration" for quite some time. And it proved to be serviceable in this regard, for at last accounts he was still saying that the bill would never be reported out of Committee if he could help it; and the sixty-eighth Congress adjourned without seeing the bill reported, that is, not by the House Judiciary Committee, though the Senate Sub-Committee did give it a unanimous report "without recommendation."

During the next session when every effort was being made to produce a vote on the bill from the two full Judiciary Committees, the advocates of the bill were offered *still further hearings*. This offer was made by the Chairman of the

House Sub-Committee and also by a member of the Senate Judiciary Committee, both of whom gave as excuse for not coming to a conclusion on the bill after five years of consideration, that they were so "terribly busy"; the calendar in this short session was so "jammed with important legislation"; there was so much "stuff" to read about endless bills, —"I sent my secretary for the data on one the other day, and would you believe it, Mrs. Dennett, there were seven volumes," implying that he had not had time to read the report of the hearings on this bill. Yet they offered more hearings, by way of still further congesting their own calendar.

No one can deny the existence of a legislative jam in every session of Congress, or that business piles up appallingly in every short session. Three weeks from the end of the last session of the sixty-eighth Congress, Senator Stanley said on the floor of the Senate, "Congress has before it in the present session 17,946 bills, resolutions and joint resolutions. As in most Congresses, the large majority of these bills relate to private or local matters like individual pensions, buildings bridges, etc., and relatively few deal with public questions or national welfare." The conduct of members of Congress under these circumstances, and the choices made by the steering committees as to which measures shall be scheduled for attention, and allowed a chance on the floor, and also the number and character of the unscheduled measures which are taken up and passed by unanimous consent, make serious food for thought for citizens with inquiring minds.

Near the close of the session, it was obvious that the Cummins-Vaile bill would not be allowed any sort of a chance by the Senate steering committee even if reported out by the full Judiciary Committee in time for a vote on the floor without discussion. In fact the leading member of the steering committee was quite explicit in saying so. It looked as if the report ("without prejudice" as at first suggested by Senator Overman, and "without recommendation" as finally filed by Senator Spencer) had been only a sop to those who had labored for the bill, a safe tribute to their "patience" and "hard work." However, the proponents of the bill, because of the inescapable conviction that the chief reason for Congressional inaction had been the "general distaste" of members for dealing with it openly, decided upon a plan for possibly getting a favorable vote from the full Judiciary Committee of Senate before adjournment, as a means of helping to break down the inhibitions of the other members of the Senate, and so to pave the way in the next Congress for easier and quicker passage of the bill.

Senator Cummins, then Chairman of the Judiciary Committee, said he would call for a vote of the Committee on the bill at any time before the end of the session if a majority were willing to vote for a favorable report. It would require nine votes to win the report. The plan adopted was an unusual and informal one, a sort of layman-citizen's way of cutting through the tangle of business. There were but twenty-six days left in the session including Sundays. The carrying out of this plan was described as follows in The Birth Control Herald (March 10, 1925) under these headlines: "A Mental Daily Dozen Prescribed for the Judiciary Committee by the V. P. L. as an Aid to Action on Cummins-Vaile Bill; Method Urged as Congressional Minute-Saver in Legislative Rush Toward Close of Session":

Not to Walter Camp's records, but to the tune of facts and reasoning arranged by the Voluntary Parenthood Director, the members of the Judiciary Committee in both Senate and House, were urged to stimulate healthy thought on the Cummins-Vaile Bill, with a view to reaching a Committee decision by the time the twelfth mental exercise was finished.

This dozen of "setting up" exercises were prescribed as an aid toward overcoming the paralysis of the reasoning faculties, induced by the embarrassment of sex consciousness, which seem to rise to the surface in the minds of most of the members, when dealing with the "birth control" bill.

The "dozen" consisted of a daily sequence of notes to each member, each note covering a single point for the bill, and so short that it would take no more than two minutes to read. The plan was offered as a first aid to minute-saving in the legislative rush toward the close of the session. One reason a day keeps the "no-time-for-consideration" argument away. There are spare minutes despite the legislative jam,—observation from the galleries proves it, says Director Dennett, after her long experience in watching the members of Congress write, talk with each other, swap jokes, or have forty winks, while their colleagues deliver themselves of their views, at great length on the floor.

The twelve notes are given below. To save space the introductory and closing words of each note are omitted.

February 6, 1925.

POINT ONE.—Accepting the probability that there will not be time, before the close of the present session, to have the Cummins-Vaile Bill discussed at length, either in the Judiciary Committee or on the floor, we are asking each member of the Judiciary Committee to consider *informally,* the very few simple points in the bill, with a view to securing, if possible, a vote in committee without appreciable debate.

We sympathetically recognize the fact that, under the existing Congressional system, *thorough* consideration for all bills is a physical impossibility for the individual Congressman, no matter how conscientious he may be; also that group consideration in Committee or by the whole House, is subject to great limitation.

For these very reasons we ask that, as practicable procedure, a decision on this bill be arrived at by the above suggested method of informal discussion, with us and with other committee members, one by one, as leisure moments during House sessions permit.

Just as we sympathize with you in your impossible legislative obligations, we assume your sympathy with us, a group of representative citizens, who after nearly six years of effort, are rightly asking action from the only body that can give it. So we ask your tolerant and cooperative reception of the memoranda of single points which will be presented to you in sequence during the next ten days.

The first one is given herewith, namely, the marked article in the enclosed paper, showing that the main principle involved in the Cummins-Vaile Bill has been previously well argued by two distinguished members of the Senate Judiciary Committee.

(The enclosure was a copy of the Birth Control Herald of January 20, giving exerpts from the arguments of Sen. Borah and Sen. Stanley on suppressing information about betting. See Appendix No. 13.)

February 7, 1925.

POINT TWO.—Constitutionally guaranteed, old-fashioned American liberty is the issue in the bill. "Birth control" is not. The latter is properly a question for individual decision in private life. The bill simply removes the legal barrier to knowledge as to what birth control may be. In other words, it is a question of freedom of speech and of the press.

Members of the Judiciary Committee are credited with judicial minds, and the ability to disassociate relevant from irrelevant argument. Much of the previous discussion, both informally and at the two Hearings, has been irrelevant; i.e., about birth control.

The few facts which constitute the relevant arguments, have, so far as I know, never been denied by any member of the Committee.

February 9, 1925.

POINT THREE.—No law exists which defines information as to the control of conception as, per se, obscene, indecent or in any way immoral.

This information therefore should not be legally classed with penalized obscenity, indecency and immorality. The Cummins-Vaile Bill removes it from this classification. But the bill leaves the five statutes in question, amply empowered to suppress any particular instance of this information, which is given in a way that warrants judicial decision that it is obscene, indecent or of immoral import.

The existing laws originally aimed at obscenity, not at science, but because of hasty enactment, the scientific information was prohibited also. The Cummins-Vaile Bill removes the error.

February 10, 1925.

POINT FOUR.—The control of parenthood by the utilization of contraceptive knowledge is an act which is entirely lawful, throughout the whole United States (with the single exception of Connecticut, where an obsolete law making it a crime still remains on the books,—the only instance of the sort in the world).

But *to secure or to give* this knowledge, via any public carrier, is a crime under Federal law (and also under the laws of twenty-four States whose obscenity statutes have been modelled closely on the Federal statutes).

To deny to citizens the use of public carriers to convey knowledge regarding an act which is in itself lawful, is a legal abnormality that should long ago have been corrected. The Cummins-Vaile Bill will do it.

February 11, 1925.

POINT FIVE.—There is no denying that the control of parenthood is already a general practice among educated Americans, including of course members of Congress, as it is among educated people in all countries.

Our prohibitive laws obviously therefore do not reflect the policy of what we call our best people. When the universal trend of intelligent people is to get and make use of the contraceptive knowledge which the laws forbid,—that is, to become lawbreakers,—is it not high time to change the laws?

The Washington Post, in an editorial recently said, "The first duty of Congress is to ascertain the will of the people. The second is to enforce and obey it."

February 12, 1925.

POINT SIX.—The portions of the present laws which the Cummins-Vaile Bill will repeal, are unenforced and unenforceable.

The prohibition of the dissemination of contraceptive knowledge is probably the most broken of all the laws on the statute books. The existing traffic in contraceptives is appalling, from the point of view of law enforcement.

If Congress does not believe in the existing laws enough to even protest against the utter laxity of the authorities, whose duty it is to enforce the laws, it surely should hasten to remove from the authorities the obligations which they will not and can not fulfill.

February 13, 1925.

POINT SEVEN.—One of the most shocking features of the unenforceability of the present laws prohibiting the circulation of contraceptive knowledge is the great and rapidly increasing volume of underground information and means which circulates despite the laws.

This information is almost wholly unauthorized by reputable scientists, is largely unreliable and inadequate, is considerably harmful and dangerous, and alas, is even vulgar and smutty in its form. The means, which are camouflaged as for other purposes, are an opportunity for conscienceless profiteering, and, like the information, are uncertified by proper authorities.

The only effective antidote possible is to make the circulation lawful, so that it can be properly inspected and made subject to the Drugs Act; and so that the first class medical experts may have a lawful and decent opportunity to denounce the quacks and profiteers, and to supplant their abominations with dignified, reliable, scientific, hygienic information.

The Cummins-Vaile Bill opens the way for this tremendously needed effort on the part of our best doctors, who are now tied hand and foot by the laws, or are obliged to resort to the undignified process of boot-legging their scientific teaching.

The doctors can save the day, if they are given a chance. Is it fair for Congress to hinder any longer?

February 14, 1925.

POINT EIGHT.—The St. Louis Times recently published the leading editorial, which follows:

"A Bill for Moral Health

"Nothing comes closer to the minds and hearts of healthy Americans than the begetting, bearing and rearing of children. Unfortunately this subject has been relegated to the limbo of the unclean, the indecent, the nasty jokesmith; and much teaching and thinking has made it so.

"A long step toward cleansing the people's minds and hearts of the prevalent false standards, clearing the visions and correcting conclusions, has been taken by the Voluntary Parenthood League. But it has taken this organization of influential citizens five years to overcome the paralyzing fears that beset both rulers and people, and get the Cummins-Vaile bill into Congress.

"Honorable physicians and scientists have been blocked from circulating wholesome information on contraception. Nevertheless, charlatans flourish like weeds. Practically every boy and girl can talk glibly of the subject, and their misinformation has come principally from foul sources.

"It is time to protect physicians and social workers, and save our children from false, foolish and foul ideas of life, to make the human body and its functions clean subjects of definite knowledge and control.

"Congress should pass the Cummins-Vaile Bill unanimously in the interest of public health, morals and decency."

February 16, 1925.

POINT NINE.—As a member of the Senate Judiciary Committee has recently brought up a point which frequently occurs in discussion, it may be well to call it to the attention of the other members; i.e., that the control of parenthood can be achieved without the utilization of any scientific knowledge,—merely by abstinence from the relationship which results in conception.

This is offered as a reason for retaining the law which bans knowledge of scientific methods.

Apart from the question of the constitutionality, justice or propriety of such prohibitive legislation, it must be remembered that in the marital relation abstinence does not have the sanction of law. In many States refusal to cohabit, as an element of desertion or of cruelty and indignity is ground for divorce. Hence abstinence thus penalized is no free or practicable alternative for the compulsory ignorance decreed by the statute.

Thus it follows that the only sort of parenthood which has the thorough sanction of American laws is the irresponsible, unintentional sort,—parenthood of no higher standard than that of the wild animals.

Is it not high time to make the laws catch up with civilization?

February 18, 1925.

POINT TEN.—Government officials themselves are guilty of flagrant violations of statutes prohibiting circulation of contraceptive knowledge. But they are not indicted for their crimes,—one more evidence that the government makes no valid effort to enforce the laws on this subject.

The following recent instances are noteworthy:

1. The Library of the Surgeon General has received and is loaning to readers the November issue of the American Journal of ———— published by the ———— Company of ————. It contains a report by Dr. ———— on methods of controlling conception,—the report being the result of research by the New York Committee on ————.

To mail the magazine from ———— to receive and loan it in Washington are criminal acts under the law.

2. The Congressional Library has received from England and has loaned to readers the new volume entitled ———— by Dr. ————, published by ———— London. It is a "Manual for the Medical and Legal Professions," and is considered one of the best and most comprehensive works on the subject in the world.

To pass the book through the customs, to transport it to Washington, to list it in the library catalogue, and to lend it to readers are criminal acts under the law.

The same volume has been borrowed by several members of the Judiciary Committee,—again a criminal act.

3. In considering these instances of official crime it is well to note the recent utilization of the laws on this subject, to secure the imprisonment of Carlo Tresca, who published in his Italian paper in New York a two line advertisement of a book on birth control. He was notified by the post office that his paper was thereby made unmailable. The two lines were deleted and the edition was mailed. But he was subsequently convicted for the offense. President Coolidge yesterday commuted the sentence, after reviewing evidence showing that Tresca had first been arrested on another charge instigated by those who objected to his political views, but who, unable to jail him for those, resorted then to the charge of violation of the laws prohibiting circulation of birth control knowledge.

Do not such facts point conclusively to the obligation of Congress to repeal these laws which are not and can not be justly enforced? To accomplish this repeal is the object of the Cummins-Vaile Bill.

NOTE: The names of the publishers and authors in the above letter cannot be printed without infringing the Federal law.

February 19, 1925.

POINT ELEVEN.—Fear to trust the people, especially young people, with access to contraceptive knowledge, is practically the only objection now offered to this bill, by members of Congress.

Can it possibly be a sound objection in view of the following points:

a. This country is founded upon faith in the people. Does Congress wish to maintain laws which repudiate that faith.

b. Can any member of Congress who expects, and rightly, that the people should have faith in him to the extent of electing him, turn around and distrust them? Surely every member of Congress would trust himself with any known or yet to be discovered facts as to the control of conception. Surely also he would not consider himself unique in such trustworthiness. The American people can not be divided into sheep and goats in this matter, with the assumption that the majority are goats.

c. One member of the Committee recently gave it as his opinion that the large majority of young women in this country refrain from illicit sexual relations only from fear of pregnancy.   On being asked if he would be willing to state this opinion publicly to his constituents, he answered, "No, I do not think it would be wise to do so." Does not the fact that alarm is felt almost exclusively in regard to young women and does not include young men, indicate that the concern may be merely for conventions instead of for character?

d. Even if the assumption were tenable that most young women are "straight" through fear only, the indictment would fall primarily on the parents, clergy and teachers who would have to stand convicted of failure as sources of education, example and inspiration. Can any member of Congress seriously hold an utter distrust of the educational and moral facts in our civilization?

As an opportunity for clean faith in the people this bill is unexcelled.   Can you be counted on to be one who will meet it squarely?

February 20, 1925.

POINT TWELVE.—It has been repeatedly stated by many members of Congress that the main reason why action on the bill has been delayed is because of distaste for legislating on any subject that brings sex considerations to mind.   Granted the existence of a certain embarrassment, does the Judiciary Committee wish any longer to stand before the public as a body which will permit embarrassment to displace reason and responsibility to the people?

Members have told us that dread of being conspicuous in this matter has inhibited them.   Such feeling is somewhat natural, and may have been more or less excusable as a reason for not acting when this legislation was first proposed in 1919.   But now in view of all the data submitted, the long delay, and the fact that no substantial arguments against the bill have been advanced by anyone, is it not time to cast aside feeling and let common sense win?   "Eventually, why not now?"

We wish to honor each member of the Committee with the assumption that he will prefer to base his stand upon a courageous sense of decency and justice to the people, rather than on either embarrassment or fear.

Regardless of whether there may or may not be opportunity for action on the Floor during the session, are you not willing now to state whether, in your individual opinion, the bill should have at least favorable report from the committee on the merit of the question?

We respectfully request your statement as to what your own stand is, and enclose for your convenience, a slip and an addressed envelope. If our twelve points for the bill, which have been submitted in single notes since February 6th, are not now at hand, and you wish duplicates of any or all of them for review, we will gladly supply them on your request. The series will be made public, together with a report on the stand of the members of the Committee.

The Enclosure:

I stand for a favorable report on the Cummins-Vaile Bill (S. 2290 H. R. 6542).

I am opposed to a favorable report on the Cummins-Vaile Bill (S. 2290 H. R. 6542).

I am not ready to state my stand on the Cummins-Vaile Bill (S. 2290 H. R. 6542).

(Kindly mark which line represents your opinion.)

Signed ....

Member of Judiciary Committee.

The nine necessary votes in the Senate Judiciary Committee could not be marshalled before the close of the session. One of the chief reasons was that word had gone the rounds, emanating apparently from the small group which controls the Senate program, that this bill was not to be included among those scheduled for attention at this session, so the Judiciary members felt little concern about deciding their own position on the legislation. Above everything was the sheer distaste which most of the members feel for dealing with this bill, officially. It touches upon sex, which induces embarrassment, which creates inhibition, which resulted in leaving the bill "on the table" where it was placed after the report "without recommendation" by the Judiciary Sub-Committee of three, before whom the two Hearings were held last Spring.

In the House Judiciary Committee the situation was

about the same. The Chairman of the Sub-Committee before which the Hearings had been held stated that he was sure that "not a single member of his committee *wanted* to vote on the bill." He did not undertake to say whether they approved or disapproved the bill, but merely that they did not want to vote on it. He said he was not ready to express his own opinion on this measure, that he had not yet made up his mind, and was "too busy" to do so. But he offered to arrange *another* Hearing if it were desired. He was entirely agreeable to anything except action. But as to that he said, "I don't see the use of trying to make reluctant men act."

CHAPTER V

WHY CONGRESS HAS BEEN SO SLOW

No one answer covers all reasons: Quiet request to Congress for repeal might have succeeded twenty years ago, before sensational law-breaking created prejudice: Laws defied without first attempting their repeal: Speeches and writings of early agitation not calculated to induce Congressional initiative: Struggle announced in advance as likely to be long and bitter "fight": Shortage of funds for publicity on behalf of bill the second reason for slowness of Congress: Third and most dominant reason found to be general embarrassment over subject: Distaste, inhibition and fear, in varying degrees almost universal among Congressmen: Striking instances: Fears covered careers, colleagues, families and constituents: Fear on behalf of young girls greatest of all: Political opposition to birth control legislation mis-interpreted by "radicals": Abortive attempt in Harding presidential campaign to use his tentative interest in this bill against him: Club women afflicted with inhibitions similar to those of members of Congress: It is leaders, not members who hold back endorsement by large organizations: Organized labor women endorse repeal ahead of club women.

NO one comprehensive answer can be given to the question as to why Congressmen have not yet acted on the removal of the chief of a set of laws which all of them know will inevitably be removed, and which all of them admit are not enforced now and never could be, and which they themselves, like most of the educated and privileged folk everywhere, have proceeded to break with impunity.

However, the answer is not a complicated one. Part of the answer probably is that Congress was not quietly asked to do this thing many years ago, say fifteen or twenty, before the birth control movement had become a defiantly agitational matter, abounding in spectacular law-breaking, denunciatory meetings, jail sentences, hunger strikes, and general hullabaloo of the sort toward which most men in politics feel a stiff aversion if not actual antagonism. The birth control movement, as most of the Congressmen of the present generation have witnessed it, did not begin with any request for a change in the laws, but burst into flame about ten years ago with a sensational campaign to induce defiance of the laws on a large scale. It cannot be wondered at, since no one went to Washington then and concretely asked that a bill be introduced to change the laws, that Congressmen did not step forward on their own initiative and offer to do it. Their minds did not work that way. Instead, they merely looked upon all the "noise," so far as they thought about it at all, as something with which they wanted to having nothing to do.

It seems a fair guess that if in 1905 or thereabouts, when the effort of the seventies to repeal the entire Comstock obscenity statutes was well in the past, some group of "solid citizens," lawyers, doctors, ministers and the like,— had gone to Washington and laid before Congress the fact that Comstock had obviously blundered when he included contraceptive information in the obscenity law, and that it was a very simple matter to correct the blunder,—it might have been done forthwith, without any particular self-consciousness or any struggle. But, of course, such a guess is incapable of proof, since no one tried the experiment at that time. And when it was tried in 1919, the later developments in the birth control movement had already stimulated and aggravated the aversion and inhibition on the part of the members of Congress which has ever since been the most serious barrier to progress.

In looking back at some of the writings and utterances which appeared a decade ago, it is perhaps not surprising that many members of Congress looked askance when in 1919 they were asked to tackle the birth control question. For instance, "The Woman Rebel," the paper which Margaret Sanger published and edited in 1914 in New York as her first message to the public, contained the following editorial announcements:

"The aim of this paper will be to stimulate working women to think for themselves and to build up a conscious fighting character.

"It will also be the aim of the Woman Rebel to advocate the prevention of conception and to impart such knowledge in the columns of this paper.

"As is well known, a law exists forbidding the imparting of information on this subject, the penalty being several years' imprisonment. Is it not time to defy this Law? And what fitter place could be found than in the pages of the Woman Rebel?"

These items were in the opening issue of the paper and were unaccompanied by any request to Congress or the New York Legislature to change the laws, or any appeal to the public to try to have them changed. The launching of this message was also linked with other matters, which were far from an inducement to average legislators to volunteer to remedy the laws relating to birth control. For example in that same first issue of the paper was this by the editor:

A Woman's Duty.—To look the whole world in the face with a go-to-hell look in the eyes; to have an ideal; to speak and act in defiance of convention.

Also this: *"The Rebel Women Claim:*

> The right to be lazy,
> The right to be an unmarried mother,
> The right to destroy,
> The right to create,
> The right to love,
> The right to live.

And this by a contributor, J. Edward Morgan:

> *My Song*—a prose poem.
> I dwelt apart in a world of song,
> But did not sing.
> Biding my time, I listened to all
> songs that I might sing, when my soul
> should find its song.
> . . . .
> . . . .
> . . . .
> One note clear, pure, lucid,
> telling all, answering all, unanswerable,
> the Song of Songs,
> My Song,
> the Song of the Bomb.

This issue also published the I. W. W. preamble, which in those days had more power to alarm than it has had since. The July number contained "A Defense of Assassination" by Herbert A. Thorpe. Also this editorial:

> The rich man places his wife on a pedestal and serves her with docility in order that she may be admired and he, be envied. He has raised her to the rank of queen. This deified woman is one of the new idols at whose feet plundering plutocracy lays the shining gold wrung from the sweat and blood of the toiling long-suffering masses. . . .
> If we do not strike the fetters off ourselves, we shall be knocked about till we forget the fetters. . . . We have done with your civilization and your gods. . . . Let us turn a deaf ear to the trumpet-tongued liars clamoring for Protection, Patriotism, Prisons, Police, Workhouses and Large Families. Leave them to vomit their own filth, and let us take the good things mother earth daily offers unheeded, to us her children.

In the July issue there was also the announcement of the forming of a Birth Control League, one of the objects of which was "to agitate vigorously for the repeal of State and Federal laws against the spreading of knowledge relative to methods for the prevention of conception." But no officers were announced other than a secretary; no later notice of a program appeared; and the organization seems never to have functioned enough even to begin carrying out any legislative program. The magazine lasted less than a year, and over half the issues printed were declared "unmailable" by the Post Office authorities.

The strident tone which had characterized this publication was somewhat modified by 1917 when Mrs. Sanger started the Birth Control Review and became its editor, but her chief message was still to break the laws rather than to get them changed. For instance in the opening number of the new magazine, two signed editorials contained these statements:

No law is too sacred to break. Throughout all the ages, the beacon lights of human progress have been lit by the law-breaker.

The law to-day is absolute and inexorable.

The race has progressed but the law has remained stationary— a senseless stumbling block in the pathway of humanity, a self perpetuating institution, dead to the vital needs of the people.

Against the State, against the Church, against the silence of the medical profession, against the whole machinery of dead institutions of the past, the woman of to-day arises.

She no longer pleads. She no longer implores. She no longer petitions. She is here to assert herself, to take back those rights which were formerly hers and hers alone.

If she must break the law to establish her right to voluntary motherhood, then the law shall be broken.

Shall the millions of women in this State bow their heads to the yoke of slavery imposed by this law?

Shall we sit quietly with folded hands and wait,—wait for our gentlemen law-makers to consider our right to voluntary motherhood?

Shall we not instead violate so brutal a law and thereby teach our law-makers that, if they wish women to obey their man-made laws, they must make such laws as women can respect?

Assailing and defying the laws without taking steps to change them, naturally induced a more dramatic situation than any quiet business-like expedition to Washington or

Albany could have brought about.   And as it is drama which attracts newspaper publicity, it was inevitable that the birth control movement should have developed an atmosphere of violence.   And it was inevitable too, that Congressmen, without having any accurate or consecutive knowledge of the events in this drama, should sense the atmosphere of it, and stiffen accordingly, and should retain an impression which was very difficult to antidote later, when they were asked to use their common sense about repealing the law.   Common sense does not readily over-leap prejudice.

Another factor in the atmosphere of the movement which was developed at this same time, and which also seeped into Congress, and with quite as much damaging reaction, was the cultivation of the idea that the struggle was bound to be a very long and bitter one.   In launching the Birth Control Review, Mrs. Sanger addressed this broadside "To the Men and Women of the United States:

Birth control is the most vital issue before the country to-day. The people are waking to the fact that there is no need for them to bring their children into the world haphazard, but that clean and harmless means are known whereby children may come when they are desired, and not as the helpless victims of blind chance.

Conscious of this fact, heretofore *concealed from them by the forces of oppression,* the men and women of America are demanding that this vitally needed knowledge be no longer withheld from them, that the doors to health, happiness and liberty be thrown open, and they be allowed to mould their lives, not at the arbitrary command of church or State, but as their conscience and judgment may dictate.

But those to whose advantage it is that the people breed abundantly, well intrenched in our social and political order, *are not going to surrender easily to the popular will. Already they are organizing their resistance and preparing their mighty engines of repression to stop the march of progress while it is yet time. The spirit of the Inquisition is abroad in the land. Its gaunt hand may even now be seen reaching out over bench and bar, making pawns of clergy and medical profession alike.*

The struggle will be bitter. It may be long. All methods known to tyranny will be used to force the people back into the darkness from which they are striving to emerge.

The time has come when those who would cast off the bondage of involuntary parenthood must have a voice, one that shall speak their protest and enforce their demands. Too long have they been silent on this most vital of all questions in human existence. The time has come for an organ devoted to the *fight for birth control in America* . . .

If you welcome this Review, if you believe that it will aid you in *your fight,* make it yours. . . .

Raise your voice, strong, clear, fearless, unconditionally to the protection of womanhood, *uncompromisingly opposed to those who, to serve selfish ends, would keep her in ignorance* and exploit her finest instincts.

(The italics are ours.)

The work of the birth control movement was here laid down in terms of "fight"; bitterness and tyranny were predicted; the picture of a long struggle was outlined. These were the days when Mrs. Sanger at her many meetings was saying, "I have dedicated my life to this fight." The newspaper headlines were quick to reflect the tone of this kind of thought. It unconsciously became more or less the habit of mind of the thousands who read the newspapers, particularly of those whose reading was limited mostly to headlines. And it was not at all unnatural that it also became the view-point of many of those who were active in the movement. For, sad but true, the world not only "loves a lover," but loves a fight. The instinct to dramatize life is so compelling and so universal that it often leads to the overstating and even mis-stating of a situation, and to action that produces excitement and complication, which tends to postpone rather than facilitate a solution. The leaders of movements as well as play-wrights are sometimes not immune to the temptation to make a four act play out of a one act plot.

To appeal for preparations for a "long-fight" against the tyranny of the "man-made laws" before the law-makers had been so much as asked specifically to change the laws would seem to be not only the cart before the horse, but a

fairly sure way of prejudicing the case in advance in the
minds of the law-makers.   And this tendency was strength-
ened by the fact that so much was read into the retention
of these old Comstock laws that was not really there.
Granted that the attitude of legislators on this subject has
warranted severe criticism, ever since 1919, when it was
first put squarely up to Congress to do the thing that was
fundamentally needed, it was simply "seein' things" in 1917
before any legislative effort had been made at all, except
the feeblest sort of a beginning in New York legislature to
describe the retention of the Comstock laws, as evidence
of the "forces of oppression" which were "organizing their
resistance and preparing their mighty engines of repression
to stop the march of progress," and to predict that "all the
methods known to tyranny will be used to force the people
back into the darkness from which they are striving to
emerge."

The actual average legislator, when talked with face
to face, proved to be the farthest removed from Mrs.
Sanger's vision of the "spirit of the Inquisition" whose
"gaunt hand may even now be seen reaching out over bench
and bar, making pawns of clergy and medical profession
alike."   Instead he was merely repelled by the racket of the
birth control movement, prejudiced because it had been
linked with revolutionary "radicalism" in general, and embarrassed by the fact that the subject touched upon sex.
Moreover he was found to be ridiculously ignorant as to
just what the Comstock laws provided anyhow.   It never
occurred to him to demand their enforcement, and he was
quite willing to infringe them himself, if his personal need
required it.   He did not in any way match up to the picture
of an "oppressive force."   He was just a man immersed in
politics, who had never been directly asked to repeal the
Comstock laws, and had never dreamed of doing it by himself without being asked, and who when asked, hastily shot

off all the "rationalizing" he could think up, to protect himself from having to take any responsibility about a "disagreeable subject." That was about all there was to it. He would make a very poor showing in the rôle of an aggressor; in fact many of them have shown rather absurd indications of wanting to run. They were not in the least interested in the enforcement of the law. They just wanted to let it alone, not because they approved it, but merely because they found it uncomfortable to do anything about it in any way.

A demonstration of law-breaking has unquestioned effectiveness as advertising for an idea; but its efficacy would seem more wisely utilized as a protest against a refusal to change the law than as a publicity appeal before any request for the change had been made.

It seems regrettable that the experiment was not at least tried of asking for the change of the laws first, and saving up the law-breaking demonstration until either the legislators had refused or had delayed, beyond reason, to act. However, it was not arranged that way in 1916, and one may only guess at what might have happened if it had been. Perhaps the illegal clinic and the jail sentences might all have been avoided, and legal freedom for contraceptive knowledge through all the natural channels for its circulation might by to-day have become a matter of course. Who knows?

However, circumstances being as they were, there was no choice but to adjust as might be to them, and antidote, as rapidly and thoroughly as possible, the prejudices which had been established. The writer's first experience in trying to do this was in Albany, when one of the evasive legislators had suggested conferring with a leading official in the State Health Department. The latter was not averse to the idea of a revision of the Comstock law. In fact he admitted all the arguments. But he was adamant when it came to recommending the Legislature to act; for he could not make himself disassociate the reasons for the repeal from his violent prejudice against the "wild" words and actions of the birth control advocates. The things he "knew" about Mrs. Sanger far exceeded anything the facts warranted: he had not stopped to find out the truth, but had a settled conviction that could not be budged, until at the very end of an hour's earnest talk, when he managed to admit that the proposition to revise the laws should be considered on its own merit, regardless of anything else.

Similarly in Washington, when various members of Congress cited the "wild radicals" who had "agitated about this thing," they had to be laboriously diverted to the consideration of the fact that there was nothing wild at all about the control of parenthood, that the most conservative classes were those who had achieved it first and most, and that Congress was being asked only to correct Comstock's blunder of banning science along with indecency, so that the law would reflect the belief and practice of the educated normal men and women of the country. It was far slower and harder work than it would otherwise have been, just because of the "fighting" psychology which had been established in the birth control movement.

All of which leads to the second part of the answer to the question as to why Congress has been so slow to act, and that is, that the group working for the Cummins-Kissel and Cummins-Vaile Bills did not have adequate funds for the constructive publicity work necessary to offset the prejudices and dissipate the inhibitions of the members of Congress.

But the third and last part of the answer is by far the dominant part, and that is, as had doubtless been evident through all the previous pages of this book, that the subject is embarrassing. It brings sex considerations and sex consciousness to the surface. And this creates varying degrees of fear and inhibition. It would have done that to a certain degree, no doubt, even if the proposition had come to Congress before the birth control movement flared into a sensational affair ten years ago. But with the background of the modern movement as it has been, the tendency has been greatly augmented, so that the fear of being conspicuous in the matter has been the outstanding obstacle. The inhibition has been very powerful in many instances. But there is much reason for concluding that the six years of effort directly with the members of Congress, together with the greatly increased articulateness of the public, has worn the inhibitions so thin and lessened the fears so much that they should evaporate in the very near future, and let the latent common-sense of the majority of the members have an unimpeded chance to function.

An assertion of this sort, that sex consciousness and fear have been the chief reason for the delay in Congress, needs the backing of proof, especially as one dislikes to believe it and would prefer to assume it to be impossible. It must be said at the outset, that probably the same reaction would have been found among any other 435 men, if placed in a similar position. The members of Congress are presumably representative of American life and feeling. They are not unique. The attitude of almost any average citizen with regard to birth control is that he wants the information, but he does not want to make himself conspicuous in getting it. Just so with members of Congress. And the sticking point with them was that they would have to be conspicuous in regard to it, if they sponsored the bill or voted it out of Committee.

In giving various instances of the evidence of the fear and distaste which have been so chronic among the members of Congress it is best, for the purposes of this book, that they shall stand just as instances, without names. It makes relatively little difference what particular Senator or Representative said or did this or that. The only matter of consequence is that this inhibition has been notably prevalent, and that it is the one thing which has chiefly held back the bill from passage.

The general policy of the Voluntary Parenthood League has been to report in its paper the character and episodes of the blockading of the bill, and all official action regarding it, but not to make public the revealing interviews with the individual members of Congress. The one exception to this custom was at the close of the 68th Congress in March, 1925, when a report on the stand of each member of both Judiciary Committees was given in the Birth Control Herald (March 10). It was prefaced as follows:

"The following résumé of the stand of the members of the Senate and House Judiciary Committee on the Cummins-Vaile Bill is compiled from their own statements either in interviews or in letters. The interviews have been promptly and carefully recorded immediately after their occurrence, and are now on file in three volumes in the office of the Voluntary Parenthood League.

"When the League began its work in Congress in the summer of 1919, no publicity was given to the interviews with the various members. It seemed a wise policy at that time, for many reasons. But now that nearly six full years have elapsed, and Congress still chooses to delay action on the bill, and is willing to be a party to the maintenance of laws which misrepresent the established practice and policy of the people, it seems only fair to those who have given their support to the bill, to present to them the record of the Committee members up to date, so that responsibility, praise and blame may be the more accurately allocated.

"Since the first introduction of the bill, each member of both Judiciary Committees has received from the V. P. L. about fifty separate letters or publications in regard to the bill, beside the many letters and telegrams which have been sent by individuals from all parts of the country. They have all received the Report of the two Hearings on the bill. They have all been interviewed, some of them so repeatedly that the records cover many pages in the interview books." (*The Birth Control Herald.*)

Senator Cummins, as noted in a previous chapter, repeatedly said that undue sex consciousness was the reason the men on the Committee tried to shelve the bill and to avoid a vote on it. Senator Dillingham, who died in 1923, said there was no question but that embarrassment was the major difficulty which prevented the men from doing justice by the bill. Space forbids even the jotting down of all the indications of this fact, which were accumulated in the observation of Congress in six years, but the following bits will serve as examples.

The two Senators who returned literature sent to them, and marked it "Refused." The Senator who declined interviews on the ground that he "would not discuss this bill with any *woman.*" The Senator who evaded interviews for over two years, and who then vibrated between declaring that he would not "say a word previous to a public hearing," and explaining his general fear of the whole question of birth control, and who wound up a hectic dissertation on the subject, with this remark: "If I were the Creator and were making the universe all over again, I would leave sex out. It is too powerful, too dangerous." The Senator who said, "The whole subject is so damn nasty, I can't bear to talk of it or even think of it." The Senator who said "This bill is practically an invitation to lechery." The Representative who construed it as a personal insult that a digest had been made from the autobiographies in the Congressional Directory showing the average number of children in the families of the members of Congress, and who confessed in the middle of a long tirade, that the reason Congress didn't act on the bill, was that the members were "afraid of it."

The evidences of fear were found to be numerous and various but all of them seemed quite clearly due, directly or indirectly, to some form or other of distrust of human capacity to integrate this phase of sex knowledge into life, with safety, to morals or regard for decorum. These fears were almost wholly in regard to or on behalf of other people, not themselves; and the range of the fears covered their colleagues in Congress, their families, their constituents, the Catholics, the public in general, but most of all the

young people.   The high school girl who is guaranteed to
go to the devil from learning what birth control information
is, has been by all means the most vivid character in the
whole realm of birth control phantasy.   Judging by the
extent of the expression of alarm felt on her behalf, it would
seem as if she constituted about seven-eighths of the entire
population.   At any rate she has seemed to fill the whole
horizon of many of the members of Congress.   No such concern was expressed regarding the young boys.

The one fear, however, which did relate to the member
of Congress himself, was as to his own career, and the effect which taking an interest in the bill might have upon
it.   In discussing the extent of this fear, one of the senior
Senators ventured the opinion that "there never was a man
in public life who did not consider his career first,—he has
to, if he is going to get anywhere."   More than one Senator
refused to sponsor the bill on the ground that it would give
too good an opportunity to political opponents to "have
fun" at his expense.   The type of "fun" they anticipated
was apparently somewhat like that in which some of the
Congressmen indulged when Mr. Kissel first introduced the
bill.   A story which then went the rounds of Congressional
gossip was that "Kissel, being a lame duck, will be out of a
job in two months and so he has introduced the birth control
bill to pave the way for getting rich by manufacturing contraceptives."   Mr. Kissel shed the jollying with good grace,
and when one of his colleagues inquired why he "wanted
to do a thing like sponsoring that bill" he came back cheer-
fully with, "because there were 434 of you others who
wouldn't."   But there was a more serious side to the possi-
bilities of this sort of fun, as recognized by one of the representatives who was facing a re-election campaign at the
time when he was asked to consider sponsoring the bill.   He
was very candid in saying that he did not intend to be defeated, and that he knew he had political enemies who would

not scruple to use this bill against him by circulating stories which it would cost him more to contradict and explain than he cared to spend. And he added, "Maybe you will call that political cowardice, and maybe it is, but anyway that is where I stand."

There seemed to be general agreement that "anything sexy" had special power to damn a man in public life. "I can't afford to touch it" was an often heard remark, from men who thoroughly approved the bill. The dread of facetious or vulgar comment from other members of Congress was a very real and often indicated dread. A Senator who was defeated for re-election, was horrified at the suggestion that he might help the bill along as a service in the last session of his term. "If I were to vote for this bill, my people wouldn't let me come home," he said. Another Senator who sincerely wanted the bill to pass felt very cramped in his advocacy of it, because of the fears of his family, who thought the thing "not nice," and that it was not good for his reputation to have anything to do with it. In the case of one Representative his fears loomed so large that they encompassed the whole population. "Why," he said, "if Congress should do such a thing (as to pass the bill) the population would rise like a mob, and the only reason they are not doing it now is because they don't know it is under consideration." A Senator whose fear regarding "the fourteen year old girls" was well nigh an obsession and who said, "You want to make everybody prostitutes," —was able when speaking seriously, to modify his fears only to the extent of saying, "If this information could be confined to the intelligent and cultured people, and kept out of the hands of the vicious and ignorant, it might be another matter, but that can't be done." From that, he argued that no one should be allowed to have it, although he had admitted previously in the same conversation that information did circulate anyway in spite of the law.

The most striking element in the expression of all these fears has been the way in which the fear, and the sex consciousness which is back of it, seeems to prevent the use of the mind in an ordinary logical fashion. Two and two do not make four, but a hundred, or any preposterous number. No conclusion is too absurd to jump at, when impelled by this fuddled embarrassment and vague terror. Some of the most squeamish members have taken refuge in the stout declaration that they have never heard of the bill and don't know anything about it, or about the subject of birth control; and this in spite of the fact that they had received many letters and much literature for over five years. They have been so occupied in devising ways to wriggle out of discussing the bill at all, that they failed to realize how they gave themselves away, within a few minutes after they knew "nothing about it," by telling of how they had talked the matter over with other members and they all agreed that "nothing can be done about it in this session."

The general tendency of the members who have been beset with fear, has been to avoid all talk and consideration as much as possible. But one member of the House Judiciary Committee was an exception; he leaned to loquacity. As his remarks give a vivid picture of the lengths to which fear and super sex-consciousness can distort an otherwise reasonable mind, the substance of one of the recorded interviews with him is given here.

"Hon. Mr. X of ————————,

"I hear you are going to make a speech against the bill, Mr. X." "Yes, if necessary I am, though I expect to kill the bill in Committee. But I shall make a speech on the floor if I have to." "It is a great advantage to be a lawyer, if you are going to work against this bill, Mr. X." He agreed heartily to that, said it was an advantage on any bill to be a lawyer.

"Yes, for you will have the sort of mind that whittles away all the irrelevant stuff, and puts attention on the real points of the bill, and those are very simple as well as important." "I see what you are driving at, Mrs. D———, but to my mind the most important consideration is the danger which this bill would make for young girls, and I am against it for that reason."

"Do you then really distrust the majority of young girls?" He thought he did,—that he had to, as a practical man, knowing the world and its ways.

"If you had been a lawyer, as I have, and tried quantities of bastardy cases, you would see why." Asked if he didn't think a lawyer's experience was like a doctor's, limited largely to the pathological side of life, and that one had to consider the great fairly normal majority. Well, he felt the majority were weak and could be safeguarded only by their fear of "getting in a family way."

"Would you be willing to say that publicly, Mr. X? It is a pretty serious thing for a man in public life, representing the people, to say he distrusts them. I can understand your talking that way privately, but would you want to say it openly." "Yes, I would, for I believe it."

"Suppose there were a public meeting in your district, Mr. X, and you stood before an audience of your own constituents, and told them that you believed that most of the young folks were better off ignorant than with knowledge on this subject, because they couldn't withstand the temptation to misuse it, and so the laws that tried to keep them from knowing were good laws. Then suppose someone else were standing beside you, saying just the reverse, another Congressman who might say, 'My dear young friends, I believe in you. I know you are human, with all the impulses that sway live people, and I know that some people are swayed when they ought not to be, but I believe the majority have the strength of mind and character to go right, even if they do know how to go wrong and cover it up, and so I am against all laws that try to keep knowledge away from you.' Which man do you think would get the response of the audience?"

"Oh, of course it would be the one who said he believed in them, that's natural. They would want to believe in themselves, too, but think how it would be that night, when the young girl goes out with the boy, and she can't help thinking, what difference will it make if nothing ever shows? And then she will forget all about character, and will let herself go, whereas if she was afraid of the practical results, she wouldn't. Yes, there are thousands of girls that are held back just that way."

Then I asked if he didn't know that there was such a lot of contraceptive knowledge in circulation—and most of it bad too—

that the number of girls that could be protected by their ignorance was diminishing every hour, and that there was absolutely no effort at enforcement of the laws? He said people argued that way about enforcing the prohibition laws, but he thought it ought to be enforced and could be. He insisted he was "just being practical, that's all." I insisted that I was the more practical, as I had faith in knowledge and strength which were dynamic, and not in just fences, which are dead. "Well, you certainly are a pretty talker, Mrs. D——— and I may be wrong. Of course, if you can convince me . . ." "I don't think I can convince you, but I think you can convince yourself, if you make a business of turning your face toward the light instead of to the darkness."

"Well anyhow, you think what would happen in all these government boarding houses over here," pointing out the window to the wartime buildings which still house hundreds of women clerks, "a lot of them are confirmed old maids too, but I wouldn't trust what would happen to them, if they all knew they could do what they pleased and no one would be the wiser."

The above instance is given, not because it represents the state of mind of the average member of Congress, for it does not. It is an extreme case. But it does give in exaggerated fashion, an indication of what is the background of feeling and thought among a very large number of members, though in a much milder and more dilute form. This particular Congressman may prove to be pugnacious to the last, but the majority show strong evidence that their fears and inhibitions can be melted away by the sunlight of wholesome public opinion, frankly expressed.

It can not be too emphatically stated that the average member of Congress would probably much rather be reasonable in this matter than not, but he has not quite reached the point where it is as easy to be reasonable as it is to be evasive. However, it has not been altogether rare to find a perfectly untrammelled mind like that of one of the leading Senators, who sailed into brisk consideration of the bill, like a fresh breeze on a muggy day; "Of course, I don't see how anyone could vote against it." On being told that some of the Senators on the Judiciary Committee seemed too inhibited to want the bill reported out, he said, "H'm, —prudes, are they?" and ran his eye over the list of Committee members to locate the prudes. "There are Senator So-and-so, and So-and-so, surely they will be for it,—just plain common sense." "And decency," added the interviewer. "A combination of both, yes." He would speak to some of the members. He saw "no reason on earth why it should not pass."

As the fear about the young people has been the most persistent of all fears expressed by member of Congress, and the one about which their minds have been most rutty, a special answer to it was prepared and sent to every member of both Houses. *It* was entitled; *"Yes, but won't it increase immorality? Isn't letting down the bars dangerous?"* and the substance of it was as follows:

When Congressmen say, "Yes, but won't this letting down the bars, mean that the unmarried and the young will have nothing to deter them from illicit relations?" We, in turn, make these queries:

"Well, will it?"

"Do you really believe that most people have no positive standards of conduct?"

"Are they kept what is called 'straight' only by their ignorance of the fact that sex relations need not result in parenthood unless so intended?"

"Is it your sober opinion that fear of 'results' and ignorance as the control of conception are the only deterrents from general promiscuity?"

When a Congressman voices this wholesale distrust of his fellow citizens in regard to contraceptive knowledge, is it irrelevant to inquire if the expressions of faith in the people such as appear in pre-election campaign speeches are all mere platitudes: "If you do really consider most people intrinsically unworthy in this regard are you ready to go before your constituents and tell them so? Are you willing to explain to them that your hesitation about the Cummins-Vaile Bill is because you think they are so weak or so vicious that they would abuse contraceptive knowledge if it were made easily accessible?"

A fair test of the validity, and even the sincerity, for any such generalization as this, is to apply the idea to our own selves. Surely we assume that our own lives are decently guided by something beside mere fear of "consequences." We can hardly consider ourselves unique in this regard, either. We cannot think that we have any personal monopoly of principles, moral standards or good taste. We surely cannot picture ourselves as standing alone in the world on a pedestal of superiority, with all the others below in a morass of moral obliquity. If we dare trust ourselves with this knowledge, and we know we do, must we not also dare to trust others?

All these disconcerting inquiries are seldom pressed home, however, with most Congressmen, for they usually think twice rather quickly, and they admit that the tendency of a few to abuse knowledge is no reason for trying to keep the mass of people ignorant.

They admit when they stop to think, that knowledge of all kinds can be abused and that it is abused every day by some people. Even reading, writing and arithmetic are abused, by forgers, embezzlers and the like, but that is no reason for not teaching these pre-requisites of civilization to everyone. The elements and natural forces can be dangerous for mankind as well as beneficent. Fire, water and electricity can all do frightful damage if they get out of hand, but under proper human control, they are blessings and fundamental necessities.

But it is the case of the young that stays longest in the mind of the doubting Congressman as a cause of apprehension. Usually it is the young girl whose "virtue" he thinks can be safeguarded by keeping her ignorant. If he is asked, "Why the sex distinction?" he is apt to admit that what is being safeguarded is convention rather than virtue, as the girl's lapse would become known while the boy's need not.

However he is almost certain to end by admitting that it is a poor kind of saint that does not know how to sin; that ignorance is not synonymous with character; that it is an insult to young people in general to assume that they cannot be trusted with knowledge; that if he would not so insult his own children, he should not be ready to insult other people's children; that such protection as ignorance may provide is ephemeral, for knowledge may reach the young person any day; that it is primarily the fault of the older generation if children have been so poorly reared that they naturally "go wrong" instead of right; that finally it is better that those who insist on promiscuity should not further add to the situation by bringing innocent babies into the world.

It is becoming more and more evident that those people, young or older, who are strongly impelled to irregular relations are the sort who most readily find ways to secure the forbidden information, and it is folly to try to deprive the millions of wholesome, needy and responsible parents who should have this knowledge, in a vain effort to keep the irresponsible uninformed. Indeed, with birth control knowledge, the undesirable elements in the population will tend to die out faster than they otherwise would, by virtue of the fact that they will not be reproducing their kind.

In the last analysis, might it not be better for the race, if birth control knowledge could be given to only one class of people, that it should be made available first of all to the generally promiscuous? They make very poor parents, and the sooner they die out the better.

It can hardly be doubted that the people who bring up this immorality bogie, as an excuse for holding back contraceptive knowledge from the public, are unconsciously trying to divert their minds from their own sense of discomfort and uncertainty regarding matters pertaining to sex. They are advancing what the modern psychologist calls "good reasons but not real reason." They are "rationalizing." They can quite well fool themselves, too, into believing that they are animated by a disinterested concern for social welfare. But presently, if they are willing to think the thing through, they may see that what they are really doing is trying to avoid or postpone the responsibility which faces all normal adults, to meet the fundamental problems of life squarely, and to help educate the human race into a triumphant and thorough solution of them.

The hope of the world lies on the far side, not the near side of knowledge.

A few years ago there was much heated assertion current among "radicals" about how church and State, and especially how "big business" wanted to suppress the knowledge of birth control; how the church (meaning mostly the Roman Catholic church) wanted more souls born, at no matter what cost, so they could be counted in the fold; how the militarists wanted more "cannon-fodder"; how the "interests" wanted more "wage-slaves" to exploit; and how the "government" wanted more millions of citizens to build up and fight for a State that would be dominant in the world; and how "politics," the servant of all these "tyrannies," was the force which would hold birth control progress back, in any attempted effort at legislation.

But "politics," as represented by the men in Congress, whose views have been sampled in the last six years, does not act at all in accord with the pattern laid out for it by the "radical." Politics, that is, political organization, re-acts just about as the individual men do. It squirms at the idea of any constructive service regarding the release of birth control information from legal ban, and the only use it has for the subject at all is a means of damning a political opponent, or rather to threaten to use it thus, in the event that other ammunition fails. If the hypothesis of the "radicals" had been sound, there would surely have been some evidence of it among the 435 men who constitute Congress. Some interest would have been shown in having the present suppressive laws enforced, but as a matter of fact, not a vestige of any such interest has been found, and there has been a general admission that the laws do not and cannot work. Occasional, feeble and ignorant remarks about race suicide are the nearest approach to an interest in making the laws effective, that has been discernible in Congress.

An extreme example of this false assumption as to why politics has thus far balked at helping to repeal the suppressive laws, is found in an editorial signed by Margaret Sanger, in the Birth Control Review of May, 1921. It was written after the first short effort to induce the New York Legislature to pass a "doctors only" bill, and was apropos of the facts that one Assemblyman who had promised to introduce the bill had backed out, "after consulting with some of the leaders of the Assembly who strongly advised" him not to do it, as it would do him "an injury" that he "could not overcome for some time"; that another Assemblyman, who was a physician, had "refused on the ground of levity from his associates"; and that a third had decided against doing it "after consulting with party leaders in New York." Part of this editorial comment was as follows:

To expect aid or even intelligent understanding of birth control from the typical Albany politician; to be disappointed because of the ignorance of these so-called "legislators"; to be discouraged because of their failure to remove the coercive and criminally obscene insult to American womanhood from the statute books [1]—this would be to succumb to emotion rather than to profit by the invaluable knowledge we have gained from our experience at Albany. The great fact is this. We can expect nothing from the politician of today. If we must use the weapon of politics to further the progress of birth control, it must be the politics created by ourselves.

When the first birth control clinic in America was declared a "public nuisance" by the courts, we were advised by well-meaning friends that the legal way, the political way, the legislative way, was the only safe and sane method of propaganda. This has now been put to the test. And we discover that the successful politician is not only mentally unable to understand the aim of birth control, but moreover he himself is the very product of those sinister forces we are aiming to eradicate from human society.

Your successful politician is the demagogue who knows the best tricks to catch the greatest number of votes. He is the hypnotist of great, docile, submissive, sheep-like majorities. He is interested in number, not intelligence. Therefore to expect such masters, who by hook or crook, ride roughshod into public office or slide into seats of the State Legislature to understand or support a program which aims at the creation of self-reliant, self-governing,[2] independent men and women, would be to neglect one of the most important factors among the resources of our opponents. But we did expect something more among men elected to public office than the embarrassed giggle of the adolescent, the cynical indecency of the gangster, in the consideration of a serious sexual and social problem.

---

[1] The bill which Mrs. Sanger was then trying to have introduced *did not remove the subject from the obscenities,* except in the case of the doctor. For all others it still remained an indecency.

[2] The bill proposed did not allow self-government as to the control of conception, but only physician-government. The person applying could get instruction only if the doctor chose to give it, not otherwise.

Perhaps, moreover, we failed to take into consideration the vast power wielded today by the politician in control and administration of the public charities, hospitals, and "correctional" institutions for the support and maintenance of the victims of compulsory motherhood.

"Our politicians today profit from human misery. They have an interest, direct or indirect, in the production through uncontrolled fecundity, of the unfit, the underfed, the feebleminded and the incurably diseased. Their interest, financially, is in the increase of our institution populations, with their insistent demands for appropriations from the City and State. Most eugenists dub the victims of our legal and social barbarism "the unfit." The victims are not the "unfit" but these blind leaders of the blind—the politician, the profiteer, the war-making patriot, the criminal moralist, who is urging men and women to "increase and multiply."

Statements of this sort were repeatedly made at public meetings for a number of years. They came to be so widely circulated that they were generally accepted among many of the groups which were agitating for social revolution or reconstruction, without much of any analysis to find out whether or not they were an accurate interpretation of the opposition of "politics" to changing the laws affecting birth control information. It is perhaps not strange that this sort of talk became common, but it had two serious disadvantages, one that it shot wide of the mark, and the other that it served to increase the prejudice of law makers against the whole program for correcting the laws, and added perceptibly to their distaste for taking a personal part in that program.

Every bit of direct experience with legislators augments the conclusion that the chief reason the individual legislator hangs back is because he is afraid it will "queer him" to stand for any action, and the reason that "political leaders" advise the legislators to let the subject alone is precisely the same. The subject is embarrassing, that's all. As one of them advised another, "Whatever you do, don't get mixed up in any sex stuff. No man in politics can afford that."

A striking proof of the foregoing point was an occurrence in the presidential campaign in 1920. Senator Harding, when a member of the Public Health Committee of the Senate (since abolished) had written to the Director of Voluntary Parenthood League saying, "I have not had time to study carefully the provisions of your bill, but at first reading I find myself very much inclined in its favor." This statement was given to the press. Presently it was taken up by some of the opposition campaign speakers who ran short of thunder, and they began spreading the news that if Harding were elected president, "government means would be used to enforce birth control." No details were given but it was insinuated that the project would be an unheard of intrusion into private life. A representative from the Democratic Headquarters was sent to the office of the Voluntary Parenthood League to secure a photostat copy of the note which Mr. Harding had written. The young man who bore the message happened to be interested in the work of the League, and he frankly admitted that the errand was distasteful to him, as the distorted use it was planned to make of this note was such as would not only reflect discredit upon Mr. Harding, but upon the League. He said he considered it most unwise campaign tactics, and he was the more disturbed over it, because some of the campaign managers had admitted that they themselves approved the bill, but as they considered it a good handle for slurring Harding, they were perfectly willing to use it in that manner for campaign purposes. Their plan, however, was checkmated by some of the levelheaded women then active in the Democratic campaign; they instantly notified the men that it would never, never do. They reminded the men that no matter how relatively silent the organized women of the country might have been on this subject, there was no doubt whatever that they believed in controlled parenthood; obviously, for they had achieved it; and any discreditable slam at birth control would be nothing but a boomerang for the Democratic campaigners. The whole idea was promptly abandoned.

It has been frequently said, inside of Congress and out, that if the "club women" had endorsed the Cummins-Vaile Bill, it would have been passed by the last Congress. There is clearly no way to prove it, but there are certain facts to be stated which throw some light on the subject. In the first place the club women have not been completely silent. In the next place, it is just as obvious that the club women believe in the control of parenthood as that Congressmen do, and that they have not and will not observe the laws which forbid access to the information. The birth rate in both groups is prima facie evidence, which no candid person would deny, as it is out of the question to assume that the educated and more or less privileged class to which both groups belong, are made up of people who are for the most part either ascetic or sterile. The only possible inference is that control of the growth of the family has been achieved by the utilization of contraceptive knowledge. Congressmen are just as able to take note of this situation as any other observers, but when they talk of waiting for the club women to voice their opinions officially in a body, they are merely exercising their ingenuity in thinking up one more form of excuse for not acting.

And the women, to the extent that have been backward about acknowledging what their lives prove, seem to be motivated by exactly the same sort of embarrassments and inhibitions as afflict the members of Congress. And similarly also, their inhibitions are wearing thinner all the time, and there is good reason to believe that ere long the organized women who belong to the more or less privileged class will follow the lead of the organized labor women who, in June, 1922, passed the following resolution at the annual convention of the National Women's Trade Union League:

Whereas the effect of certain laws of the United States, both State and Federal, is to withhold contraceptive information from the women of the working classes, while it is in most cases readily available to the well to do; and

Whereas it is important that in this, as in other matters, the best scientific information should be available to the peoples' need, regardless of their economic standing: Therefore be it

Resolved, That we, the National Women's Trade-Union League, in convention assembled, go on record as opposed to all laws, State and Federal, which in effect establish censorship over knowledge which, if open to one, should be open to all who care to secure it.

However in fairness to the rank and file of the club women it must be stated that two years earlier, in June 1920, they gave every evidence of being willing and even glad to pass a resolution of protest against the barriers to contraceptive knowledge, and it was only the timidity of the leaders which prevented their having full opportunity to do so. This circumstance occurred at the Biennial Convention of the General Federation of Women's Clubs at Des Moines, and was reported as follows in the Birth Control Herald:

At the Des Moines Convention in 1920, at the close of Mrs. Dennett's address to the Health Conference on "Children by Chance or by Choice," the delegates began a rapid fire of questions. Mrs. Dennett asked if she might put just one question to the delegates, namely, as to how many of them wanted the prohibitive laws of this country regarding contraceptive knowledge to remain as they are now without change. Not a hand was raised, whereupon Mrs. Dennett said "That is interesting in view of the fact that your Resolutions Committee has declined to report out a resolution on that question." Instantly a delegate asked the Chairman, Mrs. Elmer Blair, to have the resolution read. The delegates listened hard. A second slow reading, was asked for. Then without pause someone moved the adoption of the resolution and it was carried *unanimously* with a rising vote of thanks to the speaker. Over 500 delegates were present, constituting about a third of the whole Convention.

The wording of the resolution was as follows:

Whereas one of the primary necessities for family and therefore

for public health, is an intelligently determined interval between
pregnancies, to be secured by regulating the inception of life and not
by interfering with life after it starts, and

Whereas the lack of knowledge as to how to secure such an interval frequently results in serious disaster for mothers and babies
and indirectly for the entire family and community.

Be It Resolved that this Conference on Public Health urges
the speedy removal of all barriers, due to legal restrictions, tradi-
tion, prejudice or ignorance, which now prevents parents from access
to such scientific knowledge on this subject as is possessed by the
medical profession.

Of course it was evident that any resolution which was carried unanimously by a third of the delegates would carry
by at least a good majority if submitted to all the delegates,
and the rebuke thus administered to the resolutions committee created quite a bit of consternation among the officers
of the Federation.   But the resolution was not submitted
to the whole convention, nor has one been allowed to come
forth at any subsequent convention, although considerable
effort has been made to have it done.   The nearest approach to it has been the making of a recommendation by
the officers, that the whole subject of birth control be
"studied by the clubs."

If, as some of the Club women say, the chief reason for not
endorsing voluntary parenthood is because the Catholic members are
opposed, it would seem a perfectly simple matter to remind the
Catholic women in the first place that they are a very small minority,
and in the second place, that there is nothing compulsory about
the use of contraceptive knowledge.   If Catholics wish to remain
ignorant on the subject, they are, and should be entirely free to do
so, but they should not seek to enforce ignorance on others. (*B. C.
Herald.*)

It is said that the Catholic Clubs have threatened to
secede from the Federation if a birth control resolution
were passed, and that the leaders are so concerned to keep
up the membership in the federation that they, like the
political party leaders, have put organization first and left

fair play to the mass of citizens to take care of itself as best it might. But there seems also evidence that the excuse about the Catholics is in part at any rate, a cover for the underlying excuse of embarrassment about dealing with the subject at all.

Practically all roads of investigation in this matter lead back to this one difficulty. If that were overcome, the minor obstacles would seem inconsequential. A situation similar to that found in the women's clubs has developed in public welfare organizations of many sorts. The members were ready to move, but the leaders and officials were full of doubts and excuses. Ever since 1918, various members of the Social Work Conference, which annually gathers together representatives from nearly all the public welfare organizations of the country, who have been clamoring to have the question of birth control placed on the official program of the Conference, but thus far it has been relegated to "side show" meetings. In 1922 the request was formally made in a resolution passed with but one feeble dissenting vote, at a meeting with several hundred delegates present, but the officers have still held back at all the subsequent Conferences.

This inhibition of leaders has been so persistent that a definite effort was made by the Director of the Voluntary Parenthood League to try to help them break through it, and release their naturally helpful instincts so they could function without hindrance. It took the form of a semi-open letter, which was marked, "Not for publication—at present," and read as follows:

Dear Citizen:

The Cummins-Vaile Bill has wide-spread, splendid and rapidly increasing endorsement. But there are still some persons of consequence, who believe in the aims of the legislation, who say, "I do not feel free to express my opinion, on account of my position." They explain that as they are officially connected with this or that organization, they are obliged to forego giving any endorsement, though "personally in hearty sympathy." They are fearful lest their individual opinions should be deemed official.

This attitude is noticeably frequent among leaders of women's organizations and welfare groups. They say, "Until my organization speaks, I cannot do so." But large organizations, as such, speak their views only at annual, or even biennial conventions. So they are often precluded from giving timely assistance to important moves for social welfare. Thus the leaders are prevented from letting their individual opinions be of service at critical moments.

Granted that it is a real problem for officials to determine what is absolute wisdom in working out the dual functions of personal and public life, is it not a mistake to assume that an officer of an organization is of necessity so submerged in the office, as to lose all personal identity and freedom of opinion? Officers are seldom chosen unless they are persons of significance *apart* from the position. Office-holding should not be allowed to obliterate that significance.

In regard to removing the drastic laws which prohibit access to birth control knowledge, I believe there are very few leaders of fine mind and good heart like yourself, who can be satisfied to remain silent any longer, if they realize the good they may do by speaking out.

And further, I believe that an analysis of the probable other reasons that doubtless account in many instances, for the silence up to date, may make it easier to help in this important matter.

Are you willing to think it out with me?

Looked at quite simply, it seems to be just matter of generous spirit.

It is plain that not only leaders, but a large majority of members of social, civic and welfare organizations, are of the well-to-do educated class which has already obtained and utilized birth control knowledge, despite the laws. The birth rate in families of this class is clear proof that the majority believe in family limitation. Otherwise they would not so universally have achieved it. To assume that sophisticated people who have learned enough of this legally forbidden knowledge for the effective use in their own lives, are not willing to let the millions of unsophisticated poor have legal access to similar knowledge, is to assume a degree of conscious selfishness that is unwarranted. They would not shut their hearts against the multitudes of mothers, such as the wife of the rural delivery letter carrier, who writes as follows:

"I have searched far and wide for knowledge. I have been given advice how to produce abortion, but life was too dear to risk that. So I have stumbled along hoping some day to gain the desired knowledge. In my thirteen years of married life I have given birth to eight children, beside one miscarriage following an attack of flu-pneumonia. I have five girls and two boys living, the oldest girl is past twelve, just ready to pass into womanhood. It makes me shudder to think of the possibility of her going through what I have. I have tried to find out from doctors some preventive measure, but a sneer is my answer. I am now only thirty-six years old, far from being too old for pregnancy, but I feel I cannot possibly bring any more into the world to suffer I know not what. If I had not had one of the best husbands God ever made, I believe I would not have been able to bear up under it all. With only an R. F. D. carrier's salary for living, it has been a struggle for us both. But God willing, I am going to persevere till I find out how to prevent pregnancy occurring so often, not only for myself, but for my five girls, and also for countless other girls to take our places in the future."

The consciousness of belonging to the privileged class which has obtained at least some of this knowledge in spite of the laws, should be enough, I sincerely believe, to make the leaders who have till now held back their endorsement, feel that any further holding back is unworthy of their true responsibility as leaders. A leader is one who finding the way good and right opens that way to others.

But something seems to inhibit this natural and generous response to human need, something beside holding office. What is it?

Let me tell you the situation, as we who are shouldering this work for birth control legislation, have found it. I think that the elusive something may be discovered and the barrier eliminated.

In the first place officers are by no means consistent in refusing to express opinions because subjects are outside the direct scope of their organizations. So is it not a reasonable inference that, when this excuse is offered in regard to birth control legislation, it is unconsciously used to cover some other reason?

The leaders often tell us that they would have had this subject presented to their organizations, but they feel that "the time is not yet ripe," that "the members are not ready," etc. Yet they well know that the members believe in family limitation and spaced births, as they achieve both.

Is not this inconsistency and excuse what the psychologists call a "defense mechanism"? And is not that mechanism unconsciously

built up to cover embarrassment?   Sex taboo is still far reaching
in spite of modern education.   So it is not uncommon to find people
who have long ago accepted and acted upon the principle of controlled parenthood in their own lives, but who shrink from the
possibility of having that acceptance made publicly noticeable.   They
even dread a discussion of the dire need of contraceptive knowledge
among the ignorant, lest it be too compelling.

In other words, sex consciousness overwhelms conscience, which
otherwise would be sensitive to human need and responsive to public
welfare.

If this seems to you a precipitate inference, just run over the
following résumé of our experience in various organizations.

It has been repeatedly proved at conventions that the members
were ready to adopt endorsing resolutions, if only the leaders would
permit their being discussed and voted upon.   The story of the ways
in which organization opinion has been actually suppressed by leaders
is a significant phase of social history in this country.

At one great convention, when the large and representative
resolutions committee had decided to recommend a resolution, the
officers, by dint of prolonged effort into the small hours of the night,
coerced the committee into reversing its decision.   At another, when
it became evident that a resolution would be carried if discussed on
the floor, the officers, by appealing to administration loyalty, succeeded
in preventing a vote to permit discussion.   At another, after being
refused by a small resolutions committee and the board of directors,
the resolution was brought up from the floor when a full third of
the delegates were present, and was carried unanimously.   At
another, after the resolution had been carried by a sizable majority
of the members, the leaders manoeuvered a vote to rescind.   At
another, over six hundred delegates voted to ask their directors to
put this subject on the official program of the next year's convention.
It has not yet been done, though two years have elapsed.

Over and over at meetings of various sorts, the audience has been
asked, "How many of those present want the laws suppressing birth
control information retained."   And hardly a hand has been raised.
"How many want them repealed?"   And nearly every hand has
come up.

Ironically enough, on several occasions, the very leaders who
have prevented any convention endorsements of legislation to free
birth control knowledge or even the recognition of the principle
of controlled parenthood, have not hesitated to come to the Director

of the Voluntary Parenthood League, with this sort of request. "Do you mind telling me what are the most up-to-date contraceptives, and what doctors give the best scientific instructions on methods?" They hasten to add that personally they are in full sympathy with our movement, and usually they want the information for a daughter or a friend, or some one near and dear, whom they wish to have the best knowledge.

The above is a sad story, and the only reason for telling it is to understand what it implies.

In the light of modern psychology, it is understandable why groups, i.e., audiences and delegates, are ready to vote for a resolution, while leaders are loath to initiate or permit action. Whenever any question induces the sort of embarrassment that emanates from sex conciousness, it is inevitably easier to act as one of a group than to act by one's self. Yet leaders, just because they are such, have exceptional opportunity to let their opinions be of service to humanity. And is not the obligation of mature minds to see to it that, so far as possible, such inhibitions are not allowed to interfere with being just and generous to one's fellows?

The Congressmen who are now being asked to pass the Cummins-Vaile Bill are tempted to move all too slowly, because they have precisely these same inhibitions that have afflicted the leaders of organizations. The one thing that will most easily inspire Congressmen to move quickly in this matter, is to be relieved in their own minds, by assurance from just such leaders as you, that they will be doing wisely and well to vote for this bill. By shedding your own inhibitions for the sake of others, you will distinctly help Congressmen to shed theirs.

The tests to which some of the leaders have been put, especially among the women's organizations, have brought forth some ludicrous moments. For instance the National League of Women Voters has circulated "A Pledge For Conscientious Citizens," written by its President, Mrs. Maud Wood Park, which included this item: "To obey the law even when I am not in sympathy with all its provisions."

This pledge, if applied to the laws prohibiting access to contraceptive knowledge, looks comic indeed, for the National League of Women Voters is made up of women who very obviously have not the remotest intention of abiding by those laws.   They belong for the most part to the same general class as that which formed the basis of the report issued by the Bureau of Social Hygiene, of which Dr. Katherine Bement Davis is the executive secretary; this report gave answers to a questionnaire sent to 1000 married women, mostly college graduates, in which 74% said they used contraceptive methods.

When a National Conference on Law Enforcement was called in Washington in 1924, in which representatives of all the leading women's organizations took part, inquiry was made of the program committee as to whether there would be discussion of the enforcement of the law which is more broken than any other in the United States, not excepting the prohibition law, namely, the law forbidding access to contraceptive knowledge.   The inquiry produced consternation.   The enforcement of that law was not so much as mentioned on the program.   The laxity of officials and the indifference and criminality of citizens regarding other laws came in for due attention, but not this one—horrors, no!   It reminds one of the little girl who had been brought up in luxury, and who had never experienced any method of transportation except her little perambulator and the family limousine.   She was making her first trip with her father in a street car, a very crowded one, and she piped up, "Father, there are too many people in this car."   "Yes, my dear, shall we get out?"   "Oh, no, father, not *us.*" So the conscientious women wanted thorough-going discussion of law enforcement, but not that one.   Perish the thought!

CHAPTER VI

A "DOCTORS ONLY" FEDERAL BILL

"Doctors only" Federal bill followed straight repeal bill just as limited bills in States followed straight repeal bills: Advocated on Margaret Sanger's initiative: Provides medical monopoly of extreme type: Arguments in its behalf analyzed and answered: Proponents of "doctors only" bill do not live up to own demands for limiting contraceptive instruction to personal service by doctors: Birth control periodical carries thinly veiled advertisements for contraceptives: Improved type of "doctors only" bill drafted by George Worthington: Not so many loop-holes and inconsistencies as in first bill proposed, but still a special privilege bill and still leaves subject classed with obscenity: Worthless as means of curbing abuse of contraceptive knowledge: Clause permitting "reprints" from medical and scientific journals practically breaks down all restrictions: Makes pretense at limitation a farce.

FOUR years after the first petition slips were circulated asking for the repeal of the Comstock laws which ban contraceptive knowledge the first "doctors only" bill was proposed. Three years after the first State repeal bill was actually introduced, the first State "doctors only" bill was introduced. A somewhat similar sequence occurred as to Federal legislation. The first petitions to Congress for a straight repeal were circulated in 1915, and the Federal "doctors only" proposition first appeared in 1924; the first bill for a straight Federal repeal was actually introduced in 1923, and by the time these words are read a Federal "doctors only" bill may be before Congress. At the present writing it is announced as a definite plan. The limited legislation has in all these instances been initiated by Margaret Sanger.

It is a wide reach from her position of ten years ago, when breaking, not correcting, the laws was urged, to her position of to-day when limited, permissive legislation is being recommended to State legislatures, to Congress and to the public. The former policy was one of vehement scorn of the indecent laws and the object was to get contraceptive information directly to the people in the quickest way possible by published information and clinical service,—regardless of the law; a striking contrast to the propositions of the last two years for laws to keep the subject of contraception still classed with obscenity and to let no one have it except those who personally apply to physicians and to let no one give it except physicians.

To account for Mrs. Sanger's extraordinary swing of the pendulum from revolutionary defiance of all law to advocacy of special-privilege class legislation is not germane to the aim of this book. So far as the public is concerned the explanation, whatever it may be, does not matter. But what does matter is that there is destined to be wide-spread appeal for this type of legislation, because the organization which is back of it has more funds for publicity than have ever been had before by any groups in this country working for birth control progress; and the time is at hand for American citizens to put on their spectacles and look thoughtfully at the basically different types of legislation which they are urged to support, and to decide what they want, with their eyes wide open.

The main points for the straight repeal type of legislation have been given in the previous chapters on the Cummins-Vaile Bill which has been before Congress for over two years. The points for the proposed "doctors only" type will be given as far as possible by excerpts from the written or published words of the proponents, together with some comparisons which may be of aid to the reader in making a sort of mental parallel column for convenience in surveying the differences between the two types.

The first formulation of a Federal "doctors only" bill was announced in the Birth Control Review of March, 1924, as the official stand of the President (Margaret Sanger) and the Board of Directors of the American Birth Control League.

The Bill was drawn up for the League by Mr. Robert E. Goldsby with the aid of Dr. J. P. Chamberlin of the Columbia Law School. Its provisions cover communications from doctors to each other and to their patients, and also the transport of Birth Control material from manufacturer to dealer, and from wholesaler to retailer, and to physicians.

It adds to Section 211 of the Criminal Code the following amendment:

Any article, instrument, substance, drug, or thing designed, adapted or intended for preventing conception, or any written or printed information or advice concerning the prevention of conception is not non-mailable under this section when mailed by a duly licensed physician (a) to another person known to him to be a duly licensed physician or (b) to one of his bonafide patients in the course of his professional practice.

Any article, instrument, substance, drug or thing designed, adapted or intended for preventing conception is not non-mailable under this section when mailed in the regular course of legitimate business by:

a. An importer to a manufacturer or wholesale dealer in drugs, or by a manufacturer or wholesale dealer in drugs to an importer;

b. A manufacturer to a wholesale dealer in drugs or by such wholesale dealer to a manufacturer;

c. A wholesale dealer in drugs to another such wholesale dealer or a retail dealer in drugs, or by such retail dealer to such wholesale dealer;

d. A retail dealer in drugs to a duly licensed physician or to another person upon the written prescription of a duly li-

censed physician, or by such physician or person to such
retail dealer.

The proposed bill contains similar provisions for the amendment
of Section 245.

This bill would thus amend but two of the five Federal
statutes which prohibit the circulation of contraceptive information or means.   The Cummins-Vaile Bill amends all
five (as shown on page 97).

It leaves the control of conception still classed with
obscenity but makes the information or means mailable under certain limitations, or as the bill puts it, makes them
"not non-mailable."   The Cummins-Vaile bill entirely removes the subject, per se, from all legal connections with
obscenity.   The article in the Birth Control Review an-
nouncing the bill makes no mention of the fact that the proposed new bill leaves the subject still classed with indecency.
Great emphasis is laid upon the advantages of making the
doctors free to give the information, but nothing is said
about the fact that while the bill would permit the doctor
to dispense the obscene information without penalty, the
person who received it could not send that same information
to anyone else without being criminally indecent.

This is frankly a "doctors only" bill of a most extreme
sort, as it would not only render illegal for circulation all
contraceptive information or means except such as were
obtained personally from a physician or on his direct prescription, but would create a complete medical monopoly
of the dispensing of the information; would give doctors an
economic privilege denied to anyone else; would treat this
one phase of science as no other is treated, that is, make it
inaccessible to the public, except as doled out via a doctor's
prescription, as if the need for the knowledge were a disease.   It is the greatest possible contrast to the Cummins-
Vaile Bill which requires medical certification of methods,
but creates no medical monopoly to teach or sell, and which

frees this item of science so it can take its place in the world of science, like any other phase of hygiene.

The editor of the Birth Control Review sets forth the reasons for preferring fences to freedom as follows:

The American Birth Control League, from its inception, has set itself against the indiscriminate dissemination of so-called Birth Control information. It holds that responsible controlled motherhood can only be attained if women first receive practical scientific education in the means of Birth Control. Scientific education implies the individual treatment of each woman according to her physiological needs, and this is impossible if she depends on advertisements or printed matter which may or may not have been written with a thorough knowledge of anatomy and physiology, of the biological factors in conception, and of the nature and action of drugs and medicines.

The implication seems to be that the repeal of the Federal ban would release *only* unreliable information, whereas it would likewise release all the best and most authoritative information. All knowledge has to compete with ignorance, and no laws can prevent the struggle. What knowledge needs is an open field in which to make its effort to overcome ignorance.

Holding this view, the American Birth Control League was convinced that a campaign for the repeal of these Federal laws was of secondary importance until some educational work had been done. The first object was to remove in the public mind the idea that Birth Control implied one simple method that could be told by one person to another over the back fence, that it was the same for everybody, and that once told, nothing further remained to be done.

It would surely seem as though a better demonstration of the futility of unsuitable methods could be made if it were made lawful to discuss and compare methods than if, as at present, it is a crime to circulate anything which even names them.

For the last two and a half years The American Birth Control League has been working by means of conferences and of the *Review* to educate the public in the many aspects of the subject—sociological, economic, social, biological, physiological and psychical. It has worked for the establishment of Birth Control clinics in New York State under the limitations of the New York law, which permits the giving of Birth Control information in cases of disease, and in other States where the State laws do not place this restriction on the medical profession.

The Federal law does not affect the internal affairs of the individual States. It does not prohibit the establishment of Birth Control Clinics or the giving of advice and prescriptions by doctors in their public and private practice.

But the Federal law does most emphatically "affect the internal affairs of the individual States," by making a precedent for classing contraceptive information with obscenity. This precedent directly affects 24 States, as shown in Chapter One of Part I. The Chicago Health Commissioner held up the license of the Parenthood Clinic on this very precedent, as previously described.

The *object* of the League is that all over the United States there may be established clinics at which, under skilled medical supervision, Birth Control advice and instruction will be given to all women needing this care; and that the medical profession may be freed from the restrictions now placed upon it by State enactments, so that doctors may give Birth Control information both in their private and their public practice. The Federal laws do not directly affect this State legislation, and if all Federal restrictions on the use of the mails and on common carriers and express companies were removed, the medical profession would still, in all the States, having anti-Birth Control laws on their statute books, be legally prevented from giving oral Birth Control advice and prescriptions to their patients.

This statement fails to include the fact that the repeal of the Federal ban would be the greatest possible incentive to the 24 States having specific prohibitions, to follow suit and repeal their own repressive laws; and that without the repeal of the Federal law, the physicians in all States would be prevented from lawfully getting the books and other publications and data on which they must base their "oral advice" and their "prescriptions."

The result would be, that while women were debarred from real scientific knowledge of the subject, they might through the mails receive information entirely unsuited to their needs.

It is an unwarranted assumption that instruction given personally would be guaranteed to be scientific, while that which came by mail in a book or a pamphlet might not be. The exact reverse might be the case in many instances. In any event the repeal of the Federal law would not in the least prevent anyone from securing personal instruction from any physician who was willing or able to give it.

From certain points of view, it has seemed to the President and Directors of the American Birth Control League that little good and even possible harm might accrue at the present stage of development from an amendment of the Federal laws, eliminating all restrictions on the carriage of Birth Control information and materials; especially if this was done before sufficient data had been gathered to justify such action, and before campaigns of education had been carried on widely throughout the States, and especially before the establishment of at least a few model Birth Control clinics, which would serve not only as object lessons on the method of treating Birth Control, but also for the collection of data necessary for the use of the medical profession.

Why progress slowly under hard and unlawful conditions, instead of progressing rapidly as would be possible under freedom from legal restriction? The latter part of the foregoing quotation is a reminder of the famous official decision to build a new school house, and to use the materials in the old one for building the new one, and to occupy the old one until the new one was finished.

The removal of the Federal restrictions would almost certainly be followed by a flood of widespread advertising, of hastily written and probably misleading books and pamphlets purporting to give Birth Control information, and of supposed preventives which might or might not prevent and which certainly could not meet the needs of the numerous women who require personal physical examinations and personal prescriptions to suit their individual idiosyncrasies.

Any hastily written, inadequate or spurious information that might be circulated would have to compete with all the best, carefully written authoritative publications from abroad, and all the writings of many excellent American physicians, who have long been ready to publish their wisdom on the subject. There are at least a dozen well known American physicians who have studied contraceptive methods for twenty-five years or so, and who are ready to do their part toward the education of the profession and of the public by publishing technical books and pamphlets for the physicians and simplified hygienic instructions for the laymen.

The enactment of the Cummins-Vaile Bill would not prevent any one from securing direct advice from a physician, such as individual needs may require, but there would be every advantage in being able to supplement the instruction of a local physician by reading good books or pamphlets on the subject by some of the world's best authorities, and vice versa. To argue as if the removal of the Federal ban would interfere with individual instruction is putting up a man of straw.

Moreover if the opinion had been consistently held by the editor of the Birth Control Review that no one should receive any contraceptive instructions except those given to the individual by a physician making a "prescription to suit the individual idiosyncrasies," and after making a "personal physical examination," the Review would not have carried, as it did for many months, advertisements of contraceptives that were so thinly veiled as to deceive no one. They were advertised as antiseptics. Five such advertisements were in the very issue which contained the announcement of the new "doctors only" bill, and the arguments that no one should have instructions except personally from a doctor. Any reader of the magazine could order these contraceptives by mail from the firms which advertised them, and the orders would be filled, with no "personal prescription" or "physical examination" and with no medical endorsement of the methods. All five of the methods thus advertised may be very inadequate unless used in certain circumstances and combined with other safeguards. Yet the Review allowed its readers to run the risks, and took the profit from the advertisements. These advertisements were presently discontinued, after the magazine had been seriously criticized for publishing them.

And further, one of these contraceptives was recommended by name in Mrs. Sanger's pamphlet on family limitation, in which she described various methods. Since 1914 ten editions of this pamphlet have been sold or distributed. Many thousands of them have been sent through the mail. Mrs. Sanger herself stated at her Carnegie Hall meeting on her return from the Orient, that she had arranged to have an edition of this pamphlet printed in China. The Birth Control Review reported the publication of it in England also, and protested most vigorously because it had been suppressed under the British obscenity law. In all this widespread circulation of contraceptive advertisement and instruction, there was not even the endorsement of any physician quoted, say nothing of "personal prescription." If the theory that there should be no information allowed except via a doctor's prescription for the individual, has been so little adhered to by the very people who advance it, is it not futile to try at the eleventh hour to embody that theory in legislation? If the very people who advocate "doctors only" information are not willing to live up to it, who else could be expected to do so? How could anyone expect such legislation to be enforced?

To begin the work for Birth Control by campaigning for unrestricted use of the mails would seem more like sinking Birth Control to a hopelessly commercial and empirical level than establishing it on a firm scientific basis, with the prospect of ever-increasing developments and improvements until the ideal contraceptives are obtained.

As the government does not attempt to regulate by law what shall and what shall not circulate about other scientific subjects, there is no tenable reason why it should undertake to guide or protect this one part of science. Other scientific truths are not "reduced to a hopelessly commercial and empirical level" by being free from governmental barriers. A fair field and no favor is all that science needs.

Now the League has reached a point where some amendment of the Federal law may aid rather than hinder its work. It has not worked to have restrictions on the mails and express companies swept away. But it does desire to free the medical profession for the new duties that it is anxious to see the doctors undertake, by making it possible for them to communicate freely with each other concerning facts and data of Birth Control, and also by enabling them to secure the material necessary for their prescriptions.

Are laws made to "aid" the work of any particular organization, or are they for the benefit of the whole people?

To meet this new situation, which is developing out of the establishment of clinics in various States, it has secured the drawing up of a bill which, while not opening the mails to the commercial exploitation of Birth Control, would free the hands of the medical profession and enable the clinical data to be passed from one group of doctors to another.

It would facilitate the establishment and working of Birth Control clinics, and it would aid the doctors in assuming the new duty of giving Birth Control advice and prescriptions.

What does the medical profession really want, an opportunity for professional exploitation of birth control knowledge, or simply medical and scientific freedom?

It would leave the law as it now stands with regard to promiscuous dissemination of Birth Control advice and the advertising of supposed means of contraception.

The use of the word "promiscuous" and the word "indiscriminate" (in the first paragraph of this article, as above quoted) seems to connote some other attitude than merely the desire that each person who needs it should have individual medical advice. These two terms have been frequently used by those who oppose or who are fearful about freedom of access to contraceptive knowledge. The use of such words seems markedly inappropriate in discussing contraceptive knowledge from the point of view of health. Contraceptive methods are a part of hygiene, and the public should have access to knowledge about them just as to any other phases of hygiene. Instructions as to certain methods of brushing the teeth or as to certain diets to produce certain effects, could just as rightly be termed "promiscuous" and "indiscriminate." But no one would dream of using such language in that connection.

But to return to the text of this proposed bill. Under its provisions, no publishing of contraceptive knowledge or data would be practicable. A doctor would not personally undertake the expense of printing books and pamphlets, if he could send them only to other physicians or to his patients. Nor would publishers, medical or otherwise, issue books on the subject; because, being neither doctors nor "dealers in drugs," they could not ship their books to customers, not even if the customers were physicians. A ridiculous situation in which the publishers couldn't and the physicians wouldn't publish the data, without which the medical profession as a whole can not adequately study contraceptive science. Physicians would be deprived not only of what American publishers are ready to print (when the laws will permit) but they could not import the excellent books which are published abroad. (Sec. 102 of the Criminal Code and Sec. 305 of the Tariff Act prohibit all importations and these sections are not amended by the proposed bill.)

On detailed analysis the absurdity grows. The doctor

could mail instructions, a prescription or a contraceptive to his patient, but patients could not recommend the doctor in a letter to any one else, for that would be an "obscenity." No magazines, not even medical journals, could name the doctors who are good authorities on this subject, for that too would be "obscene." No scientists or health authorities or welfare workers could write even privately to people in dire need, listing the physicians who have made a specialty of studying methods. No hospital or clinics could mail announcements of their contraceptive service, for it would all be "obscene." The general public would have no way of ascertaining who the experts were except by the very limited way of verbal inquiry. The bill would permit importers, manufacturers and dealers in drugs to transport contraceptives, though the importer could not import them!

But the final beneficiary of this traffic would be the physician. The whole commerce would have no other lawful outlet than via the doctor's prescriptions. If the dealers should fill retail orders for any one who is not a doctor or who does not present a doctor's direct prescription, they would be criminals under the obscenity laws.

Obviously the dealers would not keep their business within any such prescribed lines. Even under the present laws dealers sell contraceptives in ever increasing quantity. They are either camouflaged as protection against venereal infection and as treatment for local ailments, or are sold on a plain boot-legging basis. Any attempt to keep this traffic within the bounds of this proposed bill would be just so much paper. No responsible legislators could be expected to take it seriously. The country is burdened with enough unenforceable laws already.

Not only will dealers sell contraceptives anyhow, but the one thing individuals can be counted upon to do is to spread the news as to what doctors give good advice, to repeat and copy their prescriptions ad infin. Information exclusively by the doctor-to-patient system is ruined at the start. No possible laws could enforce it.

Due either to the criticisms on this proposed legislation or to unaided sober second thought, this bill has recently been supplanted by another "doctors only" bill, which is now supported not only by the officers of the American Birth Control League, but by the New York Committee on Maternal Health, a group made up mostly of physicians under whose auspices, research work in contraceptive method is being carried on. Dr. Robert L. Dickinson is its Chairman. This new bill is somewhat less restrictive, and has fewer inconsistencies and loopholes than the first proposed bill, but is none the less a medical monopoly bill in intent, and is none the less class and special-privilege legislation. And like the first one, it leaves the subject of the control of conception still classed in the obscenities and penalized as a criminal indecency. It also has the same stuttering provision which makes contraceptive information and means "not non-mailable" under certain conditions. These conditions are, when they come from or are sent to a doctor, a medical publisher, an importer, manufacturer or dealer, and with a final provision that the retail dealer can not send anything of the sort to any one except a physician or some one who has a written prescription from a physician. It provides for importing and exporting under similar restrictions.

This newest version of a "doctors only" bill has been drafted by George E. Worthington, Acting Director of the Department of Legal Measures of the American Social Hygiene Association. It reads as follows:

Section 211, to be amended by adding the following:
Provided that:
Standard medical and scientific journals and reprints therefrom and standard medical works which contain information with reference to the preventing of conception are not non-mailable under this section.

Provided further that:

1. Any article, instrument, substance, drug, or thing designed, adapted or intended for preventing conception, or any written or printed information or advice concerning the prevention of conception is not non-mailable under this section when mailed by a duly licensed physician to:

   a. another person known to him to be a duly licensed physician;
   b. one of his bonafide patients in the course of his professional practice;
   c. a printer or publisher, or by a bonafide printer or publisher to a duly licensed physician.

2. Any article, instrument, substance, drug or thing designed, adapted or intended for preventing conception is not non-mailable under this section when mailed in the regular course of legitimate business by:

   a. an importer to a manufacturer or wholesale dealer in drugs, or by a manufacturer or wholesale dealer in drugs to an importer;
   b. a manufacturer to a wholesale dealer in drugs or by such wholesale dealer to a manufacturer;
   c. a wholesale dealer in drugs to another such wholesale dealer or a retail dealer in drugs, or by such retail dealer to such wholesale dealer;
   d. a retail dealer in drugs to a duly licensed physician or to another person upon the written prescription of a duly licensed physician, or by such physician or person to such retail dealer.

Section 245, to be amended by adding the following:

Provided that:

Any drug, medicine, article or thing designed, adapted, or intended for preventing conception, or any written or printed matter concerning the prevention of conception may be imported into, or exported from, the United States by a duly licensed physician, or may be transported in interstate commerce within the United States if consigned by a duly licensed physician:

   a. to another person known to him to be a duly licensed physician, or

    b. to one of his bonafide patients in the course of his professional practice.

Any drug, medicine, article or thing designed, adapted, or intended for preventing conception may be imported into or exported from the United States by a person, firm, or corporation, including a manufacturer, engaged in an established legitimate business of importing and exporting drugs, or may be transported in interstate commerce within the United States, if carried or shipped in the regular course of legitimate business, by:

    a. an importer to a manufacturer or wholesale dealer in drugs, or by a manufacturer or wholesale dealer in drugs to an importer;

    b. a manufacturer to a wholesale dealer in drugs or by such wholesale dealer to a manufacturer;

    c. a wholesale dealer in drugs to another such wholesale dealer or a retail dealer in drugs, or by such retail dealer to such wholesale dealer;

    d. a retail dealer in drugs to a duly licensed physician or to another person upon the written prescription of a duly licensed physician, or by such physician or person to such retail dealer.

Section 312, to be amended by adding the following:

Provided that:

The sale, loan, gift, exhibition or offer thereof, of any article, drug, instrument or thing, designed, adapted or intended for preventing conception, or the giving, writing or supplying of any oral, written or printed information concerning the preventing of conception, by a duly licensed physician to:

    a. another person known to him to be a duly licensed physician, or to

    b. one of his bonafide patients in the course of his professional practice;

shall not be an offense under this section, nor shall it be an offense for established wholesale or retail dealers in drugs to sell, lend, supply, give away, exhibit, possess, or transfer, to one another, in the regular course of legitimate business, or to a duly licensed physician or to another person upon the written prescription of a duly licensed physician, any article, drug, instrument, or thing, designed, adapted or intended for preventing conception. Any person obtaining any such article, drug, instrument, thing, or information in pursuance of this section may lawfully possess and use the same.

The vital difference between this bill and the previous one lies in the permission granted to medical publishers, and in the fact that "reprints" from "standard medical and scientific journals" are to be made "not non-mailable," although they contain matter which is classed as obscenity in the law to which this bill would add amendments. This bill is technically much better drawn than the previous one, but while it has filled some of the gaps in the other one—such as the provisions regarding publishing and importing—and has ironed out some of the absurdities, it still contains phrases like "bona-fide patient" and "bona-fide printer or publisher" and "standard" medical works, no one of which is defined by law. The enforcement of such a bill, if enacted into law, would therefore be built upon shifting sands, which would be just about as hopeless to deal with as have been the multitudinous interpretations of "obscenity" by censors, judges and juries for generations. What is a "bona-fide printer"? And what constitutes a *"standard medical or scientific journal"*? Whose standard would the law sanction? Standards vary widely at any given moment, and from decade to decade they vary prodigiously; indeed it is not so long ago that it was not "standard" to relieve the suffering of childbirth—it was not orthodox, it was "irreligious." Perhaps there were some who deemed it "obscene." Laws should contain explicit terms, and not those whose interpretation can vary so as not only to nullify the intent of the law, but so as to result in limitless injustice to the public and to the individuals against whom they are enforced.

The inclusion in the bill of "reprints" from "standard medical and scientific journals" practically breaks down any sort of practicable restriction. For any one can make reprints. If reprints, as well as the books and journals themselves are made mailable, it means that almost any one who wants contraceptive information can get it, and anyone who wants to can give it. And if, as has probably been the case, there is any idea on the part of those who devised this form of legislation, that restrictions of this sort will prevent "the wrong people" from getting contraceptive information, or will prevent the abuse of contraceptive knowledge, they might as well abandon the idea at the start, as to try to inflict so unenforceable a statute upon American citizens, who are already staggering under a huge mass of unenforced and unenforceable laws. Those who are impelled to misuse contraceptives, and to abuse the knowledge are quite clever enough to utilize "reprints" from the best authorities on contraception. There would be no such thing as keeping the knowledge within what anyone's notion of what proper bounds may be. There is no such thing now, even with our sweeping and unqualified laws.

This proposed bill makes the effort to limit the accessibility of knowledge into a mere gesture. True it might fool many people who do not stop to think or to analyze the bill, and it may even deceive those who propose it; but can it fool all the people? And can it fool Congress? That is the question for the American public to decide. As such a statute could not possibly keep the information within the bounds of the medical profession and those to whom the doctors specially imparted it, and as information under such a statute would circulate about as much as if a straight repeal of the ban were made, why bother with a circuitous, undignified, impracticable law, when a simple straight-forward repeal is possible, one which involves no preposterous complications as to interpretation or enforcement, and one which puts the subject of the control of conception, so far as the law is concerned, on a clean and self-respecting basis?

PART III

WHAT SORT OF LAWS DO THE PEOPLE REALLY WANT?

CHAPTER I

DO PHYSICIANS WANT A "DOCTORS ONLY" BILL?

Probably most physicians have not yet thought what sort of laws they want: Resolutions by medical associations depend largely on way subject is presented and by whom: Doctors have no interest in retaining obscenity connection as such: Only few want "doctors only" bill for mercenary reasons: Endorsement proposed for American Medical Association in 1920 sidetracked in department: President of A. M. A. cordial to idea of straight repeal: American Institute of Homeopathy and various local medical associations endorse Cummins-Vaile bill: New York Academy of Medicine took "doctors only" stand on recommendation of small sub-committee when many members are for straight repeal: Conferences of doctors and lawyers in Chicago and New York advise against all limited legislation: Dr. Pusey, Ex-President of American Medical Association warns against "silly legislation": Straight repeal the only recommendation of doctors and lawyers: Unfair to attempt to hold medical profession legally responsible for moral use of contraceptives: Doctors on the whole more interested in professional prestige and credit for devising contraceptive methods than in any exclusive control of their use.

NATURALLY the off-hand answer to such a question as "Do the physicians want a 'doctors only' bill?" is that some do and some do not. There is no accurate way of estimating the proportion of each kind, but there are some significant points to be surveyed as to the reasons offered by those who do stand for it. And it is even more significant that probably the large majority of physicians have not yet thought whether they do or do not. When asked individually, they are apt to say, as did a former

President of the California State Medical Association, when he was asked for advice in the framing of a Federal bill, "Oh, I am a physician, not a law maker. I must leave that to the experts." But he emphatically believes in birth control, and in the responsibility of the medical profession toward the subject. In his retiring presidential address he said, "It is up to the profession to urge the repeal of the laws against birth control."

When the question of birth control legislation has been brought up at meetings of medical associations, it is perhaps safe to say that more resolutions have been killed in committee than have been submitted to the members for a vote, the reasons being about the same as those which have inhibited Congress, including "consideration" for the feelings of Catholic members. The vote on those which have been submitted has depended considerably on the way the resolution was worded, and somewhat on who proposed the resolution. This is no disparagement on medical associations. It might quite as truthfully be said of almost any sort of organization. It is a human failing to vote aye in meetings, on any proposition which has a generally good-sounding purpose, or which is introduced by some one in whom the people present have general confidence. It is only occasionally that resolutions are dissected with care by any large body of people and voted upon with full comprehension of their meaning. This human disability operates just as effectively one way as another, unless the question at issue is very clear-cut and the pro and con positions are very sharply defined.

It seems more than likely that many medical associations would quite readily endorse such a bill as that drafted by Mr. Worthington and described in the last chapter, if some one were to present it with a speech emphasizing the need of the people to have reliable scientific information and to be protected from all manner of quackery and commercialism, and if nothing were said about how the bill leaves the subject of contraception still a criminal indecency, and how such a law could not possibly be enforced to give the protection it is aimed to provide, or how it would establish a class privilege in the exploitation of birth control information. On the other hand it is just as likely that many medical associations would endorse the Cummins-Vaile Bill, if it were presented as a means for rescuing contraceptive science from all legal connection with indecency, and giving to the medical profession the opportunity it has long needed, to study and teach the control of conception, on the same basis that it teaches all other subjects which relate to health, that is, with freedom; and also an opportunity to put out of business, by critical publicity, the vendors of worthless or harmful contraceptives, who are now carrying on camouflaged or boot-legging operations. Indeed such endorsement has already been made by a number of medical associations, as well as by hundreds of well known individual physicians.

While resolutions in general may usually be taken with a grain of salt, it is also fair to assume that neither medical associations nor any other groups of intelligent American citizens would naturally take a stand against the principle of freedom in education, if they once recognized the issue clearly.

That there is a small percentage of the medical profession which is animated by a mercenary motive in regard to the giving of contraceptive instruction and would therefore stand for a "doctors only" bill must be regretfully admitted, but with the cheerful guess that it is a very small proportion. There is one leading obstetrician known to the writer who protested against his wife's attending a parlor meeting on birth control, on the ground that "if you encourage that sort of thing, you know our income will be cut in two." Instances are not unknown too, of physicians who have recommended a "doctors only" law, and who have profiteered quite shockingly in the contraceptives which they sell at present unlawfully to their patients. The most forthright instance known to the writer was that of a physician who was very strenuous in advocating a "doctors only" law, so much so that he was the means of having that recommendation formulated officially by a local but large and important medical association. In private conversation he admitted all the reasons for a complete repeal of the restrictive laws; he granted that the subject was not obscene, that ignorance and half knowledge made wide-spread suffering and disaster in family life, that people should be able to get reliable scientific instruction, and get it quickly. Yet he stuck to the "doctors only" idea, in its most narrow form, that is, that no information should be available except by personal consultation with a doctor. He was fearful lest the repeal of the Federal ban would produce "a flood of quackery." When asked if he did not have confidence that the medical profession would rise to the occasion, and to educate the public as it ought to be educated on this subject, just as it rose to the occasion when the war came and educated both the soldiers and the public on the matter of venereal disease, his answer was, "What do you take us for? We are not reformers. We are busy men with our livings to earn." He was unwilling for the public to have a chance for quick education on this subject by means of authoritative books and pamphlets, but insisted upon their having it exclusively dependent upon the slow process of being informed one at a time by a visit to a doctor's office. The first consideration was that nothing should lessen the doctor's opportunity for earning his living.

Contrasted with this attitude is that of physicians like Dr. Lawrence Litchfield of Pittsburgh, former President of the Pennsylvania State Medical Society, who spoke at the Hearings in Washington on the Cummins-Vaile Bill, and whose remarks have been quoted in a previous chapter. Representative similar opinions are the following:

Dr. George Blumer, of New Haven, Conn.—"It is better to enlighten people by education than by legislation. I do not feel as a matter of principle that the regulation of birth control should be entirely in the hands of physicians . . . there are many cases where the problem is not a medical one at all."

Dr. Jerome Cook of St. Louis.—"No distinction should be made between this and other forms of medical knowledge, and no restriction should be placed upon the spread of knowledge. . . ."

Dr. Alexander Forbes of Harvard Medical School.—"The one thing I feel sure of is that the principle in the present law, classifying contraceptive knowledge as obscenity, is essentially hypocritical and unsound."

Dr. A. B. Emmons 2nd, of Harvard Medical School.—"Education rather than water-tight legislation. Censorship of manufactured articles. A few good popular articles of sound advice and vigorous warning against dangers and quacks by leading medical authorities is about all that can be done. I believe in leading rather than prohibiting."

Dr. Alma Arnold of New York.—"Enlightenment by education rather than by new laws. We have too many laws now. Logic and education of the individual must take the place of snoopery by appointed guardians."

Dr. Charles S. Bacon of Chicago. "Any attempt to limit the teaching of contraception to a class will be, I think, useless. Worthless drugs and appliances will probably disappear in the course of time, because of disappointments resulting from their use. If laws regulating the sale of poisons do not suffice, they should be amended."

Dr. J. E. Wallin, Director of Clinic for Subnormal and Delinquent Children, Miami University, Ohio.—"I am unalterably opposed to any sort of monopoly limited to any particular type of practitioner . . . who would be in a position to extort unreasonable fees."

Dr. B. S. Oppenheimer, of Mt. Sinai Hospital, New York.—"No restrictive laws would work, and the education of the public by the medical profession is the only way to get bad methods suppressed and good ones adopted."

It is noteworthy that those who stand for the "doctors only" idea in legislation are on the whole remarkably unable or unwilling to state their case in any way that is analogous to that of those who stand for the principle of freedom of access to knowledge. Their reasons are hypothetical rather than specific, and seem to be based upon expediency rather than upon principle. For instance a "doctors only" physician was invited to present that side of the argument at an open meeting of the Voluntary Parenthood League, and the points made were these: that a "doctors only" law would better safeguard the public, though no proofs of the assertion were offered; that it would be more easily passed by Congress, though that also was an unsubstantiated assertion, and experience with "doctors only" bills in State legislatures certainly does not back it up; and that it would receive more general endorsement from the medical profession, which again was a supposition that has not been borne out by facts. The final point made by this "doctors only" proponent was the advice to get a limited measure through Congress first, and then to make a later separate campaign to remove the subject from the obscenity statutes. (It was promptly suggested that any one who was willing to propose *two* long hard campaigns on this project instead of one should be made chairman of a committee to finance them!)

Another of the "doctors only" physicians has explained that he takes that stand for diplomatic purposes only, that he is really a firm believer in the ideal of clearing this subject from connection with obscenity, but because "it *sounds* so safe" to say, "keep it in the hands of the doctors," he believes it better to work for that sort of law, that it would "reassure the public more," and that the chief thing to do is to get "permission to circulate medical publications," explaining how that had "a nice professional sound," which would prevent alarm, but that "of course it would amount to about the same thing as an open law, only the worried folks wouldn't know it."

The Chairman of the New York Committee on Maternal Health, Dr. Robert L. Dickinson, although he has given his written personal endorsement of the principle of a clean repeal on which the Cummins-Vaile Bill is based, has of late decided to accept as a working basis the "doctors only" bill drawn by Mr. Worthington, and is endeavoring to get it endorsed by national medical organizations, on the supposition that this is as far as they would be willing to go.   It is noteworthy in this connection that the national medical organizations have not yet been given a chance by their officers to turn down the endorsement of a freedom bill.   It would seem that the presentation of a limited bill might better follow than precede action on a freedom bill, as being a fairer treatment of the members of the organizations.   If endorsement of the freedom bill were squarely refused after full and open discussion of its provisions, the proposal to endorse limited legislation might logically follow.   That the reverse action seems to be the policy of some of the leaders is a reminder of the way the officers in the women's clubs and some of the welfare organizations have held back the submission of any resolution to the members.

In 1920 an effort was made to have a straight repeal resolution presented to the next Convention of the American Medical Association.   Dr. Frederick R. Green, Secretary of the Council on Health and Public Instruction, at that time wrote to a physician member of the Voluntary Parenthood League,

What is needed, I think, is not any positive legislation authorizing physicians to teach the public proper scientific facts on this subject, but rather the repeal of the needless legislation that has been enacted.

In referring to Comstock as the source of this needless legislation, he said:

Comstock was a fanatical social reformer who carried his views regarding purity to a ridiculous extent. In fact it is only in late years since Freud has shown the real workings of this type of mind, that we are able to understand the reason for some of Comstock's efforts.

A few months later the Director of the Voluntary Parenthood League and a physician member of the National Council had a personal conference with Dr. Green with the result that he agreed to submit as a part of the tentative report of his Council on Health and Public Instruction a resolution favoring the removal from the obscenity statutes of the ban on contraceptive knowledge. If the five other members of the Council should approve of including the resolution in the report, it would then be presented to the Convention of the whole American Medical Association, and if accepted as read would stand as the endorsement of the Association. The resolution was worded as follows:

Whereas, one of the primary necessities for family and therefore for public health, is an intelligently determined interval between pregnancies, to be secured by regulating the inception of life and not by interfering with life after it starts, and

Whereas, the prohibition of the circulation of information on the control of conception should never have been included in Federal or State "obscenity" laws,

Be It Resolved, that the House of Delegates of the American Medical Association recommends the removal of this prohibition from the "obscenity" statutes, and

Be It Further Resolved, that for the protection of the public against unhygienic information, new separate statutes be enacted, providing that all information circulated and all materials sold for the purpose of controlling conception, must bear specific endorsement by duly licensed physicians."

For some unexplained reason the resolution disappeared from consideration. The only indication of a reason was one which hardly seems to be sufficient to be the whole cause, namely, that owing to a delay in printing the tentative report, the members of the Council on Health and Public Instruction received letters from interested physician members of the Voluntary Parenthood League, urging the adoption of the resolution, previous to their receiving from the Secretary of the Council copies of the tentative report containing the resolution. It seems unlikely that an unwitting mishap of this sort would be the only thing which prevented procedure, if procedure was what was wanted. Judging by letters from the interviews with members of the Council, there was general hospitality to the idea embodied in the resolution.

When Dr. Litchfield spoke at the second Hearing on the Cummins-Vaile Bill in May, 1924, it will be remembered that he replied to Congressman Hersey's question as to "why have you not succeeded in getting them (the American Medical Association) to adopt this?" by saying,

The medical society has been very busy, but they will do this eventually. The President of the American Medical Association told me so. I met him in conference at Atlantic City, and he said all the members were in favor of birth control, and it was only a question of time when we should have it. I am not authorized to give his name, but he stands as the first man in American medicine.

When Dr. William Allen Pusey became President of the American Medical Association, he made a very forthright appeal for the utilization of contraceptive knowledge, as imperative for health and social welfare, and he is opposed to the retention of the Comstock laws. In his address at the last International Neo-Malthusian Conference, in New York, he said:

The first prerequisite to satisfactory study of any subject is free access to the knowledge of it, and that necessitates the *unrestricted* interchange of experience and information among scientific men. That is not allowed now upon the subject of methods of birth control. We are not in a position where we can freely determine the merits and demerits of the subject. It is not that methods of birth control are not discussed and practiced; they are, everywhere. But the facts—and the fiction—are passed from individual to individual, ignorantly, crudely, unsatisfactorily and in ways that are often vicious. It is only scientific decent discussion of the subject that is prevented, the sort of discussion that is necessary and can only be had, when it is *untrammeled* among self-respecting men, who can bring to its consideration knowledge and wisdom. . . . To see that this is brought about *as quickly as possible* is a thing worthy of the vigorous efforts in that direction that are now being made.

(The italics are ours.)

The American Institute of Homeopathy, the national organization of the Homeopathic School of Medicine, has already passed a resolution in favor of the straight, clean repeal as provided in the Cummins-Vaile Bill. Several State and local medical associations have done likewise. And so far as the writer knows, there have been only two instances where a medical association has gone on record in favor of "doctors only" legislation. One was the Ohio State Medical Association, the other the New York City Academy of Medicine.

The latter organization forms a rather striking instance of the way forceful leadership and minority opinions can be made to dominate a membership which is either passive or holds other views. Early in 1920, the Public Health Committee of the Academy was asked to endorse the straight repeal measure, which later became the Cummins-Kissel Bill. The Committee had twenty-nine members; the question was referred to a sub-committee of five, which presently reported against endorsing the bill, and the report was accepted by the Health Committee. The sub-committee did not approve,

On the grounds that such amendment would remove every obstacle to the indiscriminate distribution of information relating to and advertisements of methods for prevention of conception, both

from lay and professional sources; but we are in favor of amending
the existing law in such a way that it would contain the principle,
that nothing in the obscenity law shall apply to duly licensed physicians, licensed dispensaries, and to the public health authorities in
connection with the discharge of their respective duties in protecting
the health of patients and of the community.

It was known that there were many members of the
Academy who were not accurately represented by this decision, and who did want the subject removed from the
obscenity statutes, instead of merely permitting physicians
to infringe the law without being subject to penalty; indeed
some of the more prominent of the twenty-nine members of
the Health Committee had previously signed the statement
of endorsement which constituted the platform of the Voluntary Parenthood League, and which contains the following paragraphs:

We desire to help in supporting a body of public opinion, which
will lead to so amending the Federal and State laws that it will not
be a criminal offense to give out information on the subject of birth
control, and that such information will not be classed with obscenity
and indecency.

We believe that the question as to whether or not, and when a
woman should have a child is not a question for physicians to decide
—except when a woman's life is endangered—or for the clergy or
for the State legislators to decide, but a question for the individual
family concerned to decide.

For these reasons the Health Committee was asked to
reconsider, but declined, although some of the members as
individuals expressed sympathy with the broader aims of the
freedom legislation.

A few months later, the new protective clause of the
Cummins-Vaile Bill, or at least the fore-runner of it, was
formulated. This was to provide a separate statute, quite
apart from the obscenity sections, to the effect that "no

printed information as to methods of preventing conception and no ingredients compounded for the purpose of preventing conception shall be transportable through the mails or by any other public carrier in the United States except such as bear endorsement by duly licensed physicians or public health authorities." It was thought by the officers of the Voluntary Parenthood League that such an addition to the bill would meet the views of those who wanted medical restrictions for the sake of protection to the public, at the same time that it was not class or privilege legislation, and it was consistent with the main part of the bill by which the subject was removed from the obscenity laws. So once more the Health Committee of the Academy of Medicine was asked to consider. The answer this time was that the Secretary did not "believe that the Committee would care to take up the matter of amendments anew." In conversation later the secretary said that it was not the function of the Committee "to determine exact legal phraseology, but merely to express broad principles" which they had sufficiently done previously, when they adopted the report of their sub-committee. He did, however, express his own interest in the fact that the League seemed to have "come around" to the view of the Academy Committee. He evidently did not grasp the wide difference in principle and see that the Academy Committee recommendation would establish a medical monopoly of the distribution of information, while the new protective section proposed by the League would secure medical sanction for methods, but without the possibility of monopoly.

In 1921, when the first "doctors only" bill was introduced into the New York legislature, as result of Mrs. Sanger's effort, the newspapers and the Birth Control Review announced that the Health Committee of the Academy had endorsed the bill, but it was subsequently denied in the press. The original stand against freedom and for privilege and for retaining the obscenity classification seems to be the status quo, officially; but many of the members are also members of the Voluntary Parenthood League and are hearty endorsers of the freedom bill. And what is more significant still, is that many of the members of the Academy do not know what stand their own organization has taken on this legislation, and would be at a loss to define the difference between the freedom bill and the "doctors only" sort of bill.

Such inattention to organization policy is by no means peculiar to this one medical society. It seems to be a very general characteristic of all sorts of organizations, including even those for birth control. People join organizations because of the general object, and their own general interest in that object, but that is not at all the same thing as taking careful note of the means propounded for achieving that object. So it happens that a few active members like chairmen of sub-committees can commit whole organizations to a policy that would never be adopted if the individual members had all the facts in hand and took the time to weigh the merits of differing propositions. And when once a decision has been officially adopted, it is considerably difficult to have it changed. Esprit de corps is often called in to back up a decision that has been adopted by the whole body without investigation upon the recommendation of a very small minority, with the result that the latent wisdom of the membership at large does not function on the question at all.

In the instance of the New York Academy of Medicine, just described, the workings of this sort of esprit-de-corps conscience were not without a humorous side. The several members of the Health Committee who had previously signed an endorsement of the aim to remove the ban on birth control information from the obscenity laws, found themselves committed, by the adoption of the sub-committee report, to the policy of leaving the subject in the obscenity laws. Moreover the endorsement they had signed had explicitly averred that "the question as to whether or not or when a woman should have a child is not for physicians to decide," yet by the acceptance of the sub-committee report, they were committed to the idea of leaving the giving of contraceptive information to the discretion of physicians and health authorities. Loyalty to their organization superseded loyalty to their own judgment, and they proceeded to request the Voluntary Parenthood League not to quote them as endorsers. Some of them were careful to explain in private that they had not altered their views at all, but that it was not best for them to be quoted as having them or as having had them. Their request was acceded to; their names were omitted from subsequent lists of endorsers, but obviously they could not be withdrawn from lists circulated previously.

All this occurred five years ago. Since that time a marked change has seemed evident in the medical profession as a whole. A much more keen feeling of responsibility for sound legislation has developed, especially within the last year. In the late autumn of 1924 some leading doctors and lawyers had conferences on the subject, and analyzed with care all the proposed sorts of legislation which had been devised to protect the public from harmful contraceptives and to render access to sound scientific information lawful and equitable. These conferences were called to determine whether wording of the protective section of the Cummins-Vaile Bill could be improved. One of them was held in Chicago, and one in New York. Dr. Pusey was present at the former.

The consensus of opinion at both conferences was against all "doctors only" types of legislation and for straight freedom for science. The doctors as a whole were of the opinion that an unencumbered clean repeal of the contraceptive prohibition laws would give the medical profession a larger chance to serve the public well than any other proposed measure. The lawyers emphasized the fact that no possible statutes can guarantee sound instruction for the public, that only education can approximate that result, and law can not and must not prescribe education. The conferences even advised against the protective section of the Cummins-Vaile Bill, as inadequate and sure to be meaningless in many instances of its application. There was general opinion that the existing Food and Drug Act will apply effectively to suppress fraudulent contraceptives, when the ban against the circulation of contraceptives is removed. These conferences were reported in the Birth Control Herald, from which the following excerpts giving salient points are taken.

The "doctors only" type of legislation heretofore has had sincere approval from a considerable number of physicians who were unquestionably beyond the appeal of mere money making, in the giving of contraceptive instructions. They were bent upon having good methods taught, knowing full well how harmful and fraudulent methods are being secretly and illegally circulated at present.

But now, while there is far more medical interest and conscience than ever before regarding the need for authentic instruction, there is also a very widespread conclusion that the so-called "doctors only" type of legislation would be not only futile as a means of accomplishing what the best doctors most want, but that it would actually stand in the way of their giving to the public the service they would like to render.

The doctors have buckled down to considering the question of legislation as never before, and in co-operation with some of the best lawyers, the conclusion has been reached that the simple clean repeal of the words "preventing conception" is the best and biggest thing to be done, and that the Cummins-Vaile Bill should consist of just that and nothing more.

The physicians present at the Chicago conference were Dr. William Allen Pusey, President of the American Medical Association, Dr. Herman Adler, Dr. Charles Bacon, Dr. Raphael Yarros, Dr. John Favill, President of the Mississippi Branch of the American Birth Control League, and Dr. Clara Davis, head of the Pediatric Division of the Mt. Sinai Hospital in Cleveland.

Discussion was informal, but to the point. The boiled down sense of the meeting was in favor of the straight repeal to remove the subject from the obscenity statutes, leaving the protection of the public to education by the medical profession, and the Food and Drug Act.

All the chief propositions for securing substantial protection by legislation were taken up and found wanting. They were turned down as illusive and inadequate, and even as stumbling blocks to progress.

Dr. Pusey, whose forthright views on birth control became widely known when he discussed the subject in his presidential address before the Convention of the A. M. A. last June, greatly aided clear thinking on the question of legislation. He said the main point in the Cummins-Vaile Bill was the chief thing to accomplish, that is, the removal of the subject from the obscenity laws. He did not wish to say definitely that no sort of protective legislation was a possibility, for he had not had the time to consider all the alternatives to the vanishing point.

But he did lay down some general principles. He said the chief thing to remember is that all sorts of miserable, inadequate and even dangerous contraceptive information is going the rounds *now*, in spite of the absolutely sweeping prohibition of the Comstock law; that no real attempt is being made to stop it legally, and that no such attempt will ever be made. If there is such wholesale law-breaking now, it stands to reason that no sort of "doctors only" laws could be enforced. They would only serve to deceive the public. He said great care must be taken to avoid any more "silly laws" or laws that can not be enforced. "We have too many of those already."

Members of the Executive Committee and a representative group of doctors and lawyers, combined their efforts, in person and by letter at the Headquarters of the Voluntary Parenthood League, to solve the question of protective legislation.

After discussion from all angles and earnest effort for the best, the conference voted to reaffirm the main point of the Cummins-Vaile Bill, i.e., the clean removal of the words "preventing conception" from the five Federal statutes where it occurs; and to recommend the withdrawal of the present five-doctor certification section; and to appoint a committee of three to re-investigate the present

Food and Drug Act, with power to draft an amendment specifically covering contraceptives, if such were deemed necessary. The Committee chosen was Mr. Engelhard, Chairman, Dr. D. George Fournad and Mrs. Dennett, thus representing the legal and medical professions and the League.

The Committee appointed by the Conference worked at once, and formulated a report based on a thorough investigation of the powers of the Food and Drug Act. The finding coincides with a previous legal opinion, written last year by Clarence Lewis, of New York, a lawyer who was formerly on the V. P. L. Executive Committee. The opinion is that there is ample power now in the Food and Drug Act to suppress all fraudulent contraceptives which contain drugs or chemicals.

The pertinent parts of this Act are given in Appendix No. 14.

The Committee points out that while the Food and Drug Act can take care of fraud in drugs and compounds, neither it, nor any other legislation, can efficaciously apply to contraceptives as regards their harmlessness or harmfulness. For that depends upon the case. Some drugs are harmful if used in some ways, but not so in others. So also contraceptives which are not drugs or chemicals or compounds, but are articles. Their usefulness or harmfulness depends largely upon the conditions of their use. For discrimination as to methods in these particulars, the public would be dependent upon getting instructions from good scientific sources, just as they are in regard to any other matters of hygiene.

It is not the business of the law to prescribe either methods in hygiene or to prescribe the sources from which the public shall receive instruction in hygiene. But it can and does protect the public from flagrant profiteering and fraud, in drugs and the like, by means of the Food and Drug Act.

Only one physician urged the old plea for "doctors only" legislation. The Conference was heartily with her in wanting people to have only the best instruction and to have it from competent doctors, but no restrictive legislation will achieve that goal. Proposals of this sort thus far have been open to the objection of being either class privilege, unenforceable, and inadequate even as a means of making knowledge available for the doctors themselves. She conceded that she could not herself devise any "doctors only" plan that would not be special privilege legislation. The next day she telephoned that she was convinced that education would have to be the main dependence.

This doctor mentioned having consulted an English medical journal containing elaborate data on contraceptives, in the library of one of the New York Medical Societies.   "But it was illegally put there," said the conference members almost in unison.   The law forbids all importation.   "Medical boot-legging," added the chairman.

Letters were read from distant physicians, some of whose opinions have already been quoted on page 223.

Dr. Udo J. Wile, Professor of Dermatology and Syphilology, University of Michigan, wrote, "I trust nothing will come out of the conference which will confuse the main issue, namely to get the Cummins-Vaile Bill passed.   It appears to me that the matter under consideration (protective legislation) is of minor importance.

"James F. Morton (lawyer) said that all the 'doctors only' laws would be unconstitutional anyhow, and that the only legislative choice lies between the present abominable, unenforced and unenforceable laws and complete freedom of access to knowledge."

Below is given a résumé of all the chief legislative proposals to protect the public from harmful and fraudulent contraceptives, and the reasons why they were turned down by the conference, and were not considered as material to be recommended for the Cummins-Vaile Bill.

Certification of Contraceptives by Five Licensed Physicians

The protective section as it now stands in the Cummins-Vaile Bill reads as follows:

"The transportation by mail or by any public carrier in the United States or in territory subject to the jurisdiction thereof, of information respecting the means by which conception may be prevented, or of the means of preventing conception, is hereby prohibited except as to such information or such means as shall be certified by not less than five graduate physicians lawfully engaged in the practice of medicine to be not injurious to life or health."

The doctors themselves consider this a weak and unreliable safeguard because, unfortunately, medical opinions can be too easily secured.   The certification might therefore in many instances be meaningless.

Dr. W. A. Pusey, President of the American Medical Association, in this connection said:

"We are only human.   So large a body as the medical profession would be bound to contain some undesirables."

Certification by Boards of Health
(Suggested by Sen. Spencer and others.)

Government health officials are not, as such, necessarily well informed as to the merits or demerits of contraceptives.   A few might happen to have valuable judgment, but merely being a public official would be no guarantee.

There is wide-spread disapproval of anything that smacks of "State medicine" or governmental administration of the practice of medicine.

Certification by City Health Commissioners
(Suggested by one of them.)

He admitted, however, that he had very little reliable information on this subject.   Although a physician, he turned to a layman (the Director of the V. P. L.) for advice as to the best sources for knowledge about contraceptive methods.   If one of our best known Health Commissioners could be but a beginner in this study, their group would hardly seem the right one to be given exclusive jurisdiction as to the circulation of contraceptives.

Contraceptives Authorized by Medical Boards
(Suggested tentatively by Sen. Cummins and others.)

This would be class legislation which is against American principles and would rouse the antagonism of scientists who do not belong to the medical associations, whose Boards would be given such jurisdiction.

Certification by the Department of Medical and Chemical Research of the National Public Health Service
(Suggested at the Chicago Physicians' Conference.)

This received less opposition than any other proposition to vest authority in any group, but it was subject to more or less the same objection that held in regard to the proposal to vest authority in public officials or medical Boards.

MARGARET SANGER'S PROPOSED "DOCTORS ONLY" LEGISLATION

This is suggested Federal legislation by which the Obscenity Statutes would not apply to doctors giving contraceptive instructions or prescriptions to other physicians or to their bona fide patients, nor to manufacturers and dealers in drugs who execute the physician's prescriptions. This proposition was disapproved on several counts.

First, because it leaves the subject of contraceptive science still classed with obscenity.

Second, it is merely a permit to physicians to do what would be a crime under the obscenity law, for anyone else to do.

Third, it would establish a medical economic monopoly of the circulation of contraceptive knowledge.

Fourth, it would substantially deprive the medical profession of the very opportunity it purports to provide, namely, to study contraceptive science for the benefit of the public and the perfection of methods.

Fifth, it does not make medical publishing on contraceptives any more practicable than it is under the present law.

Sixth, it would not permit the importation of scientific contraceptive data from abroad.

The conference took place before Mrs. Sanger had abandoned this form of "doctors only" bill in favor of the form subsequently drafted by Mr. Worthington, as described in the previous chapter. Some of these criticisms are not applicable to the Worthington draft, but the first and second ones do apply.

Testing out all these propositions in the light of Dr. Pusey's warning that the United States should avoid any more "silly" laws on this subject, all but one are open to further objection in the ground of wholesale unenforceability. The present protective section of the Cummins-Vaile Bill is the least unenforceable, with its provision for certification of methods by at least five licensed physicians. Under that provision there would be relatively little temptation to evade the law. But all the others would be more or less unenforceable, the Sanger proposition most of all.

Out of all the dust of discussion, the straight repeal emerges clear and clean. The doctors said it was the only practicable legislation and the lawyers that it was the only sound legislation.

It has been noticeable that physicians in discussing birth control legislation if they have leaned at all toward laws to keep the imparting of information exclusively in medical hands, have done so with a view to safeguarding the people from harmful or fraudulent methods, and have not urged it as a means for regulating morals. But laymen, notably club women, quite frequently have jumped at a hasty and thoughtless conclusion that somehow if the knowledge is kept by law in the hands of the doctors only, and is given out by them according to their discretion, it will be kept from reaching those who want to utilize it in illicit relationships. This assumption is the flimsiest kind of self-deception. The notion that doctors as a whole can see to it that they give instruction only where the use of it will stand the highest test of ethics and wisdom is nonsense. The function of the medical profession is to cure and prevent disease. It is not to act as arbiter of morals and ethics. Any pretense that it should do so is built on shifting sand.

It is utterly unfair to the doctors to expect them to serve in any such capacity, and to propose laws that would impose upon them any such responsibility. Occasionally, of course, the doctor is not only physician but friend to his patient, and is therefore in a position to give moral advice without intrusion, but that relationship is incidental to his profession and not inherent in it. Laws that would try to empower physicians to act as inquisitors into the private lives of their patients and to be responsible for the ethical use of contraceptive instructions, would be an imposition both upon the physicians and upon the people.

There is no evidence that the profession wants any such spurious responsibility thrust upon it. Medical men in general are sufficiently high grade human beings to have a high regard for morals, and as individuals they can make their influence felt, but that is an entirely different thing from foisting upon them as a class a law-imposed task of managing other people's private lives. Legislators, citizens and physicians alike must recognize that the source of moral stability is individual character, and that no repressive or paternalistic laws can ever produce the desired results.

There are many indications that medical men have an instinct for protecting the status of the profession as the natural source of scientific information on this subject, and it is not exceptional to find physicians who lean toward favoring a "doctors only" bill as a recognition of medical prestige, but this impulse is not at all synonymous with a mercenary desire to have exclusive control of the dissemination of knowledge. They quite naturally want credit for devising good contraceptive methods, but relatively few are interested to retain any monopolistic advantage in the utilization of them. The writer recalls a conversation with a physician who, after some years of experiment, had devised an extremely simple and very inexpensive contraceptive. His rather inexplicable reservations in talking about it led to the frank inquiry as to whether he planned to make money by controlling the sale of his compound. His answer was a most emphatic "No, certainly not." But he added, "I do, however, want credit for it. I have worked on this thing for five years, and have proved that it is simple, harmless, efficacious and cheap. It has solved the problem for my own patients and will do the same for thousands of others. All I want is that the formula shall stand as a part of my professional record." He solidly approves the freedom idea in legislation.

Chapter II

WHAT DO THE PEOPLE WANT?

People's first individual want is reliable contraceptive informa-
tion: Strong probability that people prefer decent enforceable laws
to those which are dirty and unenforceable: Choice can not be put
up to United States town-meeting fashion: Reader asked to make
own choice by elimination of what he does not want: Do you con-
sider contraception indecent? Should laws penalize the decent ma-
jority to reach the depraved few? Should the control of conception
itself be made a criminal act by law? Abstinence as method of birth
control has no legal standing in the U. S.: Do you want unenforce-
able laws? Can "doctors only" laws accomplish their own aims?
Are they enforceable? Do all contraceptives require personal medical
instruction? Proponents of "doctors only" bill admit they do not:
English birth control organization disapproves "doctors only" stand:
Best known English authority on birth control is biologist, not M.D.:
Are laws to control improper advertising of contraceptives prac-
ticable? Average citizen too occupied to analyze legislative proposals:
Proponents of limited legislation backward about explaining their
bills to the public: They refuse to debate openly or confer privately
with the proponents of the freedom bill.

WHAT do the people want? No doubt the first conscious want of most people so far as birth control
is concerned, is simple reliable information about methods.
It is largely their own needs and wants which have made
people pay attention to and develop the birth control movement, or realize just how the laws forbid their getting what
they want. On the latter point they are apt to be much
more vague than on the former. Some people, and unfortunately they are numerous, having managed to get what

they want in spite of the laws, are prone to forget the plight of others who are not sophisticated enough or lucky enough to be successful law-breakers, and thus they feel little direct responsibility about getting the laws revamped so that they shall not stand in the way of any one who needs access to the information. But on the whole, these careless and self-centered people would, if they stopped to think about it, agree with those who have a heart for others and are public spirited, and they too would prefer decent, just and practicable laws to those which are dirty-minded, unjust and unenforceable.

Suppose a real conference of the whole people were possible, and they could put their minds on deciding what laws they wanted on this subject, after looking over the statutes we have now, and after scrutinizing all the proposals that have been made for revising them, what sort of a decision would they be likely to make? What would their conclusion be, if left entirely to their own devices, with no "experts" to tell them what to say, and with the whole responsibility on their own shoulders? They would doubtless be deficient in putting their ideas into legal phraseology—the technician might have to be called on for that; but would they be likely to vote any sort of suppression or restrictions upon themselves? Is there any precedent in history for a body of people ever doing that? Have people ever united to express their lack of faith in themselves and said, "Let us have laws to keep us from knowing this and that, as we can not trust ourselves to use the knowledge rightly"? On the contrary, whenever people unite in demands *for themselves,* are those demands not always for freedom rather than for repression?

But since a United States town-meeting on this subject is a wild hypothesis, perhaps the next best thing would be for the reader to look upon himself as the one person upon whom the answer to this question rested—with the responsible knowledge that whatever he really wanted would forthwith become the law of the land; and realizing also that what he basically wants is, probably ten to one, what most everybody else wants too.

The simplest way to reach a conclusion about this law question would seem to be by elimination. First then—do you want the laws related to birth control to remain as they are now? Do you approve the legal company the subject is in—under such law classifications as "Obscene literature," "Indecent articles," and entangled with such adjectives as "lewd," "lascivious," "filthy," and "immoral"? No? You wish it rescued? Then the bill to repeal those two words "preventing conception" from all the obscenity statutes is what you want.

But wait—it may not be so simple as that. How about those who do feel that the control of conception *is* more or less indecent, the people who have somewhat Comstocky minds, to whom *any* reminder of sex is a danger? Are they anything like a majority. If so, would you want to let the laws remain as they are in deference to their feelings? Though no one can prove it, they are probably nothing like a majority, but even if they were, should the normal, clean-minded people be penalized for their sake? And further, is it the proper function of government to maintain laws to protect people's *feelings* about sex or anything else? Those who want to may feel as indecent as they please about the control of conception. They do not need laws to help them do it. The function of law is to protect people's rights. As no one's mere feelings are an intrusion upon another's rights, it is no concern of the law to deal with them. The laws as they stand now are a gratuitous insult to the great mass of the people who do not consider the control of conception indecent. Do you want that legal insult maintained?

Then how about those whose chief interest in the control of conception is in connection with actual sex depravity and perversion and who wish the information for that purpose? Do you want the obscenity laws to remain as they are, for the sake of trying to make them apply to those people? Hardly, because they are undoubtedly a small minority anyway, and they are quite clever enough to break the laws successfully, besides; and further, any circulation of contraceptive information which is put in indecent language or involved with inducements for sex depravity would be just as subject to prosecution under the obscenity laws *after* the removal of the words "preventing conception" as it is now. The indictment would be for *obscenity,* and that can cover improper contraceptive information or anything else that the judge or jury in a given case choose to make it cover. Obscenity, throughout the whole history of law in modern times has been an extraordinarily pliable term.

Is there then any propriety or justice in keeping this subject per se, legally enmeshed with penalized obscenity? If you agree that there is none and if you want it removed from the obscenity laws, what next?

Do you, by any chance, think that the control of conception regardless of any connection with obscenity, should *itself be declared by law to be a criminal act?* This is a crucial question absurd as it may sound. There are many people who believe that the scientific control of parenthood is wrong, though not necessarily obscene. This has been the teaching of the Catholic Church, and on this ground Catholics have opposed the repeal of the legal ban on knowledge concerning it. They have not asked Congress to amend the Comstock law by making it a criminal act to control conception. But is not this the only logical thing for them to do, if they presume to ask the government to continue to deny people access to the knowledge on the ground that the utilization of the knowledge is wrong? Ought not they and any others who are like-minded, to get themselves together and tackle this question straight from the shoulder in Congress? If they consider it at all appropriate to appear at a Hearing and urge Congress to try to keep the people from knowing about this wrong thing, is it not more fitting to ask for laws which will forbid the thing itself, instead of knowledge about the thing? They can perfectly well proceed on this course if they wish to undertake it. It is noteworthy that thus far, none of them have done so. No one has gone to Congress and pointed with pride to that unique statute in Connecticut, the only one of its sort in the world— which makes it a crime to control conception—and asked to have a Federal law of the same sort enacted. But if the Catholics and what few other opponents there are, do not wish to undertake this task, and if they persist in asking for laws to prevent others from learning how to do what they—the Catholics, et al., consider wrong, they will be treading upon ground which may menace the maintenance of their own liberty to teach and preach and practice what they believe to be right. The tables are likely to be turned upon them, so that they will have to fight for the same sort of liberty which they now seck to deny to others. Indeed this is what did happen in the case of the Oregon School law, which would be in operation to-day if the United States Supreme Court had not declared it unconstitutional. (Appendix No. 15 gives further information on this subject.)

In getting at an answer to the question as to what sort of laws are really wanted, it clears the air considerably to get rid of this point about the distinction between a law which prohibits an *act* and a law which prohibits *information about an act which in itself is perfectly lawful*. The latter is the sort of law we now have, and it is not good law either for those who believe in the control of conception or for those who do not. Both groups should join to repeal it. And then those who wish to have their belief that birth control is wrong incorporated into the law of the land would have an open field in which to make the effort. That they would fail is a foregone conclusion, and they know it of course, which no doubt accounts for their rash insistence on the retention of the present law.

The next point to eliminate is that in regard to the application of the present law to the *one method* of birth control which is sanctioned by the Catholics and the few others who deem the utilization of scientific knowledge an affront to God or nature, namely, abstinence from sex relations. The writer has a letter from Rev. John A. Ryan, Director of the National Catholic Welfare Council in which he says, "There is no question of the lawfulness of birth restriction through abstinence from the relations which result in conception." This assertion has been repeatedly made by other opponents, but that it is a mistaken assertion was pointed out by Congressman Vaile and by Prof. Roswell Johnson at the Hearings on the Cummins-Vaile Bill. Mr. Vaile said: "If abstinence from the sexual relation were practiced, either spouse could get a divorce." Abstinence itself is not sanctioned by law.

According to common law precedent, the wife gives her "services" to her husband in exchange for her "necessaries." "Services" are interpreted to mean household services and "consortium," or sex-relations. "Necessaries" are interpreted to mean food, clothes and shelter.

The law does not sanction a wife's withholding her "services," either household or sexual. If she does, it is deemed desertion, and in many States desertion is a ground for divorce.

Thus it seems that abstinence is not only illegal, because it is a method of birth control, the giving of information about which is prohibited by law, but it is also illegal because it is withholding the "services" which a wife is by law bound to give in return for her "necessaries."

In other words, so far as the law is concerned, there is no room for abstinence. It follows therefore that the only sort of family which is *legally* approved in these United States is that in which there are as many children as it is physically possible for the parents to produce. This legal situation constitutes a downright poser for the so-called "purists" who advocate the abstinence of marital sex relations except for procreation.

For abstinence is one method of birth-control. It certainly prevents conception.

To teach any method for the prevention of conception is prohibited by law throughout the United States. Yet the "purists" teach their method.

Therefore the "purists" are guilty of breaking the law. Query: Why are they not prosecuted? This question then becomes a poser for the government. Silence has been the only answer.

This leads to the next point to be cleared away, in the process of finding out what laws are really wanted or what ones it is worth while to want; that is, as to enforceability. Clearly the present laws are not enforced. The government has not the remotest idea of trying to enforce them. And if it tried, it would fail. It might mean jailing at least half the population. It simply can not be done. The knowledge is circulating whether or no. The cat is out of the bag, and it is quite useless to wave the empty bag any longer, as if somehow the cat could be persuaded back. Better cast the old bag aside, as it is full of holes anyway, and let the cat be given a decent home, instead of being obliged to skulk furtively in alleys and eat from garbage pails. Moreover it is a cat that has not only the proverbial nine lives, but more nearly ninety million lives. It can not be caught or killed, much less bagged. Do you, or does anybody really want unenforceable laws? The question answers itself.

If the the principle of enforceability is a prerequisite for law, and if the present law is abandoned because it does not live up to that principle, is anything more needed than merely to put the old law in the waste basket, in other words, just to remove those two words "preventing conception" from all the obscenity statutes in which they occur? Is any further legislation needed? And if so, is there any sort which, first of all, meets this fundamental requirement of enforceability, and which also will achieve the ends for which it is desired? And if those ends are not achievable by laws which *can* be enforced, then they will have to be achieved, will they not, by some other agency than law?

The two ends to be achieved for which other legislation has been proposed are, first, that only authoritative scientific contraceptive information shall be given to the people, and second, that all information on the subject shall be kept away, so far as may be possible from those who would misuse it, or who might be tempted to misuse it, so that immorality and depravity may not be thereby increased.

Suppose, for the moment, that you feel so strongly about the desirability of both those ends that you are inclined to favor any legislation which is aimed to achieve them. Then bearing in mind the basic requirements of enforceability and efficacy, you scan with a fresh eye and a responsible spirit the legislation which has been proposed. You find in it two principles, one that all contraceptive information and means which are circulated shall bear authoritative medical certification that they be "not injurious to life or health," that is, the certification shall be by lawfully practicing physicians; the other principle, that contraceptive information may lawfully emanate only from a certain class of the people, the medical profession, and be given only to people who qualify in certain ways, that is, those who are physicians or those who receive it personally from physicians as "bona fide" patients of the same, and that contraceptive means may be sold only to those who personally present a physician's written prescription for the same.

These two principles you find are very far apart. One requires medical sanction for methods, as somewhat of a protection to the public against harmful or fraudulent contraceptives, and while it by no means guarantees wholly satisfactory protection, as it would be subject to the possible inadequacies of the certifying physicians, it would be at least enforceable, and it establishes untrammelled freedom in the access to information and the securing of means.

The other is class legislation, and establishes a monopolistic, monetary privilege for physicians in the dispensing of information and an impracticable restriction upon those who sell contraceptive means: in so doing it by no means guarantees protection against harmful or inadequate contraceptives, as it would protect only to the extent that individual physicians were competent and conscientious, and it would be even less enforceable than our present law. For if information now leaks through the bars of the present law to a very considerable extent, it stands to reason that the leakage would be greatly increased if the bars of the law are lessened at all, and if the bars are placed very far apart as they would be by the latest "doctors only" bill proposed (the Worthington draft as given on page 212) the leakage would be so great as to reduce the efficacy of the bars to the vanishing point. It would be patently absurd to expect such a sievelike law to allow all the worthy people to get information and to keep it away from all the unworthy ones, or even any tiny proportion of the unworthy ones.

So, if the final effect of this last proposed "doctors only" bill would be about the same as the freedom bill, so far as access to information is concerned, why go all round Robin Hood's barn to achieve it, instead of doing it directly and simply? Why try to fool oneself or anybody else into thinking that any law can possibly be devised that will allow many millions of people to learn certain facts, and which will at the same time keep those facts a profound secret from the balance of the people? Does not such a proposition seem to be the outcome of mental processes somewhat akin to those of the man who cut two holes in the barn door, a big one for the old cat and a little one for the kitten?

Glance back to the changes in limited legislation which have been proposed since 1881, when the first one appeared, long before the modern birth control movement. It was in New York State, and it permitted doctors to give any instructions (including by inference contraceptive instruction) to "cure or prevent disease." In 1919 began the rapid succession of limited bills by which some of the legal bars were to be removed. First doctors and nurses were to be allowed to give information. Then the bars were thickened by eliminating the nurses, leaving the doctors in sole possession of the special privilege. Then to thicken the bars still further, the doctors could give it only to the married or to those having a license to marry. Then came the first Federal "doctors only" proposition, by which doctors could inform other doctors and their "bona fide" patients, and dealers could fill contraceptive prescriptions from doctors; but no publications or importation of publications were to be allowed. Then, as the force of criticism began to be felt, and the Cummins-Vaile Bill progressed to the point of being reported out by the Senate Judiciary Sub-Committee in Congress, the bars began to be thinned out again, and in 1925 the Worthington draft appeared, which would permit doctors to inform each other and their patients, and allow dealers to fill physicians' prescriptions, and would also permit medical and "scientific" publications, and "reprints" from the same. You find that these legislative proposals have swung all the way from a tight "doctors only" bill to a bill that is framed in the language of a "doctors only" bill but which actually would not function as such.

The point has almost been reached when, by the removal of bar after bar in the "doctors only" type of bill, one might say that "things equal to the same thing are equal to each other," inasmuch as the last version of the "doctors only" idea would be practically the same in effect as the Cummins-Vaile Bill, so far as the accessibility of contraceptive information is concerned. That being the case, is not the very fact that the limited bill proposition has been pared down till it would release information about as completely as a freedom bill, a most forceful reason for scrapping it now in favor of the freedom bill? If the restrictions are so riddled with exemptions as to be only the shadow and pretense of restriction, why go through the motions of keeping them? If such pretension at restriction should fool anyone into thinking they were genuinely efficacious, it would but serve to make the law an arrant hypocrisy. If they would not so fool anybody, why bother to try to put them into law? Is it not time to bear in mind Dr. Pusey's advice to avoid framing "silly legislation," as we have more than enough of that kind on the statute books already? Why add to the welter of laws we have, when we can better achieve what we want by merely substracting errors from the existing laws. As "Life" observed:

Thirty-eight thousand eight hundred and forty-four laws were proposed in the United States last year, of which 10,809 were actually enacted. Our national sport used to be baseball.

Probably most if not all of the "doctors only" proponents would be quite willing and even glad to have this subject removed from the obscenity classification in law, if they could see a feasible way to keep the "doctors only" provision at the same time. But that would force them to propose a law that would frankly be a legal permit for class privilege. It would be too obvious to attempt with decorum. So they try to accomplish the same end by the indirect method of providing exemptions for doctors under the existing obscenity statutes. But just as a rose by another name would smell as sweet, is not a wrong by another name just as offensive?

This thought brings up the next point for consideration as to the sort of laws it is worth while to want. Even if the latest form of "doctors only" bill does break down the restrictions so that they would be a mere gesture rather than a genuine law, do you want any laws passed which are based on the idea of privilege? If so, would you be willing to be quite candid about it? Would you be willing to ask a member of Congress to introduce a bill which would be a legal permit for certain people to give contraceptive information and certain people to buy and sell contraceptives, and would forbid all other people to do the same? If you would shrink from such a blatant betrayal of democratic American principles as that, are you not in all conscience bound to stand for a law which would be true to those principles? If you were not willing to do openly and directly a thing which you knew to be unsound in principle, could you possibly persuade yourself to do it indirectly?

Suppose then you have a healthy scorn of pretentions, legal and otherwise, and you find yourself averse to any legislation that could be rightly deemed double-faced, and you proceed in your survey of legislative proposals. You may find that the point about the need for personal prescription of contraceptives which is so stressed in behalf of the "doctors only" bills, still troubles you. You wonder perhaps, if there is not some sound way to make a legal provision that would work out so as to give the people just what they individually need in the way of contraceptives and protect them from means that are unsafe or ineffective.

If so, there are these facts to consider. There is doubtless great advantage in having the personal advice of a thoroughly well informed physician as to contraceptive method. It is reassuring if nothing else, even if not imperatively needed in most cases. For average individuals with normal physique a professional prescription is by no means always necessary. But exceptional physical conditions do need special attention, such as only the doctor or an experienced nurse can give. Under the present handicap of the laws, advice from a competent physician is of especial use because he can warn his patient against the many worthless and even harmful methods which are being secretly advocated. But when publications on the subject can be openly circulated, the difference between the good and bad methods can be made clear by authoritative spokesmen, and the general public can learn the main facts about this sort of hygiene in the same natural way that they learn about dental and dietetic hygiene, and so forth. There is no need to make a medical mystery of this knowledge, or to assume that the public will be lost in hopeless ignorance unless a doctor prescribes specially for each individual. The simplicity of some of the best methods makes such an attitude an absurdity.

At the last Hearing in the New York Legislature on a "doctors only" bill, the Birth Control Review reports Mrs. Sanger as saying that "the Clinical Research Department of the American Birth Control League teaches methods so simple that once learned any mother who is intelligent enough to keep a nursing bottle clean can use them." Dr. Robert L. Dickinson, head of the New York Committee on Maternal Health has said that the method most favorably regarded does not require the instruction of a physician preceding its use. "The New Generation," one of the two outstanding birth control periodicals in England, and official organ of the Neo-Malthusian group of birth control advocates, published in January, 1925, the following editorial against the "doctors only" position.

MEDICAL MONOPOLY

We deeply sympathize with our American friends in their difficulties with the Comstock Act, but we fear that Mrs. Sanger's proposed compromise—to give the doctors a monopoly of knowledge—would only be a step from the frying pan into the fire. Mrs. Sanger thinks that contraception must in any case be a subject for medical experts, so it does not matter much whether they have a monopoly or not. There we differ from her. We cannot admit that contraception must necessarily be a medical question. We admit that the kind of contraceptive most fashionable at present has to be fitted by a doctor or nurse, but science may easily evolve a better one which will render doctors and nurses entirely needless. The results of eighteen months' experiment in Mrs. Sanger's own clinic are the best proof of this. One of the most successful devices employed there was a ———— paste which needs no doctor to fit it. Its percentage of failure was as small as that of any other tried method. From the standpoint of the public it is devoutly to be hoped that some simple method which needs no doctors will turn out to be the best. But such a result would be directly opposed to the interests of the medical profession. If the doctors had a legal monopoly of knowledge, they would be under the strongest temptation to develop and improve those methods which demand the assistance of doctors, and to discourage all research which would make doctors unnecessary.

The official stand of the Society for Constructive Birth Control and Racial Progress, in England is also against the "doctors only" position. This is the Society of which Dr. Marie C. Stopes, founder of the first English birth control clinic, is the president.

A striking bit of evidence which is related to this point is that the best known authority on this subject in England, and the one from whom many physicians both abroad and in this country have learned most of what they know about the control of conception and who has written a large volume of the subject, is a biologist, who has scientific degrees but who is not an M.D. So the framing of laws which would place the giving of information exclusively in the hands of physicians becomes an absurdity for that reason if for no other.

"Floods of advertisements" streaming through the mails, commercializing, cheapening and degrading contraceptive science—this is one of the bogies held before the eyes of the public by those who want limited legislation in place of freedom legislation. You may consider this a point well taken as a possible reason for "doctors only" legislation. Certainly decent people do not want any such thing to happen. The question is how to prevent it. Can it be achieved by law? If so, then would it not be better to have a separate statute on the subject of advertising contraceptives, than to try to accomplish the curbing of improper advertising in a round about back-handed way via a "doctors only" bill? Of course a blanket prohibition of all advertising would not be appropriate for that would rule out the publisher's announcements of the "standard medical works and reprints therefrom" which are to be allowed according to the latest form of "doctors only" bill. It is hard to see where any line could be drawn, as "standard medical" and "scientific" publications are not defined by law. What conceivably might be done is to pass laws similar to the obsolete one in Holland which forbids the display of contraceptives in shop windows, and so forth. But on the whole would it not be best to have the laws simply provide an open field, and let the dignified authoritative scientists compete with the quacks and the spurious folk, with faith that eventually the best would win, very much as the increased public knowledge of general hygiene is steadily putting quackery into the background?

The writer of this book believes whole-heartedly that the American public wants sound legislation on the subject of birth control. The difficulty in getting it lies in the fact that people in general are so concerned with each day's doings that there is scant time or opportunity to dig out from all manner of sources the few facts that are the basis of sound legislation. The tendency of busy people is to "let the experts decide." The tendency of average citizens is to vote yes on any project that claims to carry out ideas to which he gives general approval. The tendency of birth control enthusiasts is to assume that the sincere and self-sacrificing leaders of an agitation are automatically wise at framing laws on the subject. But, as Heywood Broun said in the New York World, anent another subject and a different sort of organization:

I am quite ready to be convinced that many of its members are dangerously sincere and are utterly convinced that the objects for which they work will save the Nation. What of it? Where on earth did the notion come from that sincerity was a sort of police pass which would admit the bearer through all restraining lines and permit him to pour kerosene on the conflagration? Would you have your appendix out at the hands of a sincere surgeon or ask a passionate architect to design the foundations of your cellar?

And one of the chief difficulties for the interested citizen in this particular matter is that the proponents of the "doctors only" legislation give such a small part of the salient facts to the public in asking for support for their bills. Much is omitted which might radically alter the response to the request for endorsement, if it were but known. For instance, the public is being asked in widely circulated appeals to endorse the bill drafted by Mr. George Worthington, which is to be introduced into Congress as soon as possible. It may very likely be before Congress by the time these words are read. The statement which accompanies the request for endorsement is this:

The object of this amendment (to Section 211 of the Penal Code) is to permit the mailing of contraceptive information and scientific reports by duly licensed physicians to bona fide patients, physicians and printers,—and to permit bona fide druggists, manufacturers and physicians to mail articles of contraception.

A copy of the Worthington amendment is given. That is all. There is not a word about the fact that this is an amendment to the obscenity law, and that the subject of birth control is still left, a penalized indecency in that law. There is no suggestion given that this amendment is permissive legislation for a class privilege. There is no inkling given that it is legislation that could not possibly be enforced so as to exclude others beside those listed from using the mailing privilege. There is no statement explaining that there is no such thing in law as a definition as to what constitutes a "bona fide" "patient," or "printer" or "manufacturer." The public is merely asked to say yes to what looks, at first glance, like a most desirable thing. And apparently the public is being counted upon to say it, without a second glance or a pause for thoughtful inquiry.

Indeed, on the part of some of the proponents of limited legislation there seems to be a definite intention not to let the public realize that there is or could be a choice as to the type of bills which our legislators are asked to pass. A striking example of this tendency has appeared in New Jersey. Circular letters are going the rounds asking the public to endorse a "doctors only" and married-people-only bill, as shown in Appendix No. 8. The State organizer of the American Birth Control League who has charge of this work, was asked if he had "ever considered submitting a choice of bills to the public" he was "circularizing to see which they would prefer asking the Legislature to pass, a limited measure or a simple repeal act?" He answered thus: "It is a hard enough job to educate the public to see the necessity for birth control as a general proposition, without confusing the issue by asking them to express an opinion or choice as between two possible measures, about neither of which they know very much. Even if such a questionnaire were possible, I would not make it." It is noticeable that the letters which are being circulated asking for endorsement do not inform the New Jersey people much of anything even about the limited bill proposed. Yet the endorsement which these New Jersey citizens send in will be used to convince the Legislature that the people want this particular bill, as proved by their endorsements. It goes without saying that those who collect the endorsements will not then state that they did not trust the people to know what they wanted themselves.

Further indication of unwillingness on the part of the "doctors only" group to have the public get a full and free comprehension of the two radically different types of legislation that have been proposed, has been the repeated refusal of the "doctors only" proponents to debate the subject in open meeting. The proponents of the freedom bill on the other hand have made many efforts to pool the points held in common between the two groups, and to iron out the differences so that a sound joint legislative platform would be the result. It may be illuminating to the reader to see the terms of a recent effort on the part of the proponents of the freedom bill to get together with the proponents of the exemption bill drafted by Mr. Worthington. They are embodied in a Memorandum which was sent by the freedom bill group to the exemption bill group preliminary to a proposed conference. The exemption bill group refused to confer. The Memorandum reads as follows:

1. *Proposed legislation should be tested* for its *soundness* as law, its *enforceability,* and its *adequacy* to meet the people's need.

2. It can be assumed that everyone sincerely interested in the birth control movement, from whatever angle, will want all laws to meet these tests.

3. Conversely, it can be assumed that no one would, wittingly, approve laws which are unsound, that is, unsuitable for a democracy, or untrue to the letter or spirit of the Constitution; or laws which are unenforceable, that is, which are a mere gesture, calculated to have a discretionary or educational effect on the public, but are not intended for genuine execution; or laws which are inadequate, that is, which do not permit the widest and speediest opportunity for the largest possible number of people to have access to contraceptive knowledge.

4. It can be assumed also, that in the effort to find a legislative platform which the public and all who are specially interested in the birth control movement can be asked to support, there should be no provisions proposed which are based upon personal, organization, or professional partisanship; that the platform should represent only intrinsic merit, regardless of priority of effort, individual reputation in leadership, or of professional prestige.

5. If all concerned will agree then, as to what *not to do,* they can the more readily determine what *to do.*

6. The basic elements which all hold in common seem to be;

    a. Recognition that contraceptive knowledge is not obscenity and that it is all gain and no loss to remove it from that classification in law, and that the demand for a clean legal status for the subject is in itself a very valuable educational process for the public.

    b. Desire that all who need contraceptive instruction shall receive it from the best possible sources, and through the best possible channels. The best sources are generally conceded to be the medical and biological scientists.

7. Point *a* can easily and properly be achieved by legislation. It involves only striking out "Preventing Conception" from all the obscenity statutes, wherever they occur.

8. But point *b* presents great difficulty if not impossibility of achievement via legislation, *not, however,* via publicity and a campaign of education.

Thus far no legislative proposal on this point *b* has successfully met any of the three tests named in the first paragraph of this Memorandum as fundamental necessities.

They have either been class legislation, or permits for special privilege, or have been unenforceable, or inefficient as means for allowing the accomplishment of the desired aim.

9. Unless there is some genius who can now frame a law that is adequate to provide for point *b* and which at the same time is free from the serious legal sins noted above, is it not the part of wisdom for all who are working in the birth control movement, to join in approving legislation to achieve point *a* and then work in their many various ways to achieve point *b* by a vigorous publicity campaign, that will be so wide-spread and effective that all America will shortly know that the best way to get contraceptive instruction is to consult the best medical and biological authorities?

10. People can be successfully advised and guided along paths that no laws can *compel* them to take.

11. The *result* is what every one wants, that is *education*. Then why not concentrate on education straight, instead of trying to secure it by laws? *And why not depend on legislation for the simple purpose of removing the barriers to education?*

12. The obligation resting upon those who undertake to frame legislation is serious. They must see to it that the enthusiasm of the large groups interested in birth control is not wrongly capitalized. Most of these people are not innately law-makers, and, legally speaking, they think very superficially. They do not differentiate between enthusiasm for a humanitarian project and providing the legal processes that clear the road for the achievement of the project.

13. Knowing as we all do, that large numbers of people will endorse any sort of proposed birth control laws out of sheer enthusiasm for the big cause, it behooves the few who devise legislative procedure, to hand to the legislators and to the public, propositions that are thoroughly sound, just and efficacious. We must carefully safeguard our country, at least so far as our movement is concerned, against the addition of any more laws that are superfluous, spurious or ineffective.

14. We shall do well to bear in mind, that education is the great thing, but that it needs an open road in order to progress rapidly, which the repeal embodied in the Cummins-Vaile Bill would accomplish.

If such a thing were possible that the people really wanted, knowingly, the enactment of a "doctors only," special permit exemption bill, and also knowingly, did not want the enactment of a freedom bill, then they ought to have what they want. Democracy is government by the people. It is not necessarily good government. But at least the people should know what sort of legislation they are choosing when they sign endorsement slips and petitions. Many of these have been circulated in the past, and many are being circulated now. There is a notable difference between the two sorts. Those circulated in behalf of the freedom bill have plainly stated that the bill was to remove the ban from the obscenity laws, so that any one who signed could know that he was expressing his approval of that act. Those which are being circulated on behalf of the special-permit, exemption, "not non-mailable" bill *do not state* that the subject is being *left* in the obscenity laws. If the assumption is that the people would approve leaving the subject in the indecency classification in laws, then it would seem to be only fair and square to ask them to say so explicitly. For it is a good deal of an assumption. It needs proof before it can be believed. In justice to themselves also, should not the proponents of the limited legislation state clearly what their proposed law would do and would not do, in order that no one should have opportunity to charge them either with carelessness or with duplicity?

CHAPTER III

CAN THE PEOPLE GET WHAT THEY WANT?

Congress will do what the people want if the request is made clearly and forceably enough: Inhibitions are waning: Later generations will not bless birth control workers or Congress if legislation is bungled now: Danger of blundering as Comstock blundered: Those who mean well regarding legislation must do well: Present laws unconstitutional: First class legal opinion deems all "doctors only" laws unconstitutional also: Time to discard governmental distrust of the people.

THE people can get just what they want from Congress and the State Legislatures regarding the birth control question, if they make their wants known definitely enough. If they leave it wholly to the relatively few citizens who take the trouble to go down to Washington and worry bills through Congress, they may wake later to find that misguided enthusiasm has done for this generation what Comstock did for his generation—enacted laws which were well meant, but which have worked ill. Some senator of our day may have to warn Congress as did Senator Conkling in 1873, lest we "do something which when we come to see it in print, will not be the thing we would have done if we had understood it." It is doubtful if any thoughtful members of Congress or any clear-headed citizens could be proud if it should happen that the laws affecting birth control were amended so as to create a special privilege in access to knowledge instead of freedom for all; if they established monopoly instead of equal opportunity; or if they created paternalism instead of democracy. No one in later years would bless Congress for passing another batch of unenforceable laws. And it is safe to say also that American citizens would not bless any birth control advocates who, after endless talk and the expenditure of time and money which Congressional work requires, should persuade Congress to leave the subject of birth control still mired in the obscenity laws where Comstock (and Congress meekly acquiescing) placed it over half a century ago.

Much water has gone under the bridge since birth control corrective legislation was first proposed. Congressional inhibitions have considerably lessened. The whole subject in press, pulpit, fiction and private life is on a more wholesome plane than ever before. The time is ripe to have that improvement reflected into sound legislative action. Congress will just as willingly do the fine thing as the flimsy thing, if the people demand it. Congress will help to take birth control out of the laws, instead of putting it into further spurious laws, if the people say so.

It is up to the public to let the birth control workers know what is wanted, and for both the birth control workers and the public to let Congress know what is wanted—and wanted with the best that is in people's minds and hearts, not what is dictated by their superficial fears, their doubts and their shames.

Professor Raymond Pearl has said: "The cure for the defects of birth control, paraphrasing the old remark about democracy, is more and more democratic birth control." And surely the cure for the defects of legislation regarding birth control is more and more democratic legislation.

It has to be admitted that the American public has often been shockingly easy-going about responsibility for the sort of laws that its representatives enact, likewise that the public is often woefully pliant in accepting ready made opinions and policies without analysis. But it is to be hoped that there are enough citizens who are genuinely interested to help check misguided legislation and promote sound legislation on this subject, to prevent our country from making another great blunder in birth control legislation instead of correcting Comstock's original blunder with a clean firm sweep. Standing up and being counted as a believer in birth control is not enough. Those who are on record in birth control organizations as adherents of "the cause" must see to it that their names are not linked to endorsements of bills which they do not approve. Birth control leaders, like members of Congress, will yield to public opinion, if it is clearly enough and forcibly enough expressed.

It is time for every one who means well in this matter to do well also. The gist of the question is very simple and lucid. It has unfortunately been gummed up with all manner of excrescences. But they can all be readily scraped off by dint of the application of plain common sense and determination not to fool one's self or to attempt to fool the public or the legislators.

Also there is a considerable portion of the American public which cares about having the laws on this subject in harmony with the proud traditions of American ideals, the people to whom the guarantees of freedom of speech and of the press mean something, and who are keen to have the spirit of the Constitution lived up to, not so much because it is the Constitution as because those principles of freedom are vital to human progress and precious to human aspiration. There has always been a sizable body of opinion that all the Comstock laws are constitutional, as contrary to the United States Constitution and to the constitutions of the States. Forty-five of the forty-eight States in the Union have provisions in their constitutions or the Bill of Rights that "every man is given the right freely to write, speak and publish his opinions on all subjects, being responsible for the abuse of that privilege." Twenty-six of the States give an additional safeguard providing that "No law shall ever be passed to restrain freedom of speech or of the press." Cortlandt Palmer, in 1883 wrote a vigorous article in the "New York Observer" in criticism of the Comstock laws, in which he said:

Sometimes a mistaken method of preventing vice entails worse evils than the vice it would prevent. The Liberals oppose the methods of these postal laws (the Federal obscenity laws) because they regard them as an example of saving at the spigot and losing at the bung, an instance of expending a dollar to save a dime. The question straightway narrows itself into one issue, viz., that of method. It is agreed on all hands that obscenity should be checked, and if possible eradicated. The only point is *how*. We regard these laws as unconstitutional, useless, unnecessary, impolitic and immoral. They are unconstitutional, because the United States Constitution simply empowers Congress to establish post offices and post roads— no more. How then can these words be construed to authorize our representatives to sit in judgment on the moral quality of the parcels entrusted to the mails? The Post Office as we conceive it is a mechanical not an ethical institution. Judge Story says in his work on the Constitution that Congress can not use this power (viz., to establish post-offices and post-roads) *for any other ulterior purpose,* which means, if it means anything, that while the government may for postal reasons, or for the convenience and necessity of the service, exclude such articles as liquor and dynamite, it can not sit in judgment on the intellectual or moral quality of the communications entrusted to it.

It has many times been suggested that the matter of birth control legislation be settled by a test case taken to the supreme court on the ground of unconstitutionality. But in view of the fact that the Supreme Court declined to act on Margaret Sanger's case when it was appealed from the New York courts, and in view of various other precedents, it has not seemed a promising way to get results, certainly not quick results. It might take several years at best to carry a case through, and in the meantime Congress might be only too glad to utilize the fact that a decision was pending, to postpone its own responsibility to act on the repeal bill on which it has been asked to act for six years past. The obvious fact that the ban on the circulation of knowledge in the Comstock law is contrary to the right of freedom of the press should alone be sufficient reason for its repeal by Congress. And both birth control advocates and Congress should pay attention to the fact that there is first class legal opinion that all the "doctors only" laws, if enacted, would also be unconstitutional.

Above everything, is it not high time for Americans to discard these laws which are predicated upon the utterly undemocratic basis of governmental distrust of the people? Is it not a matter of deep concern to upstanding American citizens that they should be for over half a century the victims of the discreditable fear that animated a man like Anthony Comstock? Do not Americans trust themselves with knowledge? Are they longer willing to retain the mouldy laws which have stood for such a disgracefully extended period as a sign of distrust of the people? Are they not ready now to share the deep emotion of Walt Whitman who said, "There is to me something profoundly affecting in large masses of men following the lead of those who do not believe in men." Are they not more than ready to demand that Congress and the State Legislatures shall make all haste in purging the statute books of these old blemishes, so that the pure white light of science may shine unimpeded upon the lives of all?

———

"Study, without reflection," says Confucius, "is waste of time; reflection without study is dangerous."

APPENDICES

APPENDIX NO. 1

*The research work was done by Harriette M. Dilla, LL.B.,
Ph.D., formerly of the Department of Sociology and
Economics of Smith College.*

Twenty-four States (and Porto Rico) specifically penalize contraceptive knowledge in their obscenity laws.

Twenty-four States (and the District of Columbia,
Alaska and Hawaii) have obscenity laws, under which, because of the Federal precedent, contraceptive knowledge
may be suppressed as obscene, although it is not specifically
mentioned. Obscenity has never been defined in law. This
produces a mass of conflicting, inconsistent judicial decision,
which would be humorous, if it were not such a mortifying
revelation of the limitations and perversions of the human
mind.

Twenty-three States make it a crime to publish or advertise contraceptive information. They are as follows:
Arizona, California, Colorado, Idaho, Indiana, Iowa, Kansas, Maine, Massachusetts, Minnesota, Mississippi, Missouri, Montana, Nebraska, Nevada, New Jersey, New
York, North Dakota, Ohio, Oklahoma, Pennsylvania,
Washington, Wyoming; also Porto Rico.

Twenty-two States include in their prohibition drugs and
instruments for the prevention of conception. They are as
follows: Arizona, California, Colorado, Connecticut, Idaho,

Indiana, Iowa, Kansas, Massachusetts, Minnesota, Mississippi, Missouri, Montana, Nebraska, Nevada, New Jersey, New York, Ohio, Oklahoma, Pennsylvania, Washington, Wyoming and Porto Rico.

Eleven States make it a crime to have in one's possession any instruction for contraception. These are: Colorado, Indiana, Iowa, Minnesota, Mississippi, New Jersey, New York, North Dakota, Ohio, Pennsylvania, Wyoming.

Fourteen States make it a crime to tell anyone where or how contraceptive knowledge may be acquired. These are: Colorado, Indiana, Iowa, Massachusetts, Minnesota, Mississippi, Missouri, Montana, Nevada, New Jersey, New York, Pennsylvania, Washington, Wyoming.

Six States prohibit the offer to assist in any method whatever which would lead to knowledge by which contraception might be accomplished. These are: Arizona, California, Idaho, Montana, Nevada, Oklahoma and Porto Rico.

Eight States prohibit depositing in the Post Office any contraceptive information. These are: Colorado, Indiana, Iowa, Minnesota, New York, North Dakota, Ohio, Wyoming.[1]

One State, Colorado, prohibits the bringing into the State of any contraceptive knowledge.

Four States have laws authorizing the search for and seizure of contraceptive instructions, and these are: Colorado, Idaho, Iowa, Oklahoma. In all these States but Idaho, the laws authorize the destruction of the things seized.

---

[1] These States present a knotty legal question as to whether the repeal of the Federal prohibition relating to the mails will automatically make these State laws void. Legal opinion (as expressed by Attorneys Alfred Hayes and James F. Morton, Jr.) seems to agree that the Federal action will probably be effective, but there is authority for the assumption that under the State law police power might withhold such supposedly undesirable mail from the recipient.

Certain exemptions from the penalties of these laws are made by the States for

Medical Colleges	Medical Books	Physicians
Colorado	Colorado	Colorado
Indiana	Indiana	Indiana
Missouri	Kansas	Nevada
Nebraska	Missouri	New York
Ohio	Nebraska	Ohio
Pennsylvania	Ohio	Wyoming
Wyoming	Pennsylvania	
	Wyoming	

Druggists

Colorado, Indiana, Ohio, Wyoming.

Seventeen States prohibit any information which corrupts morals, 12 of them, as starred in the following list, particularly mentioning the morals of the young. This is an interesting point of view of the frequently offered objection to freedom of access to contraceptive knowledge, that it will demoralize the young. These States are: Colorado, Delaware,* Florida,* Iowa,* Maine,* Massachusetts,* Michigan,* Rhode Island, South Carolina, South Dakota, Tennessee, Texas,* Vermont,* Virginia,* West Virginia,* Wisconsin * and Hawaii.

Two States have no obscenity statutes, but police power in these States can suppress contraceptive knowledge as an "Obscenity" or "public nuisance," by virtue of the Federal precedent. These States are: North Carolina and New Mexico.

EFFECT OF REMOVING THE PROHIBITION OF CONTRACEPTIVE KNOWLEDGE FROM THE FEDERAL OBSCENITY LAWS

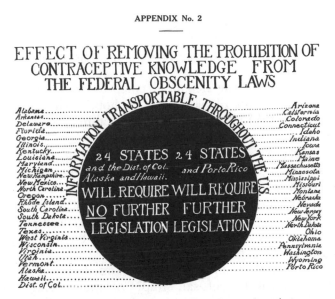

Alabama................
Arkansas................
Delaware................
Florida................
Georgia................
Illinois................
Kentucky................
Louisiana................
Maryland................
Michigan................
New Hampshire................
New Mexico................
North Carolina................
Oregon................
Rhode Island................
South Carolina................
South Dakota................
Tennessee................
Texas................
West Virginia................
Wisconsin................
Virginia................
Utah................
Vermont................
Alaska................
Hawaii................
Dist. of Col................

Arizona
California
Colorado
Connecticut
Idaho
Indiana
Iowa
Kansas
Maine
Massachusetts
Minnesota
Mississippi
Missouri
Montana
Nebraska
Nevada
New Jersey
New York
North Dakota
Ohio
Oklahoma
Pennsylvania
Washington
Wyoming
Porto Rico

INFORMATION TRANSPORTABLE THROUGHOUT THE U.S.

24 STATES and the Dist. of Col. Alaska and Hawaii. WILL REQUIRE NO FURTHER LEGISLATION

24 STATES and Porto Rico WILL REQUIRE FURTHER LEGISLATION

It will then be legal to transport contraceptive information anywhere in the United States.

It will then be legal to give verbal information in 24 states, the District of Columbia, Alaska and Hawaii, which, by precedent of the federal laws, have heretofore been justified in suppressing contraceptive information as "obscene."
With this precedent removed, the probability of such suppression will be negligible; and physicians may begin at once to teach contraception both in private practice and in clinics, hospitals and dispensaries. There are over 46,000,000 people in these states.

In the remaining 24 states, and Porto Rico, where the laws specifically prohibit giving contraceptive information, the necessary repeal acts will be more easily accomplished because of this federal example.

THIS IS THE LONGEST SINGLE STEP TOWARD ACHIEVING SELF-DETERMINED PARENTHOOD FOR THE UNITED STATES

APPENDIX NO. 3

THE ANNUAL REPORT OF THE ILLINOIS LEAGUE

In 1923, when the League decided to open a free clinic, we had wonderful plans and high hopes which were all dashed by the refusal of the Health Commissioner to grant us the necessary license. We took the matter into Court and received a decision in our favor from Judge Fisher but the case was immediately appealed. After waiting for months for a decision from the Appellate Court, we temporarily abandoned the idea of a free clinic and opened a Medical Center which does not require a license as it is operated as a private office, a small fee being charged to each patient.

When the decision was finally handed down it upheld Dr. Bundeson in his refusal, simply on the ground that the granting of licenses is a matter entirely in the discretion of the Health Commissioner. Our hopes of a free clinic being, therefore, definitely at an end, we opened in February, 1925, a second office at ———— Street, known as Medical Center No. 2. Each Center has a secretary and our Medical Staff consists of the Director, Dr. ———— and three physicians:

Dr. ....
Dr. ....
Dr. ....

all of whom have given devoted service.

There is a commonly accepted picture of our Birth Control work which represents us as standing in the midst of clamoring crowds, distributing information indiscriminately to all comers and handing leaflets and tracts destined to fall into the hands of high school children and unmarried girls, thereby doing unlimited harm. The true picture is very different. Our offices, one on the inside court of the ——— Building, the other in a small house on a quiet West Side street, have very little publicity. We do not advertise. It is difficult to get any notice of our work in the newspapers. It is not spectacular enough. The result is that our patients come slowly. We have had to build up a practice.

The first Medical Center was opened July 7, 1924, and during the first three months we had sixty patients, mostly sent to us by a few social agencies. In October we had some newspaper notices and our numbers jumped to seventy-four in one month. In November we had one hundred and twenty. From July seventh to date, ten months, we have had in all five hundred and forty patients. It may be interesting to hear some of the data on the first five hundred cases.

We are constantly asked what nationalities we reach. It would be simpler to say what nationalities we do not reach. The exact figures are as follows:

American	252	Slovakian	4
Polish	58	Canadian	2
Hebrew	42	Lithuanian	2
German	35	Austrian	2
Colored	26	Spanish	2
Bohemian	15	Belgian	1
Italian	14	Croatian	1
Swedish	11	Greek	1
English	8	Swiss	1
Irish	7	Dutch	1
Norwegian	5	Russian	1
Scotch	4	Mexican	1
Hungarian	4		

Of these, 304 were Protestants, or 6/10ths were Protestants
147 were Catholics
3 were Greek Orthodox, or 3/10ths were Catholics
46 were Jewish, or 1/10th Jewish

Women of all ages have come, from 16 to 40, the largest number (152) being between the ages of twenty-five and thirty. The young girls under twenty are not school girls, they are rather weary, discouraged little mothers with two or three children, who seem to us entitled to information which will give them a few years' rest in which to recuperate before they bear more children.

So much has been said about the selfishness of women and the growing desire of the modern woman to leave her home and go into industry that it is rather a surprise to find that 464 of the 500 patients gave their occupation as "Housewife" and only 36 were engaged in work outside their homes.

> Of these, 13 were employed as stenographers or book-keepers,
> 7 were employed as teachers,
> 5 were still students,
> 5 were in social work,
> 6 were employed by the day, cleaning and doing housework.

In almost every case, the women were working to support their families because their husbands were either ill, or drank, or gambled. In a few cases the young couple were just married and living in one or two rooms and were both obliged to work in order to support themselves and of course felt that they must postpone all thought of children until they had saved enough to take care of them.

It is impossible to classify the occupation of the husbands. They cover practically every employment:

Engineer	Musician
Laborer	Switchman
Carpenter	Teamster
Bank Cashier	Watchman
Gambler	Lawyer
Minister	Coal-miners, etc.

These people have come to us from many sources:

282 through the newspapers
 54 from the United Charities
 36 from the Infant Welfare Society
 80 from Social Agencies, Settlements, Dispensaries, Doctors, etc.
 48 from friends and patients.

Of the women, 252 have used some forms of contraceptive, some of them harmful, most of them useless. Many have resorted to abortion. The reasons given for wishing information are as difficult to classify as are the occupations of the men. In almost every case, the foundation of the trouble is economic but there are usually other complications. For instances:

Four children in four years.
Instrumental deliveries—contracted pelvis and goitre.
Caesarean operation always necessary.
Wants to wait until stronger before having any more.
Wants children but husband is just starting in business.
Six children—all tubercular.
No home, husband traveling musician.
Nine miscarriages in ten years—retroversion—cannot carry to term.

It is also very interesting to note that we have had five cases of sterility, the women willing to do anything if only they might have children.

But it means very little to read a list of reasons like this —too many factors enter into each individual case and perhaps the only way to get a real picture of the situation is to have a little story of some of these family tragedies. The cases divide quite sharply into three classes:

I. Young women just married who wish to postpone having children for a few years until they can make a home.

II. Cases in which the health of either husband or wife makes children impossible.

III. Those many cases of too large families and too little money to take care of them.

Here is *Case No. 88*—Referred—Newspaper.

The man is 59 years old, a cashier. The woman 39 years old, married at 37, Swedish-Protestant. Has had one child. Reason for wishing information is, that she has nephritis, had a difficult labor and convulsions and was unconscious for five days. The baby died at birth.

Case No. 451—Referred by Mental Hygiene Society.

The man is 37 years old, cannot work. The woman is 38 years old, American-Protestant, married at 26 and has had seven pregnancies, four children, ages ten, eight, six and four years. She teaches to support this family. The husband is insane—diagnosis dementia praecox—and has been sent home from the Elgin Asylum on probation. The wife is in terror for fear of another pregnancy.

Case No. 186—Referred—Newspaper.

The man 30 years old, not working. The woman, 30, married at 21, American-Protestant, has had four pregnancies, two miscarriages and two children. The husband has spinal trouble. The woman is very nervous. One child has rickets and the other tubercular glands.

Case No. 3.

Quite a tragic case. Man 37 years of age. The woman 36 years of age, married at 26, German-Protestant. In ten years she has had sixteen pregnancies, seven miscarriages, six induced abortions and three children. Reason—economic.

Case No. 31.

The man 62 years of age, factory sweeper. The woman 31 years of age, married at 13, Italian-Catholic. In eighteen years she has had ten children, seven living, ages ranging from seventeen years to four months.

Case No. 413.

The man is 41 years old, elevated guard. The woman is 30 years old, German-Protestant, married at 19 and has had seven children, six living. Reason—all they can support on husband's wages.

Case No. 59—Referred by United Charities and Municipal Tuberculosis Sanitarium.

The man is 54 years of age, street cleaner, Colored-Protestant. The woman is 40 years of age, married at 20 and in twenty years has had sixteen pregnancies. Of the fourteen children, whose ages range from seventeen years to eighteen months, seven died in infancy.

Case No. 241.

The man is 23 years old, laborer, no work. The woman is 19 years old, and was first married at fourteen, divorced after two months and married again at the age of sixteen. She has had three children, whose ages are four and two years and seven weeks. Reason—economic, and having children too fast.

Case No. 318—Referred—United Charities.

The man is 28 years old, laborer. The woman is 20 years old, German-Catholic, married at 19. Both feeble minded. One child feeble minded.

Case No. 471—Referred by United Charities.

The man is 31 years old, hostler, not working. The woman is 29 years old, Irish-Catholic, married at sixteen and has had nine children, seven living, ages ranging from eleven years to six months. The husband is chronic alcoholic.

This gives a clear record of the family history. The reason given by the mother for wishing information is *that she is too poor, worn out and very tired.* When one stops to think that this reason is given by a young woman of 29, it seems sad beyond words.

It is this sort of story that our doctors listen to day after day. The cases are not exceptional, there are so many almost alike that it is hard to select them.

At the moment there seem to be no legal obstacles on the horizon and we hope that we shall be able to go quietly on with our work which this year must include some meetings and talks on the West Side, in the Stock Yards' Districts, and among the colored people, for the purpose of explaining what birth control really means. Most of the women are perfectly familiar with abortion but the idea of contraception has not yet reached those who need it most. We hope to establish more Centers and so to bring the information to the people who are not accustomed to coming to Michigan Avenue for medical advice.

APPENDIX NO. 4

SENTENCES OF BIRTH CONTROL ADVOCATES

FEDERAL

Margaret Sanger, New York ...... 1914 Federal case—dismissed,
9 indictments.

Mrs. Rhea C. Kachel, Philadelphia, Pa. .... $25.00 fine

Mr. Fred Merkel, Reading, Pa. .... 25.00 fine

William Sanger, New York .... 30 days—workhouse

Emma Goldman, New York .... 15 days

Joseph Macario, San Francisco .... Freed

Emma Goldman, Portland, Ore. .... Freed

Dr. Ben L. Reitman, Portland, Ore. .... Freed

Margaret Sanger, Portland, Ore. .... Freed

Carl Rave, Portland, Ore. .... $10.00 fine

Herbert Smith, Seattle, Wash. .... 25.00 fine

Van Kleeck Allison, Boston, Mass. .... 60 days

Steven Kerr, New York .... 15 days

Peter Marner, New York .... 15 days

Bolton Hall, New York .... Freed

Jessie Ashley, New York .... $100.00 fine

Emma Goldman, New York .... Freed

Dr. Ben L. Reitman, New York .... 60 days

Ethel Byrne, New York .... 30 days
           (Pardoned during hunger strike.)

Dr. Ben L. Reitman, Cleveland, O. .... 6 mos.
           ($1000 fine and costs.)

Margaret Sanger, New York .... 30 days

Kitty Marion, New York .... 30 days—workhouse

APPENDIX NO. 5

FEDERAL STATUTES

I. A Bill to Amend
Section 211, the
Federal Penal Code.

Every obscene, lewd, or lascivious, and every filthy book, pamphlet, picture, paper, letter, writing, print, or other publication of an indecent character, and every article or thing designed, adapted, or intended for [preventing conception or] producing abortion, or for any indecent or immoral use; and every article, instrument, substance, drug, medicine, or thing which is advertised or described in a manner calculated to lead another to use or apply it for [preventing conception or] producing abortion, or for any indecent or immoral purpose; and every written or printed card, letter, circular, book, pamphlet, advertisement, or notice of any kind giving information directly or indirectly, where, or how, of whom, or by what means any of the hereinbefore-mentioned matters, articles, or things may be obtained or made, or where or by whom any act or operation of any kind for the procuring or producing of abortion will be done or performed, or how or by what means [conception may be prevented or] abortion may be produced, whether sealed or unsealed; and every letter, packet, or package, or other mail matter containing any filthy, vile, or indecent thing, device, or substance and every paper, writing, advertisement, or representation that any article, instrument, substance, drug, medicine or thing may, or can be, used or applied, for [preventing conception or] producing abortion, or for any indecent or immoral purpose; and every description calculated to induce or incite a person to so use or apply any such article, instrument, substance, drug, medicine, or thing, is hereby declared to be non-mailable matter and shall not be conveyed in the mails or delivered from any post office or by any letter carrier. Whoever shall knowingly deposit or cause to be deposited for mailing or delivery, anything declared by this section to be non-mailable, or shall knowingly take, or cause the same to be taken, from the mails for the purpose of circulating or disposing thereof, or of aiding in the circulation or disposition thereof, shall be fined not more than five thousand dollars, or imprisoned not more than five years, or both. *But no book, magazine, pamphlet, paper, letter, writing or publication is obscene, lewd, or lascivious, or of an indecent character, or non-mailable by reason of the fact that it mentions, discusses or recommends prevention of conception, or gives information concerning methods or means for the prevention of conception: or tells how, where, or in what manner such information or such means can be obtained: and no article, instrument, substance or drug is non-mailable by reason of the fact that it is designed or adapted for the prevention of conception, or is advertised or otherwise represented to be so designed or adapted.*

(Matter in brackets omitted; matter in italics new.)

II. A Bill to Amend
Section 245, The
Federal Penal Code.

Whoever shall bring or cause to be brought into the United States or any place subject to the jurisdiction thereof from any foreign country or shall therein knowingly deposit or cause to be deposited with any express company or other common carrier for carriage from one State, territory or district of the United States, or in place non-contiguous to, but subject to the jurisdiction thereof, or from any place in or subject to the jurisdiction of the United States through a foreign country to any place in or subject to the jurisdiction of the United States, any obscene, lewd or lascivious or any filthy book, pamphlet, picture, paper, letter, writing, print, or other matter of indecent character, of any drug, medicine, article or thing designed, adapted or intended for [preventing conception or] producing abortion, or for any indecent or immoral use, or any written or printed card, letter, circular, book, pamphlet, advertisement or notice of any kind, giving information directly or indirectly, where, how, or of whom, or by what means any of the hereinbefore-mentioned articles, matters, or things may be obtained or made, or whoever shall knowingly take or cause to be taken from such express company or common carrier, any matter or thing, the depositing of which for carriage is herein made unlawful, shall be fined not more than five thousand dollars or imprisoned not more than five years or both. *But no book, pamphlet, paper, letter, writing, circular, advertisement, notice or print is obscene, lewd, lascivious or filthy, by reason of the fact that it mentions, discusses or recommends prevention of conception, or gives information concerning methods or means for the prevention of conception: or tells how, where, or in what manner such information or such means can be obtained: and no drug, medicine, article or thing shall be for indecent or immoral use because it is designed, adapted or intended for the prevention of conception.*

(Matter in brackets omitted; matter in italics new.)

NEW YORK STATUTES

PENAL LAW.

Section 1141.—A person who sells, lends, gives away or shows, or offers to sell, lend, give away, or who, or has in his possession with intent to sell, lend, or give away, or to show or advertises in any manner, or who otherwise offers for loan, gift, sale or distribution, any obscene, lewd, lascivious, filthy, indecent or disgusting book, magazine, pamphlet, newspaper, story paper, writing paper, picture, drawing, photograph, figure, or image, or any written or printed matter of an indecent character; or any article or instrument of indecent or immoral use, or purporting to be for indecent or immoral use or purpose, or who designs, copies, draws, photographs, prints, utters, publishes, or in any manner manufactures, or prepares any such book, picture, drawing, magazine, pamphlet, newspaper, story paper, writing paper, figure, image, matter, article, or thing, or who writes, prints, publishes, or utters, or causes to be written, printed, published or uttered any advertisement or notice of any kind, giving information, directly or indirectly, stating, or purporting so to do, where, how, of whom, or by what means any, or what purports to be any, obscene, lewd, lascivious, filthy, disgusting or indecent book, picture, writing, paper, figure, image, matter, article, or thing named in this section can be purchased, obtained, or had or who has in his possession any slot machine or other mechanical contrivances with moving pictures of nude or partly denuded female figures which pictures are lewd, obscene, indecent or immoral, or other lewd, obscene, indecent or immoral drawing, image article or object or who shows, advertises or exhibits the same, or causes the same to be shown, advertised, or exhibited, or who brings, owns or holds any such ma-

chine with the intent to show, advertise, or in any manner exhibit
the same, . . . is guilty of a misdemeanor, and upon conviction,
shall be sentenced to not less than ten days nor more than one year
imprisonment, or be fined not less than fifty dollars nor more than
one thousand dollars, or both fine and imprisonment for each offense.

(Section 1141 will be unchanged by the proposed legislation.)

Section 1141-b (New).—A book, magazine, pamphlet, newspaper, or other printed, typewritten or written matter is not obscene,
lewd, lascivious, filthy, indecent, or disgusting, or of an indecent
character, within this article, by reason of the fact that it mentions,
discusses, recommends, or gives information concerning prevention
of conception or methods or means for the prevention of conception
or gives information as to where, how or of whom advice concerning,
or articles, drugs or instruments for the prevention of conception
can be obtained; and an article is not of indecent or immoral use
or purpose, within this article, because it is adapted or designed, or
is advertised or represented to be adapted or designed for the prevention of conception.

(Section 1141-b is all new matter.)

Section 1142: INDECENT ARTICLES.—A person who sells, lends,
gives away, or in any manner exhibits or offers to sell, lend or give
away, or has in his possession with intent to sell, lend or give away,
or advertises or offers for sale, loan or distribution any instrument
or article, or any recipe, drug, or medicine, [for the prevention of
conception or] for causing unlawful abortion, or purporting to be
[for the prevention of conception, or] for causing unlawful abortion,
or advertises, or holds out representations that it can be so used or
applied, or any such description as will be calculated to lead another
to so use or apply any such article, recipe, drug, medicine or instrument, or who writes or prints, or causes to be written or printed, a
card, circular, pamphlet, advertisement, or notice of any kind, or gives
information orally, stating when, where, how, of whom, or by what
means such an instrument, article, recipe, drug or medicine can be
purchased or obtained, or who manufactures any such instrument,
article, recipe, drug or medicine, is guilty of a misdemeanor, and shall
be liable to the same penalties as provided in Section eleven hundred
and forty-one in this chapter.

(Matter in brackets omitted.)

APPENDIX NO. 6

BILL INTRODUCED IN NEW YORK LEGISLATURE IN 1923

Drafted by Samuel McCune Lindsey of the Legislative Bureau of Columbia University

Section 1145 of the Penal Code to be amended to read as follows:

PHYSICIANS, INSTRUMENTS AND ADVICE. An article or instrument, used or applied by physicians lawfully practicing or by their direction or prescription, for the cure or prevention of disease, is not an article of indecent or immoral nature or use, within this article. The supplying of such articles to such physicians or by their direction or prescription, is not an offense under this article. *The giving by a physician lawfully practicing, to any person, married or having a license entitling him or her to be married duly and lawfully obtained by him or her, of any information or advice in regard to the prevention of conception, on the application of such person to such physician; or the supplying to such physician or by any one on the written prescription of such physician to any such person of any article, instrument, drug, recipe or medicine for the prevention of conception, is not an offense under this article.*

Explanation. The portions in italics are new.

APPENDIX NO. 7

The Connecticut Law and the Amendment Proposed by the American Birth Control League

The present statute, enacted in 1878, reads as follows:

General Statutes, Section 6399. Use of Drugs or Instruments to Prevent Conception. Every person who shall use any drug, medicinal article or instrument for the purpose of preventing conception shall be fined not less than $50.00 or imprisoned not less than 60 days nor more than one year or both.

The proposed bill would repeal the above section, and enact the following new section.

The giving by a physician licensed to practice or by a duly registered nurse to any person applying to him or her, of information or advice in regard to, or the supplying by such physician or nurse, or on a prescription signed legibly by him or her, of any article or medicine for the prevention of conception shall not be a violation of the statutes of this State.

APPENDIX NO. 8

NEW JERSEY LAW

AND

Amendment Proposed by the American Birth Control League

AN ACT to amend an act entitled "an act for the punishment of crimes (Revision of 1898), approved June Fourteenth, one thousand and eight hundred and ninety-eight.

BE IT ENACTED by the Senate and General Assembly of the State of New Jersey:

1. Section fifty-three of the act to which this act is amendatory be and hereby is amended so as to read as follows:

53. Any person who without just cause, shall utter or expose to the view of another, or to have in his possession, with intent so to utter or expose to view, or to sell the same, any obscene or indecent book, pamphlet, picture, or other representation, however made; or any instrument, medicine, or other thing, designed or purporting to be designed for the prevention of conception, or the procuring of abortion, or who shall in any wise advertise, or aid, or assist in advertising the same, or in any manner, whether by recommendation against its use or otherwise, give or cause to be given, or aid in giving any information how or where any of the same may be had or seen, bought or sold, shall be guilty of a misdemeanor, THE CONTRACEPTIVE TREATMENT OF MARRIED PERSONS BY DULY PRACTICING PHYSICIANS, OR UPON THEIR WRITTEN PRESCRIPTION, shall be deemed a just cause hereunder.

The underlined clause is the amendment desired by the American Birth Control League.

APPENDIX NO. 9

CALIFORNIA LAW

AND

Amendment Introduced in 1917 by Senator Chamberlain and Assemblyman Wishard

The California law is Section 317 of the Penal Code under the Chapter Heading, "INDECENT EXPOSURE, OBSCENE EXHIBITIONS, BOOKS AND PRINTS, AND BAWDY AND OTHER DISORDERLY HOUSES."

The bill introduced by Senator Chamberlain and Assemblyman Wishard amended the Section by striking out the words "or for the prevention of conception." The wording of the Section is as follows:

317. ADVERTISING TO PRODUCE MISCARRIAGE. Every person who wilfully writes, composes or publishes any notice or advertisement of any medicine or means for producing or facilitating a miscarriage or abortion, or for the prevention of conception, or who offers his services by any notice, advertisement, or otherwise, to assist in the accomplishment of any such purpose, is guilty of a felony.

APPENDIX NO. 10

Indications of Opposition of Birth Control Advocates to Removing Ban on Contraceptive Information from Federal Obscenity Laws

At the first American Birth Control Conference when the American Birth Control League was organized in November, 1921, the following resolution was submitted, but the Conference was not allowed to vote upon it:

Whereas, the proposition has been laid before Post Master General Hays by the Voluntary Parenthood League, that he recommend to Congress the revision of the Federal law so that contraceptive knowledge shall not be included among the penalized indecencies which are now declared unmailable.

Be It Resolved, that this American Conference for birth control urges Post Master General Hays to act favorably on this proposition as a matter of postal progress and as a service to modern science, welfare and justice.

A "doctors only" proponent, speaking from the floor against allowing a vote on this resolution to be taken by the Conference said, "If we could have the Federal bill passed *to-day,* we would not want it."

Excerpts from an Editorial in the Birth Control Review of March, 1921

In contrast to the State legislation is the proposed repeal of the Federal law, aiming to open the United States mails to the distribution of birth control knowledge by amateurs.

We are told that the repeal of the Federal law would be the quickest and shortest way to achieve our goal. But there is no such royal road! We might flood the country with tons of good books and pamphlets on the subject by recognized authorities on hygiene, psychology and sociology, but with no appreciable effect. (A poor woman once said to me, "I have read your book from cover to cover; and yet I am pregnant again.") To offer a pamphlet to a woman who can not read or is too tired and weary to understand its directions, is like offering a printed bill of fare to a starving man.

Yet the repeal of the Federal law would accomplish practically no more than this. Nevertheless, to some it seems of primary importance; and those who think so are best qualified to throw their energies into that work.

Much as we wish that one fine gesture would sweep aside these obsolete and ridiculous anti-contraceptive laws, both Federal and State, experience has shown us the emptiness of legal and legislative victories unless followed up vigorously by concerted action. Remember that in England there is no law preventing the spread of birth control knowledge; yet we see there, that the removal of legal restriction in the use of the mails is not enough. Our interests and our activity must be positive, fundamental, dynamic, constructive. Let us beware of the futility of striving after vain victories and theoretical triumphs—which may, indeed, stimulate in us a fine glow of egotistical satisfaction, but also divert and distract our attention and interest from the hard, thankless, detailed work of helping overburdened mothers. Let us not be led into the trap of believing that the mere repeal of a Federal law will change the course of ancient human habits or the most deep-rooted of instincts.

APPENDIX NO. 11

NOTE: The words "preventing conception" are removed from the five Sections of the Federal Statutes which appear in the Bill.

1st Session.
68th CONGRESS,

S. 2290

IN THE SENATE OF THE UNITED STATES

JANUARY 28 (calendar day, JANUARY 30), 1924.

Mr. Cummins introduced the following bill; which was read twice and referred to the Committee on the Judiciary.

A BILL

To remove the prohibition of the circulation of contraceptive knowledge and means by amending sections 102, 211, 245, and 312 of the Criminal Code; and section 305, paragraphs (a) and (b), of the Tariff Act of 1922; and to safeguard the circulation of proper contraceptive knowledge and means by the enactment of a new section for the Criminal Code.

Be it enacted by the Senate and House of Representatives of the United States of America in Congress assembled, That section 102 of the Criminal Code be amended to read as follows:

"SEC. 102. Whoever, being an officer, agent, or employee of the Government of the United States, shall knowingly aid or abet any person engaged in violating any provision of law prohibiting importing, advertising, dealing in, exhibiting, or sending or receiving by mail obscene or indecent publications or representations, or means for producing abortion, or other article of indecent or immoral use or tendency, shall be fined not more than $5000 or imprisoned not more than ten years or both."

SEC. 2. That section 211 of the Criminal Code be amended to read as follows:

290

"SEC. 211. Every obscene, lewd, or lascivious and filthy book, pamphlet, picture, paper, letter, writing, print, or other publication of an indecent character; and every article or thing designed, adapted, or intended for producing abortion, or for any indecent or immoral use; and every article, instrument, substance, drug, medicine, or thing which is advertised or described in a manner calculated to lead another to use or apply it for producing abortion, or for any indecent or immoral purpose; and every written or printed card, letter, circular, book, pamphlet, advertisement, or notice of any kind giving information, directly or indirectly, where or how or from whom or by what means any of the hereinbefore-mentioned matters, articles, or things may be obtained or made, or where or by whom any act or operation of any kind for the procuring or producing of abortion will be done or performed, or how or by what means abortion may be produced, whether sealed or unsealed; and every letter, packet, or package, or other mail matter containing any filthy, vile, or indecent thing, device, or substance; and every paper, writing, advertisement, or representation that any article, instrument, substance, drug, medicine, or thing may or can be used or applied for producing abortion, or for any indecent or immoral purpose; and every description calculated to induce or incite a person to so use or apply any such article, instrument, substance, drug, medicine, or thing is hereby declared to be non-mailable matter and shall not be conveyed in the mails or delivered from any post office or by any letter carrier. Whoever shall knowingly deposit, or cause to be deposited for mailing or delivery, anything declared by this section to be non-mailable, or shall knowingly take, or cause the same to be taken, from the mails for the purpose of circulating or disposing thereof, or of aiding in the circulation or disposition thereof, shall be fined not more than $5000, or imprisoned not more than five years, or both. And the term "indecent" within the intendment of this section shall include matter of a character tending to incite arson, murder, or assassination."

SEC. 3. That section 245 of the Criminal Code be amended to read as follows:

"SEC. 245. Whoever shall bring or cause to be brought into the United States or any place subject to the jurisdiction thereof, from any foreign country, or shall therein knowingly deposit or cause to be deposited with any express company or other common carrier, for carriage from one State, Territory, or District of the United States, or place noncontiguous to, but subject to the jurisdiction thereof, to any other State, Territory, or District of the United States, or place noncontiguous to but subject to the jurisdiction thereof, or from any place in or subject to the jurisdiction of the United States through a foreign country to any place in or subject to the jurisdiction thereof, or from any place in or subject to the jurisdiction of the United States to a foreign country, any obscene, lewd, lascivious, or filthy book, pamphlet, picture, paper, letter, writing, print, or other matter of indecent character; or any drug, medicine, article, or thing designed, adapted, or intended for producing abortion, or for any indecent or immoral use; or any written or printed card, letter, circular, book, pamphlet, advertisement, or notice of any kind giving information, directly or indirectly, where, how, or of whom or by what means any of the hereinbefore-mentioned articles, matters, or things may be obtained or made; or whoever shall knowingly take or cause to be taken from such express company or other common carrier any matter or thing, the depositing of which for carriage is herein made unlawful, shall be fined not more than $5000, or imprisoned not more than five years, or both."

SEC. 4. That section 312 of the Criminal Code be amended to read as follows:

"SEC. 312. Whoever shall sell, lend, give away, or in any manner exhibit, or offer to sell, lend, give away, or in any manner exhibit, or shall otherwise publish or offer to publish in any manner, or shall have in his possession for any such purpose, any obscene book, pamphlet, paper, writing, advertisement, circular, print, picture, drawing, or other representation, figure, or image on or of paper or other material, or any cast, instrument, or other article of an immoral nature, or any drug or medicine, or any article whatever for causing unlawful abortion, or shall advertise the same for sale, or shall write or print, or cause to be written or printed, any card, circular, book, pamphlet, advertisement, or notice of any kind, stating when, where, how, or of whom, or by what means, any of the articles above mentioned can be purchased or obtained, or shall manufacture, draw, or print, or in anywise make any of such articles, shall be fined not more than $2000, or imprisoned not more than five years or both."

SEC. 5. That section 305, paragraphs (a) and (b), of the Tariff Act of 1922 be amended to read as follows:

"SEC. 305. (a) That all persons are prohibited from importing into the United States from any foreign country any obscene book, pamphlet, paper, writing, advertisement, circular, print, picture, drawing, or other representation, figure, or image on or of paper or other material, or any cast, instrument, or other article of an immoral nature, or any drug or medicine, or any article whatever, for causing unlawful abortion, or any lottery ticket, or any printed paper that may be used as a lottery ticket, or any advertisement of any lottery. No such articles, whether imported separately or contained in packages with other goods entitled to entry, shall be admitted to entry; and all such articles shall be proceeded against, seized, and forfeited by due course of law. All such prohibited articles and the package in which they are contained shall be detained by the officer of customs, and proceedings taken against the same as hereinafter prescribed, unless it appears to the satisfaction of the collector that the obscene articles contained in the package were inclosed therein without the knowledge or consent of the importer, owner, agent, or consignee: *Provided,* That the drugs hereinbefore mentioned, when imported in bulk and not put up for any of the purposes hereinbefore specified, are excepted from the operation of this sub-section.

"(b) That any officer, agent, or employee of the Government of the United States who shall knowingly aid or abet any person engaged in any violation of any of the provisions of law prohibiting importing, advertising, dealing in, exhibiting, or sending or receiving by mail obscene or indecent publications or representations, or means for procuring abortion, or other articles of indecent or immoral use or tendency, shall be deemed guilty of a misdemeanor, and shall for every offense be punishable by a fine of not more than $5000 or by imprisonment at hard labor for not more than ten years, or both."

SEC. 6. The transportation by mail or by any public carrier in the United States or in territory subject to the jurisdiction thereof, of information respecting the means by which conception may be prevented, or of the means of preventing conception, is hereby prohibited, except as to such information or such means as shall be certified by not less than five graduate physicians lawfully engaged in the practice of medicine to be not injurious to life or health. Whoever shall knowingly aid or abet in any transportation prohibited by this Act shall be deemed guilty of a felony, and, upon conviction thereof, shall be fined not more than $5000 or imprisoned for not more than five years, or shall be punished by both such fine and imprisonment.

APPENDIX NO. 12

CONDENSED CHRONOLOGICAL STORY OF THE FEDERAL BILL TO RE-
MOVE THE BAN ON CONTRACEPTIVE KNOWLEDGE FROM
THE OBSCENITY LAWS

1919. July 24. Began preliminary interviews with Senators and
Congressmen with a view to discovering the right sponsor
for the bill, and to create a good atmosphere for its introduction.

Sept. 24. Asked Senator France of Maryland to introduce
it, he being chairman of the Committee on Public Health,
a physician and heartily in favor of the bill. He agreed
to consider it.

Oct. 21. Senator France doubted the wisdom of his being
sponsor. He suggested Senator Norris of Nebraska.

Oct. 22. Senator Norris was wholly favorable to the measure, but said the prejudice of the Judiciary Committee
against other measures for which he stood would hurt his
sponsorship and he hadn't the advantage of being a physician.

Oct. 23. As Senator France was most desirable, the sponsorship was again put up to him and he said he would again
consider it.

1920. Jan. 19. After nearly three months of prodding by letters
and interviews, Senator France wrote that he did not feel
ready to shoulder our bill ahead of others to which he was
already committed. He did not decline, but thought it
unfair to keep us waiting further.

Jan. 21. Took it back to Senator Norris, who agonized over
it conscientiously, but decided he had better not. He had
sounded Senator Ball, the only other physician in the Senate beside France. Found him rather skeptical. He then
suggested asking Senator Nelson, chairman of the Judiciary
Committee to do it as proof of his repentance for having
been an abusive opponent (one of the very few we have
met).

Jan. 22.   Senator Nelson's repentance went to the extent of recommending that the bill be referred first to the Committee on Public Health and implied that the Judiciary Committee would concur if the report should be favorable.

During the next few weeks, besides hunting for a sponsor we interviewed the Health Committee.   Seven out of eleven were wholly in favor or inclined favorably toward the bill.

Senator Ball was seen several times, in the hope that he would prove to be the right sort for a sponsor.   He was slow in coming to a conclusion as to the merits of the bill.

Meanwhile two other Senators were asked.

Jan. 29.   Senator Sterling of South Dakota, first.   The discussion convinced him as to the merits of the bill, and he finally agreed to consider sponsoring it.

Feb. 18.   Urged his decision.   He did not refuse, but said he would be relieved to be released from consideration.   Promised to work for the measure in Committee and on the floor.

Mar. 5.   After conferring with Senators France and Norris, whose advice has always been helpful, took the bill to Senator Dillingham of Vermont.   He is wholly in favor but considered himself unsuitable sponsor.   He is the *only* Senator who has not kept us waiting for his decision.   He urged Ball as best sponsor.

Mar. 6.   As Senator Ball had announced on February 20th, that he was convinced by our data—on the advice of Dillingham, France and Norris, he was asked by letter to introduce the bill.

Mar. 11.   Went to Washington for his decision.   Found him; he had not even read the letter carefully enough to realize he was being asked.   Said "No."   Then reconsidered and agreed to talk it over with France.

Mar. 19.   *He promised to sponsor the bill.*   He asked for "a few days of grace" before introducing it, to recover from influenza and attend to the suffrage crisis in Delaware.

Apr. 21.   Introduction still hanging.   Said he "hadn't had time."   Meanwhile the comment of the other Senators had begun to disconcert him.   He turned us over to Major Parkinson of the bill drafting service to discuss phraseology and work out an opposition-proof bill.   Everything was settled to our satisfaction.   It was the Senator's next move.

Apr. 24. He "hadn't had time to see Parkinson," and asked for a few days more of patience. We reminded him that we had waited over a month. He said he would surely do it during this session. We insisted on something definite. He finally promised "some day next week" and that he would wire us what day.

May 25. No word, despite letters from our office and many from the supporters of the League.

Letters, telegrams, personal interviews with Senator Ball in Washington were all unavailing. He did nothing but reiterate promises.

June. 5. *The Senate adjourned and the bill was not introduced.*

Dec. 6. With the opening of the last session of Congress, we began the sponsor hunt again. Nine Senators in succession have been asked to sponsor the bill, as follows:

Sen. Capper of Kansas. For the bill, but too submerged in his agricultural relief bills to take ours on.

Sen. Townsend of Mich. (Member of Health Com.) Favors the bill, but declined on grounds that he was too ignorant on the data to face debate, and too busy to get primed.

Sen. Kenyon of Iowa. (Had reputation of being chief welfare advocate of Senate.) Too busy with his "packer" bill. Might consider it at next session.

Sen. McCumber of S. D. Admitted merit of bill, but thought he better not imperil his re-election (in 1923) by sponsoring it. Suggested that it be introduced by Health Com. as a whole, without individual sponsorship, so no one would "be the goat."

Sen. Sheppard of Texas. (Sponsor of Sheppard-Towner Maternity Bill.) Recognized necessity of our bill to complete the service provided by his bill, but could not consider sponsoring ours till next session anyway, and probably not then, as he thinks it should come from a Republican.

Sen. Fletcher of Fla. (Member of Health Com.) Heartily approves bill, but considers himself unsuitable sponsor because he is a Democrat.

Sen. Frelinghuysen of N. J. (Member of Health Com.) Frankly said he would be "afraid" to do it, but he feels favorably toward the bill.

Sen. Owen of Okla. (Member of Health Com.) Like Senator France, author of bill for Federal Health Dept.—unqualifiedly in favor, but sure bill should not be sponsored from Democratic side.

Dec. 31. Proposed to Senator France that the bill be introduced by the Health Committee without individual sponsorship.

1921. Jan. 5. Senator France declined the proposition on the ground that the burden of the bill would fall on him just the same.

Jan. 13. After thorough consultation with Senator France, took bill back to Senator Sterling.

Jan. 27. Senator Sterling answered that he was "too busy to do it at this session."

Feb. 11. Senator Kenyon was asked to reconsider. He replied, "I'm mighty sorry, but I am just loaded down with bills that are taking every minute of my time, and I must ask you to secure some other Senator to take care of this legislation for you."

Mar. 1. Senator Borah was asked to sponsor the bill. He did not see his way to doing it.

Aug. 19. Post Master General Hays had put himself on record as not believing in the maintenance of Post Office censorship laws. He was accordingly asked to consider recommending to Congress the removal of the censorship law regarding birth control knowledge. He was most hospitable to the suggestion—said it was timely, that he was interested and had about come to the conclusion that he ought to ask Congress to revise all the laws bearing on Post Office censorship power. He asked for a compilation of pertinent data, which was promptly provided. He had the matter under consideration till he resigned office the following March. But he made no recommendation to Congress.

The sponsor hunt began again.

Senator Borah suggested the possibility that he might slip in our bill as an amendment to the bill proposing to extend Post Office censorship to information about race track betting tips, if it was reported out of committee and reached the floor for discussion. The bill was killed in Committee, due in part to Senator Borah's opposition to it.

1922. Dec.   Sponsors found in both Houses.   Senator Cummins in the Senate, and Congressman John Kissel of New York in the House.   The latter responded to a circular letter asking for a volunteer statesman for the task.

1923. Jan. 10.   Bill introduced in both Houses.

Jan. 22.   Sen. Nelson, Chairman of the Judiciary Committee appointed Sub-Committee of three to consider the bill— Senators Cummins, Colt and Ashurst.   Senator Cummins was ill and went to Florida.   Committee action was stalled.

Strenuous effort was made to get substitute Chairman so action could proceed.   Norris was added to Committee but not as Chairman.

Feb. 6.   Sen. Colt declined to act as Chairman.

Feb. 8.   Sen. Colt asked to be excused from the Committee.

Feb. 13.   Sen. Cummins returned.

Feb. 19.   Sen. Cummins tried to get vote of full Judiciary, as conditions had not permitted a Hearing and report from the Sub-Committee.   Meeting adjourned without action. They "did not get to the bill."

Feb. 26.   Sen. Cummins tried again to get a vote.   Announced that he would call for it before adjournment, again. The members slipped out one by one, so no quorum was present.   The Senator said, "They just faded away."

1924. Jan. 30.   Bill reintroduced by Senator Cummins.

Feb. 1.   Bill introduced in House by Congressman William N. Vaile of Colorado.

Mar. 7.   Bill referred to Senate Sub-Committee, consisting of Senators Spencer, Norris and Overman.

Mar. 22.   Bill referred to House Sub-Committee of seven, Congressmen Yates, Hersey, Perlman, Larson, Thomas, Major and O'Sullivan.

Apr. 8.   Joint Hearing held before both Sub-Committees. Ten spoke for the bill, and five against.

May 9.   Hearing reopened at request of the Catholics.

June 7.   Congress adjourned.   Neither Committee reported the bill.

1925. Dec.   Senator Cummins made Chairman of the Judiciary Committee.

Jan. 20.   Senate Sub-Committee unanimously reported Cummins-Vaile Bill "without recommendation."

House Sub-Committee evaded making a report.

Mar. 4.   Congress adjourned.

APPENDIX NO. 13

SENATORS BORAH AND STANLEY ARGUED BEFORE THE JUDICIARY
COMMITTEE IN 1921 FOR THE PRINCIPLES ON WHICH THE
CUMMINS-VAILE BILL IS BASED, BUT REGARDING
ANOTHER BILL

The following excerpts from the Hearing, with editorial comment, are taken from the Birth Control Herald of January 20, 1925.

The Bill on which the Hearing was held had passed the House in October, 1921. It aimed primarily to make race track betting tips unmailable, but section No. 5 to which Senators Stanley and Borah objected most strenuously was a sweeping infringement of the freedom of the press, by which nothing could go through the mails that gives any information as to bets or wagers on any contest of speed, strength or skill. The bill was referred to a Sub-Committee of the Judiciary consisting of Senator Sterling, Chairman, and Senators Borah and Overman.

The measure has never been reported out by the full committee, and it seems evident that the vigorous opposition of the two Senators who argued on principle, and the disapproval of powerful newspaper associations, have resulted in the burying of the bill.

At the time of this Hearing (January, 1922), Senator Stanley was not on the Judiciary Committee but he was so interested in preserving the right of free press from further encroachment that he appeared at the Hearing as an opponent of the bill, and as a pleader for fundamental liberty. At present, however, he is a member of the Judiciary Committee, with the best of opportunities to make his convictions count effectively for the Cummins-Vaile Bill, in which precisely the same principle is at stake, namely, the freedom of the press and the right of the individual to have access to knowledge.

The V. P. L. Director was originally indebted to Senator Borah for her copy of the report of this Hearing. He has never faltered in his opposition to the principle of censorship. And Senator Sterling, the Chairman before whom this Hearing was held, was already at that time committed to support of the Cummins-Vaile Bill. He gave his word that he would work for the Bill in the Judiciary Committee and on the floor of the Senate.

In the 113 pages of the Report of the two Hearings on the bill to exclude gambling information from the mails, there are many more analogies to the principle involved in the Cummins-Vaile Bill than there is room to recount, so the excerpts below are only samples.

At the very start there is similarity of circumstance. At the first Hearing Senator Stanley spoke "especially of the section that was added in the last hour of debate, about which I am advised comparatively few members of Congress knew anything at the time of its passage." That the House should have inadvertently passed a measure on the strength of its moral sounding aim, but which contained an unwarranted suppression of constitutional rights is exactly what happened in 1873, when the Comstock bill was hastily passed, aimed at obscenity, just as this bill was aimed at gambling, but blundering into suppression not only of crime, but of freedom.

Sen. Stanley (speaking on behalf of representatives of the chief metropolitan newspapers) : "These great papers wish an opportunity to show that the gambling evil is not best remedied—especially by a government of delegated powers—by an unwarranted restriction of the freedom of the press or the freedom of speech."

(Similarly, the abuse of contraceptive information is not to be remedied by laws forbidding access to that information. Ed.)

Sen. Stanley (at the second Hearing) : "Despotic governments have always viewed and always will view freedom of speech with apprehension and alarm. When you have placed a censorship or arbitrary inhibition or prohibition upon either the freedom of speech or the freedom of the press, you have not invaded one constitutional right, but have imperilled or desolated them all."

Sen. Borah: "Do you attack this as unconstitutional, or simply the policy of it?"

Sen. Stanley: "Both. I maintain that it is not necessary to show that it is unconstitutional, because of its folly and its unwisdom. It is absolutely a violation of the spirit of the Constitution."

Sen. Sterling: "If you think race-track gambling is an evil, do you think that advice or suggestions in regard to wagers and bets should be prevented?"

Sen. Stanley: "May I answer that question by asking another? Does the Chairman believe that the Federal government should pass a law prohibiting anything that is morally or industrially wrong?"

Sen. Sterling: "Oh no, there are limitations of course upon the power of the Federal government to do those things."

Sen. Stanley: "Yes, . . . I had begun to doubt it."

Sen. Sterling: "This prohibits the use of the mails for certain purposes.

Sen. Stanley: "Yes."

Sen. Sterling: "And we have passed laws relative to the use of the mails . . . prohibiting certain written or printed matter. . . .

Sen. Stanley: "And Mr. Chairman, that is the worst vice, the worst phase of this legislative itch with which the country is infected, for the Federal and sumptuary regulation of all the activities of the people, moral, intellectual and industrial. It is gaining. One bad law breeds a million."

Sen. Borah: "Well, Mr. Stanley, you do not have to make any argument to me that we have no power to establish a censorship."

Sen. Stanley: "This is as fine an instance, Mr. Chairman, as I know, of the abortive birth and progress of this character of half baked legislation. A bill, honest, and perhaps advised in the main, was introduced. . . . As it passed a Representative took a shot at it on the fly and inserted this section 5. The Postmaster General (Hays) in a letter to Chairman Nelson of this Committee very pertinently observed: 'This particular section 5 makes it an offense for newspapers to publish racing news. I favor the bill, but am opposed to this section 5. I was not consulted about it, and I hope this section does not pass. The whole bill had better be defeated in my opinion, than to add this additional curtailment of the freedom of the press. There has been a very strong tendency of late in that direction, and I am sure it is essential that such tendency be checked. I am reminded of Voltaire's statement, "I wholly disapprove what you say and will defend with my life your right to say it." ' "

Sen. Borah: "It is not necessary to proceed any further then, is it?"

Sen. Stanley: "Senator, I think there is more in this than this bill. I have no fear that this bill will pass. This is too much. Neither the minds nor the stomachs of the people are prepared to endure it. But I wish to emphasize its evils in order that this character of legislation may be discouraged, that this persistent and pernicious effort to control the freedom of the press may find an end somewhere at some time."

(The Cummins-Vaile Bill will also help to end it. Ed.)

Sen. Borah: "Well, Senator Stanley, as I think you know from personal conversation, I am quite in sympathy with your view, but I am unable to construe this letter (from Postmaster General Hays, quoted above) in harmony with a number of statutes that are already upon the statute books, and already in force."

(The Comstock law, for instance. Ed.)

Sen. Stanley: "It is unfortunately true."

Sen. Borah: "Indicating that we are taking a step back to constitutional government."

Sen. Stanley: "Buckle says that all civilization for five hundred years consisted in repealing laws. I wish Buckle were eligible for a seat in the Senate now."

(Hear, hear! Ed.)

"Mr. Chairman, the greatest influence for good—and it may be greatest power for evil—is the power of the press. There is no free government without it. There are no free men without it. There is no free thought without it. I commend to your attention just a little paragraph from that great defense of free institutions, with (one) possible exception, the greatest in the English tongue: 'Though all the winds of doctrine were let loose to play upon the earth, so Truth be in the field, we do ingloriously by licensing and prohibiting to misdoubt her strength. Let her and Falsehood grapple; who ever knew Truth put to the worse in a free and open encounter?'"

Sen. Stanley continuing: "Now let us see what this bill prohibits. Section 5 reads: 'No newspaper, postcard, letter, circular, or other written or printed matter containing information, or statements, by way of advice of suggestions, purporting to give the odds at which bets or wagers are being laid or waged, upon the outcome of speed, strength or skill, or setting forth the bets,'—now get this,— 'made or offered to be made, or the sums of money won or lost upon the outcome or result of such contest,' etc.

"If a school boy at college should write to his mother that his room-mate had bet five cents on a foot-ball game, he could be sent to the penitentiary for five years and fined $5000.

"Put in force this act and then endeavor to convince a civilized world that this is the land of the free and the home of the brave."

(Compare the wording of this proposed law with that of the old Comstock law by which "every book, pamphlet . . . paper, letter, writing . . . or notice of any kind giving information directly or indirectly where, how or of whom or by what means," etc., conception may be controlled is unmailable. Then parallel Sen. Stanley's instance of the college boy and his five cent bet on the foot-ball game with the fact that no mother can now lawfully write to her married daughter any information even in a private letter as to how she may space the births of her babies. Ed.)

Sen. Stanley: "The evil of attempting to restrict the freedom of the press in discussing this matter more than counterbalances any possible ultimate good. It is purely problematical whether it would stop any racing or not, or deter it. It is an actual fact that it would be another step in the wrong direction—that is of a pernicious, vexacious, inquisitorial censorship of the press.

"It would of course be argued that the boy would not be sent to prison for five years or fined $5000. And why? Because judges have more sense and more humanity and more decency than the Senate, and that they would refrain from doing what they are authorized to do. Now you enact this bill, and how do you know that somewhere, sometime, you are not going to find a Judge that has just as little sense of proportion and propriety and justice as the Senate of the United States?

(For instance the Judge who sent Carlo Tresca to jail for a small unwitting infringement of the Comstock act, which government officials as a whole make not the slightest attempt to enforce. Ed.)

Sen. Stanley, satirically: "Because Congress has gone very near the end of its constitutional tether, it should cut the tether and go the whole length: because it has regulated the freedom of the press in a few respects, it should now proceed to regulate them in all respects."

Sen. Borah: "I think, Senator Stanley, that the argument that we will have to rely upon finally is whether we are going any further. There are plenty of precedents for this law on the statute books. . . . They are bad precedents, but they are there."

Sen. Stanley: "Exactly, Senator Borah."

Sen. Borah: "I would like to repeal many of them."

Sen. Stanley: "I would like to join you in that. . . .

"No man of course is in favor of moral uncleanness. . . . But that is no reason why the Federal Government should act as a spy and as a supervisor of the private relations between men and women in the several States. . . .

"Race gambling no one doubts is an evil. Of course it is. But intemperance is a bad thing. Therefore the papers must not encourage intemperance by mentioning the concomitants of an alcoholic drink; the other day an officer tried to stop the Cincinnati Inquirer from making reference to a copper can because they said some copper cans were used for distilling! That is a fact. Where are we going to stop?

"Burglary is a bad thing. Think of it, there are millions of men who do not know that a simple flat piece of steel, called a jimmy, can be used to open doors that are locked. . . . Suppose the papers tell of how a man gets into a house by means of a jimmy . . . some fellow reads that and gets a jimmy and breaks into a house. Are you going to stop all mention of that? . . . I want to stop now, any further advance as Senator Borah has said, in this pernicious practice of regulating the morals of the people by prescribing what the press shall say about their morals, whether in their domestic relations, their gaming practices, or anything else. . . .

"You pass this act, and by virtue of its precedent and those others of its kind that now deface the statute books of a free country, within a few short years, with a little ingenuity, I can keep anything out of the columns of the press except an account of a school picnic or a pink tea. I thank you, Mr. Chairman."

(And this paper thanks the Senator. Ed.)

APPENDIX NO. 14

SECTIONS OF THE FOOD AND DRUG ACT WHICH ARE PERTINENT TO MATERIALS USED FOR THE PREVENTION OF CONCEPTION

Manufacture:

Sec. 8717: It shall be unlawful for any person to manufacture within any territory or the District of Columbia any article of food or drug which is adulterated or misbranded, within the meaning of this Act.

Importation:

Sec. 8718: The introduction into any State or Territory or the District of Columbia from any other State or Territory or the District of Columbia, or from any foreign country of any article of food or drugs which is adulterated or misbranded, within the meaning of this Act, is hereby prohibited.

Definition of Drug Includes Compounds:

Sec. 8722: The term "drug," as used in this Act, shall include all medicines and preparations recognized in the United States Pharmacopoeia or National Formulary for internal or external use, and any substance or mixture of substances intended to be used for the cure, mitigation, or prevention of disease of either man or other animals.

Adulteration:

Sec. 8723: For the purposes of this Act an article shall be deemed to be adulterated:

In case of drugs:

First: If, when a drug is sold under or by a name recognized in the United States Pharmacopoeia or National Formulary, it differs from the standard of strength, quality, or purity as determined by the test laid down in the United States Pharmacopoeia or National Formulary official at the time of investigation.

Second: If its strength or purity fall below the professed standard of quality under which it is sold.

305

Misbranding:

Sec. 8724: The term "misbranded," as used herein, shall apply to all drugs, or articles of food, or articles which enter into the composition of food, the package or label of which shall bear any statement, design, or device regarding such article, or the ingredients or substances contained therein which shall be false or misleading in any particular, and to any food or drug product which is falsely branded as to be the State, Territory, or country in which it is manufactured or produced.

That for the purposes of this Act an article shall also be deemed to be misbranded.

In case of drugs:

First: If it be an imitation of or offered for sale under the name of another article.

Second: (Not pertinent.)

Third: If its package or label shall bear or contain any statement, design, or device regarding the curative or therapeutic effect of such article or any of the ingredients or substances contained therein, which is false and fraudulent.

Fourth: If the package containing it or its label shall bear any statement, design, or device regarding the ingredients or the substances contained therein, which statement, design, or device shall be false or misleading in any particular.

APPENDIX NO. 15

FREEDOM OF ACCESS TO KNOWLEDGE OF THEIR OWN CHOOSING DENIED TO CATHOLICS BY OREGON SCHOOL LAW, AND SERIOUSLY THREATENED IN OTHER STATES

SAME PRINCIPLE AT STAKE AS THAT IN CUMMINS-VAILE BILL

The following letter was sent by the Director of the Voluntary Parenthood League to every Catholic member of Congress. There are 37 Catholic members in the House, and 5 in the Senate.

January 16, 1925.

DEAR SIR:

Am I correct in thinking that you are one of the thirty-seven Roman Catholic members of the House? If so, may I not assume both your special interest in the recently attempted anti-Catholic legislation in several States, and in the possibly anti-Catholic tendencies of certain proposed Federal measures, and your common concern with all liberty loving Americans at these new menaces to certain of our fundamental rights.

Among the proposals to which I refer are those made in Oregon, California, Washington, Michigan and Alabama to restrict Catholic teaching and learning. The laws proposed have not attempted directly to prohibit Catholic schools, but they indirectly achieve that end, by compelling all children of certain ages to attend public schools during all the hours of all the school days through out the year. What is perhaps the most preposterous of these attempts, actually became law in Oregon in 1922. Its provisions are incredible to upholders of a supposedly free government. They create a Prussian type of surveillance and control over all private instruction, and empower a County School Superintendent, vested with absolutely autocratic authority from which there is no appeal, to decide whether such private instruction as may be allowed is being "properly" conducted and to compel children receiving such private instruction as he may disapprove to attend the public school in the district of their residence. Fortunately, protest against this outrageous law from Catholics and other citizens, has taken the questions to the courts. Equally fortunately, the Federal District Court in Oregon has pronounced against the law's constitutionality.

At Washington, it is the Sterling education bill at which lovers of our constitutional liberties, Catholics and non-Catholics alike, are looking askance as a possible gateway to Federal compulsion of public school attendance, or to other Federal interference with individual freedom in the acquisition of knowledge. In view of these legislative tendencies, then, and of the intolerant and lawless aggressiveness of certain groups which are violently anti-Catholic, and quite ready to translate their feelings into political control, may there not well be concern lest our guaranteed American freedom become a farce?

This is no time then for thoughtful Catholics to take sides against freedom. They need it to protect their own rights. Am I wrong in thinking that, on sober thought, they will not wish to line up against a bill that makes a stand for the very principle that is most dear to them, namely, their right to knowledge of their own choosing? It has been generally assumed that Catholic Representatives, as such, will vote against the Cummins-Vaile Bill, which touches inferentially upon "birth control"; but will they, can they, when they reflect that this measure only seeks to repeal the same kind of pernicious legislation as now imperils the civil liberties of all of us, but Catholics in particular, in the matter of their schools and religious instruction?

For these reasons I respectfully ask your judicial consideration of the above facts and those which follow, as they have a bearing on the decision to be made as to this bill by any Congressman who is at the same time a loyal Catholic and a conscientious legislator.

Neither the existing laws nor the provisions of the Cummins-Vaile Bill deal directly with the question of birth control. They have no right to do so. That is essentially a question for the individual conscience. But they do both affect the question indirectly. However, in so doing the laws have established tyranny, whereas the bill re-establishes individual freedom. The laws are an intrusion upon personal liberty, such as is prohibited by the constitution, and the bill simply removes that intrusion.

No Federal statutes forbid the actual control of conception. That is an entirely lawful act for the individual. But the laws do forbid the circulation by any public carrier, of any information as to how conception may be controlled. That is, they forbid the circulation of knowledge by restricting the freedom of the press, and even the freedom of individual communication by letter. Yet freedom of speech and press is constitutionally guaranteed.

Liberty to learn and to teach is a fundamental American right, which may not justly be infringed, except when the things taught are criminal acts. The control of conception is not a crime. It could not possibly be declared such, by law. It may be contrary to ethics, morality and religious teachings as claimed by the authorities of the Catholic Church, but so also it may not be. Opinion differs about it, though it is obvious that the trend of opinion, as proven by the birth rates the world over, is in its favor. However, it is a question apart from the law, and should be worked out in accord with personal conscience, and whatever educational and inspirational influence the individual wishes to accept.

So I earnestly ask you, Sir, to think this matter through, and to co-operate now with us who are working for enactment of this bill; so that freedom may be safeguarded for everyone, and each allowed to utilize it according to his own conscience. I do not ask you to believe in birth control. It would be utterly irrelevant and intrusive to do so. It is not the point of the bill. The point of the bill is one that all Americans should have in common, a love of freedom and insistence upon having it for all.

Will you stand for the Cummins-Vaile Bill on that one ground?
Yours respectfully,
MARY WARE DENNETT,
Director.